Enduring Violence

Enduring Violence

Ladina Women's Lives in Guatemala

Cecilia Menjívar

UNIVERSITY OF CALIFORNIA PRESS
Berkeley · Los Angeles · London

University of California Press, one of the most distinguished university presses in the United States, enriches lives around the world by advancing scholarship in the humanities, social sciences, and natural sciences. Its activities are supported by the UC Press Foundation and by philanthropic contributions from individuals and institutions. For more information, visit www.ucpress.edu.

University of California Press
Berkeley and Los Angeles, California

University of California Press, Ltd.
London, England

Library of Congress Cataloging-in-Publication Data

Menjívar, Cecilia
Enduring violence : Ladina women's lives in Guatemala / Cecilia Menjívar.
p. cm.
ISBN 978-0-520-26766-4 (cloth : alk. paper)
ISBN 978-0-520-26767-1 (pbk. : alk. paper)
1. Women—Guatemala—Social conditions. 2. Women—Violence against—Guatemala. 3. Ladino (Latin American people)—Violence against—Guatemala. 4. Violence—Guatemala. I. Title.
HQ1477.M46 2011
305.48'9694209728I4—dc22 2010037628

Manufactured in the United States of America

20 19 18 17 16 15 14 13 12 11
10 9 8 7 6 5 4 3 2 1

This book is printed on 50# Enterprise, a 30% post consumer waste, recycled, de-inked fiber and processed chlorine free. It is acid-free, and meets all ANSI/NISO (Z 39.48) requirements.

To
P. C. de Ch.
P. Ch. vda. de S.
J. A. Ch.
M. Ch. M.
M. A. Ch.
In Memoriam

U.N. Declaration on the Elimination of Violence against Women

ARTICLE 1:

For the purposes of this Declaration, the term "violence against women" means any act of gender-based violence that results in, or is likely to result in, physical, sexual or psychological harm or suffering to women, including threats of such acts, coercion or arbitrary deprivation of liberty, whether occurring in public or in private life.

ARTICLE 2:

Violence against women shall encompass, but is not limited to the following:

(a) Physical, sexual and psychological violence occurring in the family, including battering, sexual abuse of female children in the household, dowry-related violence, marital rape, female genital mutilation and other traditional practices harmful to women, non-spousal violence and violence related to exploitation;

(b) Physical, sexual and psychological violence occurring within the general community, including rape, sexual abuse, sexual harassment and intimidation at work, in educational institutions and elsewhere, trafficking in women and forced prostitution;

(c) Physical, sexual and psychological violence perpetrated or condoned by the state, wherever it occurs.

ARTICLE 3:

Women are entitled to the equal enjoyment and protection of all human rights and fundamental freedoms in the political, economic, social, cultural, civil or any other field. These rights include, inter alia:

(a) The right to life;

(b) The right to equality;

(c) The right to liberty and security of person;

(d) The right to equal protection under the law;

(e) The right to be free from all forms of discrimination;

(f) The right to the highest standard attainable of physical and mental health;

(g) The right to just and favourable conditions of work;

(h) The right not to be subjected to torture, or other cruel, inhuman or degrading treatment or punishment.

United Nations, General Assembly, 85th plenary meeting,
20 December 1993; A/RES/48/104
http://www.un.org/documents/ga/res/48/a48r104.htm

Contents

Acknowledgments

This project took detours and years to materialize into a book, and over the years the list of people and institutions to whom I am indebted became long. I apologize in advance for any inadvertent omissions.

I offer my most heartfelt gratitude to the women whose lives I depict in this book. Due to issues of confidentiality, only their pseudonyms will be known to others, but they have allowed me to know them by name, to come into their homes, and to learn about their lives, dreams, and joys. In the process I learned lifelong lessons about the human spirit, about kindness, and about resilience, among other qualities that enhance us as human beings. In many ways, it was the women's example and the various lessons they taught me that motivated and sustained me to complete this project. I hope that the work I have produced contributes something in return.

There are several individuals who contributed in diverse ways to this project. First, I thank Anne Pebley, who invited me to participate in her project—with her Princeton, Institute of Nutrition for Central America and Panama (INCAP), and RAND collaborators—on maternal and child mortality in Guatemala. Anne introduced me to studying Guatemala and doing fieldwork there; she provided crucial guidance, mentorship, and key resources in those important initial stages of research. Most of all, her generosity and the dignity with which she approaches the subject of her work have been models I seek to emulate in my own professional life. I am also immensely grateful to the people at INCAP for their logistic and technical support, in particular, Nora Coj, for her patience and dedication to the project. I also want to thank Dolores Acevedo García for paving the way for me to do research in the two towns where I conducted my fieldwork.

I am very grateful to institutions that provided financial support for this research endeavor. The National Institutes of Child and Human Development, through grants to Anne Pebley and her collaborators and a supplement to support my part, financed the initial stages. Arizona State University (ASU) facilitated additional fieldwork in Guatemala through a Faculty Grant-in-Aid Award, a Dean's Incentive Grant (twice), a grant from the then Center for Latin American Studies, and another one from the Women's Studies Program (now Women and Gender Studies). Funds provided to me through the Cowden Distinguished Professorship were instrumental in the last stages of this project.

During the time I was working on the book, I spent a semester visiting at the Maison des Sciences de l'Homme in Paris and another one in the Department of Sociology at Yerevan State University in Armenia. I am grateful for the institutional support I received in both places, in particular, the use of the wonderful library in Paris and the opportunity to teach a course and learn from conversations with students and colleagues in Yerevan. I would like to thank Polymia Zagefka, who welcomed me to the Institut des Hautes Études de l'Amérique Latine, Université de Paris 3, and introduced me to others working there.

Several friends and colleagues offered advice and introduced me to work that proved immensely useful. M. Gabriela Torres always has been ready to help, to share her work with me, and to give me feedback and suggestions; she also invited me to present my work at panels she organized at meetings of the Latin American Studies Association and the American Anthropological Association, both of which gave me opportunities to obtain excellent comments. Miguel Huezo Mixco immediately sent me information about writings on violence produced in Central America when I asked him. And Paula Godoy-Paiz and Nestor Rodriguez also have been quick to share their work with me whenever I have asked.

At ASU I would like to acknowledge friends and colleagues for their friendship and collegiality over the years. Mariluz Cruz-Torres, Kathy Kyle, Vera Lopez, Lisa Magaña, and Rose Weitz have been great listeners. Though I did not discuss with all of them details of what I was writing, their friendship alone meant a lot to me during the time I was writing. And my colleagues in the School of Social and Family Dynamics and the Center for Population Dynamics have created a wonderful environment conducive to research and intellectual engagement.

Several other people have been instrumental in one way or another in this project. I am grateful to my brother, Oscar Menjívar, who provided me with a place to stay in Guatemala City during the time I was doing fieldwork. My cousin Sara Menjívar de Barbón took time out of her busy schedule teaching medical students at the university in San Salvador to visit me in Guatemala; she ended up organizing field notes and making photocopies for me but also accompanying me to visit the women, which I hope made up for the mundane tasks she volunteered to undertake. And Ivette Castro, my close friend since childhood, has always been a great sounding board for my research ideas and projects.

I thank the editors of the *Latin American Research Review* and *Studies in Social Justice* for their permission to publish versions of "Violence and Women's Lives in Eastern Guatemala: A Conceptual Framework," *Latin American Research Review* 43 (3): 109–36; and "Corporeal Dimensions of Gender Violence: Women's Self and Body in Eastern Guatemala," *Studies in Social Justice* 2 (1): 12–26. Chapters 2 and 3 are based on these articles.

I would like to thank the Albright Knox Art Gallery for permission to use an image of Rufino Tamayo's painting *Mujeres de Tehuantepec* on the cover of this book, and in particular Kelly Carpenter for making sure I obtained permission.

At the University of California Press, once again Naomi Schneider took on a project of mine with professionalism, diligence, and care. This book has benefited from her remarkable editorship, and I will always be grateful to her. I also thank the reviewers for the Press for their extremely helpful comments and the production staff for taking this project to completion, in particular, Sheila Berg for once again editing my work with great care and Emily Park, for her patience and help throughout the production of this book. I am also grateful to Sandy Batalden in Tempe for her fine editing, as always.

Perhaps an indication of the multiple connections to other countries in my family, I have worked on this project in different parts of the world. During this time, I have had the good fortune to spend time with my in-laws, Sergei Gaikovich Agadjanian and Valentina Semeyonovna Guseva. Whether it is at their home in Moscow, at ours in Tempe, or during our visits in Paris and Yerevan, they have made sure that I have ample time to dedicate to my work (I miss them in Maputo!). This means that they take care of everything else around me, from cooking the delicious meals that Valentina Semeyonovna knows I like, to spending time with my son, and doing all sorts of other routine and time-consuming tasks. For all this and much more, *Bol'shoye Spasibo!* I also thank the rest of the Agadjanian (and Muradian) family, in particular, Susana and Sergei, for their kindness and hospitality during my visits to Yerevan but especially during the semester my family and I spent there.

From the very beginning of this project, my colleague, closest friend, and husband, Victor Agadjanian, has been involved in various ways. He is no doubt my toughest critic but also my main source of support. His dedication and respect for my ideas and my work have been indispensable for my professional fulfillment and fundamental to the home we have shared for two decades. Any words of appreciation fall short and prove inadequate to convey my deep gratitude to and for him. And Alexander (Sasha), our "tween," continues to bring distractions and commotion to my daily routine. His interruptions of my work to share the latest sports news or to ask for help with his Latin homework are beautiful reminders of the sheer joy of being his mother.

I dedicate this book to the long line of women on my maternal side—my great-grandmother, great-aunts, mother, and aunt—with admiration and gratitude for their generosity and example in living amazing, dignified, and out-of-the-ordinary lives.

CHAPTER 1

Approaching Violence in Eastern Guatemala

The aim of the psychological war is to win people's "hearts and minds" so that they accept the requirements of the dominant order and, consequently, accept as good and even "natural" whatever violence may be necessary to maintain it.

—Ignacio Martín-Baró, "Violence in Central America"

Rather than view violence . . . simply as a set of discrete events, which quite obviously it also can be, the perspective I am advancing seeks to unearth those entrenched processes of ordering the social world and making (or realizing) culture that themselves are forms of violence: violence that is multiple, mundane, and perhaps all the more fundamental because it is the hidden or secret violence out of which images of people are shaped, experiences of groups are coerced, and agency itself is engendered.

—Arthur Kleinman, "The Violences of Everyday Life"

Much has been written about violence in Guatemala, a country that has come to be known for the contrast between its spectacular beauty and its unspeakable suffering. This book, however, is not about the direct, political violence in the highlands (Altiplano) targeting the Maya, a form of violence for which Guatemala has long been known. It is about the everyday violence in the lives of ladinas in Oriente, eastern Guatemala, where few outsiders, either scholars or tourists, venture to visit. It is about violence not directly attributable to individual actions intended to cause harm but embedded in institutions and in quotidian aspects of life—the familiar, the routine; violence so commonplace and so much a part of life that it is often not recognized as such. In contrast to many other works about Guatemala, this book is about the violence that becomes visible only when its consequences, in the form of suffering, are talked about. It is about the violence that women *habitually* experience, which is intertwined with the other forms of violence that have held sway in Guatemala for a long time.[1]

Guatemala is a society dealing with the aftermath of nearly four decades of state terror (Grandin 2000; Manz 2004) and undergoing "civic insecurity," with high levels of violence, persistent impunity, and an inability to address the postconflict instability (Torres 2008: 2). Although it has been more than a decade since the Peace Accords were signed in 1996, Guatemalans are still experiencing the consequences of an internal armed conflict that was, in some respects, the most brutal in the region during the past century. The United Nations–sponsored Truth Commission (CEH 1999) estimated that as many as 200,000 people were killed—a majority at the hands of government forces—during the thirty-six-year war that ended in 1996. The victims were mostly unarmed civilians, and the government's methods were often extraordinarily cruel. According to the U.N. commission, the methods employed by the state could be said to constitute "acts of genocide." The armed conflict left the country awash in weapons, with webs of people trained to use them and a civil society accustomed to the horrors of violence. The conflict not only left widows, orphans, and whole communities traumatized; it also left a population distrustful of the authorities.

Therefore, recent accounts of violence (Benson, Fischer, and Thomas 2008; Snodgrass Godoy 2006; Steenkamp 2009) in postwar, "peacetime" Guatemala reveal some of the highest homicide rates in the hemisphere, daily kidnappings, extortion, robberies, lynchings, and feminicide, the new wave of killings in which women, regardless of their ethnicity, are the targets. Guatemalans now face multiple forms of violence, often at higher rates than during "wartime." Angelina Snodgrass Godoy (2005) notes that in Guatemala the boundaries between "common" and "political" crime have become blurred; thus familiar distinctions between the two no longer stand up to empirical scrutiny. Indeed, it is difficult to conceive of these as "peacetime" conditions.

Guatemala also has one of the most unequal distributions of wealth in the hemisphere, which means that structural violence shapes many aspects of life and has manifold expressions, such as multiple forms of exploitation, extreme forms of poverty, and deeply unequal access to society's benefits. But in describing Guatemala's state of affairs today, one must bear in mind that such conditions do not have roots in the recent past. They are the culmination of a long history of abuse, exploitation, and repression brought about by the legacy of Spanish colonialism, U.S. foreign policy, and recent neoliberal economic reforms, intersections that scholars of Guatemala have amply documented (Cojtí Cuxil 1997; Hale 2006; Lovell 2010; Manz 2004; Smith 1990). Thus some of the violence Guatemala has experienced is directly related to the militarization of life during the political conflict, whereas other forms are tied to long-standing structural inequalities that have assaulted the lives of the majority of Guatemalans for centuries. These sources of violence are linked: it is not a matter of tracing root causes to one or another factor but of recognizing that multiple forms of violence act on one another and are experienced all at once. As Paul Farmer (2004) notes, the systematic violation of human rights as a product of capitalism is not unrelated and indeed is made possible through the use of state-sponsored violence (see also Binford 2004). Accordingly, links among vulnerability, inequality, human rights violations, and neoliberal restructuring are key to understanding the root causes of multiple forms of violence, as evinced in the work of Benson, Fischer, and Thomas (2008) and Benson and Fischer (2009) on Guatemala, Moodie (2006) on El Salvador, and Gill (2007) on Colombia, as well as Burkhart's (2002) quantitative analysis of the relation between capitalism and human rights violations. As Benson and Fischer (2009: 153) observe in their work on Guatemala, "By implicating neoliberal ideologies and policies in the production of the new violence, we complicate simple assessments of the Peace Accords' successes and failures and challenge the guiding premise that unfettered market forces are necessary for achieving peace and security."

An examination of the multiple forms of violence in the lives of ladinas in eastern Guatemala, who live away from the zones where direct political terror was "a way of life" (see Green 1999), exposes the deep, broad, and often indirect consequences of living in a society in which the population has been brutalized and life has become fragile and cheap, depicting the "long arm of violence." In pointing to the violence in women's lives, I do not pathologize them. In fact, it would be easier to fall back on frames that focus on pathologizing individuals than to attempt to dissect the multiple systems of oppression and exclusion that generate suffering in the manner I do here. The ladinas' lives are much more complex, and a close-up look reveals those extrapersonal forces that produce suffering for them. I have strived to convey this complexity fully. And whereas women turn to others when in need, it is often those others—friends, family, husbands, and neighbors—whose actions instantiate the violence in the context in which the women live. It is for this reason that in my discussions I intersperse instances of comfort with narratives of suffering, as they intertwine in complex ways. However, my goal is to focus the analytical gaze on violence and suffering so as to retrieve them from the recesses of normality and in this way to propose alternative ways of thinking about violence,[2] perhaps, in the words of Kleinman (2000: 231), a critique "of the normal as well as of the normative social order."

MAIN OBJECTIVE OF THE BOOK

My main objective is to unearth the misrecognized violence that women routinely experience in familiar, commonplace spaces. I seek to unveil the violence that is difficult to see and to measure (and therefore often to define as violence) because it is not confined to individual acts or horrific crimes that can be reported or tabulated. I focus on, as Kleinman (2000: 226) puts it, "the effect of the *social violence* that social orders—local, national, global—bring to bear on people [original emphasis]." I bring attention to the veiled violence in forms of social control of women that result in devaluation, humiliation, a lowered gaze, the kind of violence that does not shock the observer because it is part of the everyday but that is deeply connected to the more noticeable acts that inflict physical injury because both kinds of violence arise from the same structures. Thus the forms of violence that I examine here are related to and *make possible* (though perhaps not *cause*), through the devaluation of women's lives, the more gruesome expressions that come in the form of feminicides in Guatemala, a discussion to which I return in the conclusion. The links to which I draw attention here are evident in other contexts as well, such as the cases that the journalists Nicholas D. Kristof and Sheryl WuDunn (2009) have written about from a human rights stance, based on their work in Cambodia, India, Pakistan, Congo, Ethiopia, among other countries, in which they chronicle the manifold and mutating forms of oppression and violence against women that arise from multiple structural inequalities.

In the process I aim to develop an approach to examining structures of violence grounded in women's experiences. This approach captures the suffering in the women's lives that comes from deep inequalities in access to resources based on socioeconomic position, superimposed on the humiliations and fear originating in orthodox gender ideologies that constrain women's lives, all occurring in a background of fear and insecurity. Malnourishment, lack of opportunities to secure dignified work, and unequal access to education and health care are all expressions of the forms of violence I explore. However, I also include the physical forms of interpersonal violence that are more strongly associated with the phenomenon of violence, because in real life they are intermingled. As Irina Carlota Silber (2004) notes, when women are economically vulnerable, they also become vulnerable to men's sexual violence and exploitation and are seen as culpable for their own conditions, which in turn limits their ability to seek redress for their predicament. Although my project is to make multiple sources of suffering visible in the women's lives, I do not mean to present only this aspect of their lives or to argue that everything in the women's lives is violent. I would not be doing justice to the complexity of their lives if I presented them as being spent in abject subordination or insurmountable social pathology and spirals of violence. As well, my focus on gender domination and violence should not foreclose the potential for gendered agency and survival. Thus I also highlight, in each sphere of life I examine, the women's spaces of sociability and the collective dimensions of their experiences. I do so by focusing on the presence of other women in their lives—family members, friends, coreligionists, and coworkers, among others—that allows them the potential to create oppositional spaces and responses to their conditions. At the same time, I do not mean to portray the presence of others in the women's lives in a black-and-white manner, as nothing more than sources of support devoid of complex dynamics and contradictions. These social relations also occur in a broader context of violence.

Although there are now many organized responses to the violence in the lives of women, I mention only a few of them in the conclusion in a discussion of the efforts of national and international nongovernmental organizations (NGOs) and women's groups. Thus, without ignoring these efforts or implying that women are victims, I focus on how violence is experienced and normalized in everyday life, because none of the women I met were involved in or aware of these broader efforts. The very nature of the forms of violence I examine often escapes the attention of these groups, as they are the "violent consequences of social power" (Kleinman 2000: 228).

I must note that although the violence that the women experience is often concretized in specific acts often attributed to the men in their families, the men's acts per se are not the focus of my discussion. I seek to locate analytically the forms of violence in the women's lives outside of individuals. Focusing on men as "perpetrators" or on their individual acts isolated from a broader context would lead to a facile and misguided analysis that would serve to legitimize and disguise the deeper roots of violence. As Paula Godoy-Paiz (2008: 42) notes, "Through framing violence toward women as merely interpersonal, the laws depoliticize gender-based violence." Indeed, the individuals whose actions instantiate the violence I examine here are far from its main causes. My examination unveils the intertwined nature of power inequalities that shape daily life—in Kleinman's words (2000: 228), "the violent consequences of social power . . . [,] not surprisingly, less likely to be labeled 'violence.'" But as George Kent (2006: 55) observes, "The common thread in all these forms of violence is the fulfillment of one party's purposes at the expense of others. Violence entails the use of power."

In many ways this book explores how a geography of marginalization is lived in certain areas of the periphery, by some of the most disadvantaged social groups and by some of the most vulnerable individuals. I seek to understand social processes *in relation* to the conditions in which women live, work, love, and create. Social relations are not mechanistic reactions to those conditions, nor are they free floating and independent of them. They need to be understood within larger processes of social production and reproduction, as dynamic processes, not monolithic "characteristics" of a group or of individuals. As understood from this viewpoint, an examination of social relations in an overall context of violence allows us to grasp the consequences of living in multiple hierarchies of power and how these operate jointly.

Though direct causal relationships between sources of violence and suffering are difficult to establish, especially when dealing with forms of violence that are not always recognized as such, there were palpable effects of living in a context in which multiple forms of violence came together to shape the lives of women in the Guatemalan Oriente. I will use an instance in one of my informants' narratives to illustrate what I am trying to bring attention to. Hortencia was thirty-four years old when I first met her, had never attended school but had learned to read and write in an adult literacy program, was earning an income as a street food vendor, and was a widow who had had five children (one of whom had died in infancy). She paid Q.50 (about U.S.$10 in 1995) a month for the rent of a small adobe house, plus electricity. Her small house with very low ceilings was sparsely furnished: two beds, a small armoire, one chair, and one table in the main room. Hortencia wanted to share how she had been able to buy some of the furniture in the house:

> There was a time that I didn't even have a bed, but thanks to God, the things that you see here, I owe them to the Bomberos Voluntarios [firefighters]. A year ago they had a raffle, and my little boy wanted to buy a ticket. I had just sold Q.2 of tostadas at the park, and I told him that the Q.2 was all I had. He really wanted the ticket, so I said, well, go ahead, and cooperate with the firefighters. And imagine my surprise when they announced that my little boy had won the first prize! It was a refrigerator! I thought they were pulling my leg, I even cried. I asked my neighbor, and she had heard it on the radio, so it was true. At that time I lived in a house where I didn't have [potable] water or electricity and my boy had won a refrigerator! I was shaking when I went to get the prize; I couldn't even walk. So my cousin had to accompany me. They were so nice that they even brought it to my house. They took pictures and everything. They also said, "Look, señora, if you have the need to buy other things, just sell the refrigerator and buy whatever you need. Here is all the paperwork." So I did, I sold the refrigerator. I bought the bed, armoire, and television set. I wanted to get that for my kids because they used to go watch cartoons from the windows of houses, and people sometimes would shoo them, you know how people are with poor *patojos* [kids]; they treat them worse than animals. Now in this house they can watch whatever they want, and [with the armoire] I have a place to put my clothes.

Hortencia's words, without any references to direct, physical violence or to harm inflicted by a bullet, capture the embodiment of the multisided violence in the form of poverty and lack of access to decent wages and social services, as well as the mistreatment and humiliations that the poor endure, all of which are part of the everyday experiences in the lives of the ladinas I came to know in Oriente. The violence exposed in Hortencia's words intertwines with more direct forms, such as those inflicted through insults and sometimes physical injuries. Hortencia's story, I learned, was not at all atypical.

A key point in my examination is that the different manifestations of violence are mutually constitutive. Thus the injustices that a despotic regime breeds and that are manifested in overt political conflict are manifested in the micro-processes of life, in addition to being linked to the structural violence existing in the form of profound inequalities in access to well-paid work and social services. At the same time, these inequalities feed into and shape different expressions of everyday and symbolic violence, including social exclusion, humiliation, contempt, self-depreciation, and mistreatment, and make up the very frames that individuals use to guide their actions and understand the world around them. They coalesce with gender and gendered forms of violence to create a context that gives rise to, but also naturalizes, suffering in the lives of women. It is in such a context of "social violence" (Kleinman 2000: 226) that the killings of women, the phenomenon of feminicide, *can* take place. Thus in order to understand this wave of crimes against women in Guatemala today, I argue, one needs to understand (and recognize) the multiple strands of normalized violence that shape their lives. By focusing attention on different forms of violence in several areas of women's everyday lives, my analysis can contribute to identifying sources of suffering that are so entrenched in the social milieu as to appear part of tradition. Misrecognition, Nancy Fraser (2007) notes, is fundamental to gender inequality.

THE STUDY OF VIOLENCE

Violence has been studied from different disciplinary angles and in different areas of life. At a very general level, most studies typically have centered on the physical, visible aspects of violence, such as injuries inflicted on an unwilling victim by force, although violence that leads to psychological injuries also has been examined. A focus on physical, corporeal injuries no doubt comes from the ease of recording actions that can be counted, categorized, and tabulated. Indeed, in a recent treatise on violence, Randall Collins (2008) notes that the way sociologists have understood and studied violence has been guided by the way data are collected, namely, by examining individuals and their actions. Thus, Collins observes, we have achieved an understanding of violent individuals but not of violent situations. He sees an opportunity for sociologists of micro-processes to make a key contribution to explaining violent situations across varied contexts.

In her overview of empirical studies of violence, Mary Jackman (2002: 388) notes that "a narrow, legalistic concept of agency has led scholars to highlight interpersonal violence." In Jackman's view, two dominant assumptions have guided most examinations of violence: it is conceived as being motivated by the willful intent to cause harm and is presumed to be prompted by hostility; and it is assumed to be socially or morally "deviant" from mainstream human activity. Indeed, Collins

(2008: 4) noted that "violence . . . is about . . . the intertwining of human emotions of fear, anger and excitement, in ways that run against the conventional morality of normal situations." Therefore, Jackman (2002: 388) observes, "violence has come to be viewed as comprising eruptions of hostility that have bubbled over the normal boundaries of social intercourse. When violence is motivated by positive intentions, or is the incidental by-product of other goals, or is socially accepted or lauded, it escapes our attention."

Thus examinations of violence have tended to overlook other than interpersonal forms, such as those that can reside in social and economic institutions. However concrete, observable, and measurable (see also Collins 2008) the physical injuries that have been studied, they provide only a partial picture of the wide array of injuries that human beings find consequential (Jackman 2002). As Jackman (2002: 393) insightfully notes, what is left out are sources of material injuries: "destruction, confiscation[,] . . . or loss of earnings; the psychological outcomes of fear, anxiety, anguish, shame, or diminished self-esteem; and the social consequences of public humiliation, stigmatization, exclusion, imprisonment, [and] banishment . . . are all highly consequential for human welfare." Often, the effects of nonphysical injuries are more enduring and traumatic than those caused by direct physical violence. For instance, verbal insults that humiliate and denigrate another person can inflict profound, long-lasting injuries that may alter an individual's sense of self, without there being a single punch or any other recognizable form of violence. Jackman (2002) acknowledges that social injuries are the least likely to be acknowledged in discussions of violence, although they are sometimes mentioned, as, for example, when it is argued that pornographic materials are acts of violence against women because they are demeaning to women.[3] Ignoring the often nondramatic, quieter forms of injury results in a "patchy, ad hoc conception of violence" (Jackman 2002: 395). I heed Jackman's general call to open up the optic through which we examine violence so as to include and acknowledge the power and consequential effects of indirect forms of violence. Thus I seek not only to include other *methods* that individuals can use to inflict pain on one another, such as words, threats, insults, neglect, or even the actions of abusive employers. My aim is also to open the lens to include a wide range of *sources* of pain and injury that are not found in the actions of individuals, though often they are carried out by individuals, but in the "social order of things."

To accomplish my goal I have borrowed from a number of intellectual traditions and have used a lens that is broad and inclusive. In organizing a framework to help me to make sense of my observations in the Guatemalan Oriente, I have been cognizant of the diverse forms of violence that coexist in the Guatemalan context (see Green 1999). Many of these, mostly in their political form, have been skillfully studied by several scholars, both inside and outside Guatemala (Falla 1994; Grandin 2000; Green 1999; Manz 2004; Nelson 1999; Zepeda López 2005). And though I do not build directly on this scholarship, the body of work these scholars have produced has been influential in helping me to construct my analytic lens and shape my viewpoint. I follow Philippe Bourgois (2001) in including structural, political, symbolic, and everyday interpersonal forms of violence to unravel the interrelated strands that shape the lives of the women I came to know in eastern Guatemala. I add gender and gendered forms of violence as they coalesce in everyday events of life, not only in the extraordinary events of the women's lives. Iris Young's (1990) "five faces of oppression" (exploitation, marginalization, powerlessness, cultural imperialism, and random acts of violence) come close to the different facets of violence I include in the framework I have composed. Although these illuminate my work in many ways, I have employed some of these "faces" but not others. Having composed the framework I use here inductively, I have included those aspects of oppression that allow me to grasp the experiences of Guatemalan women more fully.

I also borrow from the work of critical anthropologists, such as Nancy Scheper-Hughes, Arthur Kleinman, and Paul Farmer; and I rely on Pierre Bourdieu's reflections on violence, on Javier Auyero's and Veena Das's writings on noninterpersonal violence in other regions of the world, and on the work of intellectuals preoccupied with the different varieties of everyday political and symbolic violence that coexist in Latin America, such as that of Edelberto Torres Rivas, Ignacio Martín-Baró, and other Latin American social scientists. From these scholars' writings, I have culled an ample supply of interpretations that focus not only on interpersonal, purposeful, physical, or more evident forms of violence but also on hidden, though equally damaging, forms of violence such as abuse, ill-treatment, neglect, indignities, inequalities, and victimization that take place in the quotidian normality of life. I lay out this framework in detail in chapter 2.[4]

I also find Scheper-Hughes and Bourgois's (2004: 4) notion, "to 'trouble' distinctions between the visible and invisible, legitimate and illegitimate forms of violence in times that can best be described as neither war nor peacetime," relevant for the case I examine here. As Cynthia Cockburn (2004: 24) observes, "A gender perspective on the successive moments in the flux of peace and war is not an optional extra but a stark necessity." Indeed, Scheper-Hughes's (1997) notion of peacetime crimes to address the routinization of violence in everyday life—whether in the form of direct political violence or in the form of daily experiences of the poor and excluded—is especially appropriate for capturing the daily anguish in women's lives in eastern Guatemala.

An examination of violence that goes beyond observable forms and away from a strict focus on deviant interpretations of purposeful hostility between individuals opens up a window into everyday dynamics that normalize violence and contort human relations. To do this, however, one must look to familiar, noneventful, everyday situations. As Das (1997: 567) aptly argues, "One can see suffering not only in extraordinary events such as those of police firing on crowds of young children, but also in the routine of everyday life." But, as Carolyn Nordstrom (2004) observes, we are always more likely to be drawn to notice the physical aspects of violence, in particular of political violence, such as wounding, maiming, torture, and murder.

Eugene V. Walter's (1969: 8) definition of violence as "destructive harm[,] . . . including not only physical assaults that damage the body, but also . . . the many techniques of inflicting harm by mental or emotional means," based on his work on political violence in Africa, is also relevant for my work here. The forms of violence I examine are intricately related to the political violence that is associated with Guatemala but are left unexplored or attributed to other factors, such as tradition. Only when verbalized do these forms of violence become visible and connections to broader structures made. Thus the lens I have developed allows me to retrieve the normalized and routinized violence inscribed in social relations, often misrecognized as pathological or "abnormal," or, to use Martín-Baró's (1994: 132) term when referring to chronic difficulties and burdens, "normal abnormality."

Although my approach is relevant for the Guatemalan case because it allows exposure of the insidious effects of living in a context of generalized violence, it may have broader applications, as there are many other postwar societies that are characterized by similar forms of structural and institutional violence and injustice, such as Northern Ireland, Colombia, South Africa, and El Salvador (Silber 2004; Steenkamp 2009). The conditions of violence created by a conflict, including the proliferation of arms, a culture of institutional violence by the security forces, poverty, and profound economic inequality (Moser and McIlwaine 2001), affect the transition to peace and become key factors in postwar violence (Steenkamp 2009). These effects are not confined to the material devastation in the aftermath of political violence but extend to changes in the individuals' minds, frames of thinking, and their very being. Nordstrom (1992) notes in her research in Mozambique and Sri Lanka that in societies that used terror and brutality as a means to control communities and in which civilians, rather than soldiers, were the tactical targets, violence was normalized and became part of life. In these instances, the psychological scarring left by the conflict is not easily erased by peace accords, especially when the structures behind the terror were left intact.

For instance, Steenkamp (2009) describes reports of Iraqi children incorporating in their games make-believe hijackings and decapitations and concludes that the children have internalized these forms of violence to which they have been exposed since the U.S.-led invasion. Focusing on "postconflict" Guatemala, Diane M. Nelson (2009) argues that the way the war was waged affected the very frames of knowing and being and that therefore it continues to shape how those who lived through the conflict make sense of the violence and loss today. Given the long-term consequences of political violence on the very self, some scholars even question the use of the term *postwar* or *postconflict.* In her examination of memory in postdictatorship Chile, Macarena Gómez-Barris (2009) distinguishes between the terms *aftermath,* which refers to the economic and political legacy of political violence, and *afterlife* to capture the continued symbolic and material effects of the violence on people's lives and their social and psychic identities. Based on her comparative work on Cambodia and Guatemala, and in a call for a more inclusive lens beyond the political sphere in examinations of postwar violence, Sabine Kurtenbach (2008) argues that given the instability and fragility of these societies, a more apt descriptive term is *war-torn.* Indeed, the idea of a postwar era in a society that has been engulfed in violence for decades poses definitional challenges and questions efforts to separate conflict from postconflict violence. For instance, the crime waves observed in "postwar" societies in El Salvador, Haiti, South Africa, and Guatemala are often framed as "common crimes" or even "ordinary crimes" in a depoliticized manner that ignores structural links (Snodgrass Godoy 2006; Steenkamp 2009). As Benson, Fischer, and Thomas (2008: 39) note, "The very notion of a *postwar* era can have the effect of deflecting attention from the existence of subtler forms of violence and persistent linkages of violence to politics and the state [original emphasis]."

My fieldwork in Guatemala straddled the last years of the conflict and the first years of the postconflict era, though tellingly, for the women I came to know, this transition did not materialize in much change. A woman in eastern Guatemala told me that "the situation" was bad but that not everyone ran the same risks, for "sólo el que anda metido en algo, puede temer que algo malo le pase, ¿verdad?" (only those who are involved in something can be afraid that something bad can happen to them, right?), using the same frame to interpret political crime at the time of the conflict to make sense of the new crime wave.

Therefore, even if the case I analyze in depth is perhaps not generalizable to other contexts, some of my observations apply to experiences of violence in other so-called postwar societies. There are several examples of efforts throughout the world to examine the issue of gender-based violence, including a national conference held in Windhoek, Namibia, in June 2007 and the U.N.-sponsored international dialogue to prevent gender-based violence held in Kampala, Uganda, in September 2003. My contribution, together with observations from other contexts, invites a rethinking of the concept of violence (and peace) based on an amplified lens as key to grasping the ramifications of visible and invisible forms of violence in the lives of women around the world today.

THE STUDY OF LADINOS IN GUATEMALA

According to the Guatemalan anthropologist Claudia Dary Fuentes (1994: 55), ladinos are a "sociocultural group characterized, at a very general level, by speaking Spanish as a mother tongue, by wearing Western clothes and shoes, and by practicing an array of customs of Spanish origin that are historically intertwined and syncretized with indigenous ones. Every time one refers to ladinos it is in relation to indigenous, like a negation of the indigenous." Furthermore, she notes, it has been assumed that ladinos are a homogeneous group, and she refers to ladinos as "the most forgotten group in Guatemalan history and anthropology" (1994: 55). The term *ladino* itself has been used to categorize different social groups at various points in time, and thus the term has not meant the same thing throughout Guatemalan history. But in the end, Dary Fuentes notes, the term includes social groups with different cultures and histories whose common denominator is the language they speak.[5]

Although the focus of this book is not on issues of identity construction or racial relations in Guatemala (both towns in which I did fieldwork were quite homogeneous and thus offered few to no opportunities to observe direct interactions between indigenous Mayas and ladinos), I find it useful to briefly discuss questions about ladino identity because they have occupied center stage for scholars of Guatemala both in the country and outside, and it is ladinas on whom I focus here. The very definition of *ladino,* as well as the significance of this group for the study of race and ethnic relations in Guatemala, has a long and complicated history.[6]

Nelson (1998: 102) observes that "the word *ladino* . . . decomposes under the pressure of analysis into myriad terms that mark class, distinction, color, and history." Others, such as Robert Carmack (2001), have argued that there is a social group between indigenous and ladinos that we might call mestizos,[7] while still others (Guzmán Böckler 1975; Guzmán Böckler and Herbert 1972) have argued that ladinos are an invented group, that ladinos seek to flee both from the Indian and from themselves and thus are both nationals and foreigners in their own country, a view that highlights the ladinos' historical " 'in-between' position" (Guzmán Böckler 1975). Ladinos are discriminated against by the elite, but they in turn discriminate against Indians, Carlos Guzmán Böckler (1975) argues, which leads them to seek a closer position with the white elite and greater distance from Indians. Others do not agree with the intermediary position of ladinos in the social hierarchy of Guatemala. Arturo Tarracena Arriola (1997, and Tarracena et al. 2002) traces the historical emergence of ladinos as a social group and as a dominant class and argues that ladinos' historical role is not confined to that of mediators between the owners of coffee plantations and the indigenous workers because ladinos themselves were plantation owners. In the view of Tarracena Arriola et al. (2002: 411), the assimilation process of ladinos and the whitening of nonindigenous groups in the late nineteenth century cemented the indigenous-ladino bipolarity, which was then formalized and supported by the statistical strategy of dividing the population into ladinos and indigenous and became the basis of Guatemala's national project (416).[8] More recently, Charles Hale (2006) has examined how ladinos experience their racial ambivalence at a time when Guatemala has undergone enormous change and Mayas have made important advances for their collective rights.

Important in the debate about ladino identity and social position is how they view themselves vis-à-vis the Mayas (or Indians) and how they act on these views in the context of Guatemala's ethno-racial hierarchy. Marta Elena Casaús Arzú's (1998, 2007) survey of the views that the oligarchy, where individuals self-identified as whites, ladinos, criollos, or mestizos, have with respect to marital relations, marriage, work, and so on, with Indians provides an in-depth look into how the ruling class's different groups construct one another and what they do to sustain socially constructed divisions. Hale's (2006) study provides a key reminder of the heterogeneity of positions and views among ladinos. Analyses such as these have challenged dichotomies and constructed bipolarities and represent important road maps for examining ladinas' lives.[9] In line with these approaches and paralleling Dary Fuentes's (1994) observations, my focus on the ladinas in this study can also serve to correct the homogenizing tendencies seen in discussions about ladinos as a social group in Guatemala.

The deeply rooted racial divisions in Guatemala have led scholars to examine the divisions between ladinos and indigenous in terms of a caste or a semicaste system (Colby and van den Berghe 1969; Tumin 1952), in which the indigenous remain at the bottom. Whereas I cannot disagree with these observations, I would like to note important forms of ladino social differentiation that add complexity to the picture. For instance, whereas the overwhelming majority of ladinos are poor, it is the elite among this group who have dominated government, commerce, manufacturing, and the political and economic life of the country.[10] And even though ladinos were targets of political violence in the 1970s, when the government was targeting labor union members, students, teachers, and anyone who dared to speak up, the brutality of the campaign of terror in the highlands, as the conflict expanded, was overwhelmingly focused on the indigenous Maya, a situation that prompted researchers, many from the north, to focus their attention on Maya indigenous communities.[11]

Scholarly work and involvement in Guatemalan indigenous communities has shaped how Guatemala has been understood and presented outside Guatemala (Blacklock and Crosby 2004). The concentration on the indigenous Maya has resulted in a lopsided production of knowledge, with hundreds of volumes dedicated to the study of the Mayas, covering almost every township in the Guatemalan Altiplano and many of the twenty-one indigenous Maya groups but only a handful of books about the "other half" of the population, ladinos (Hale 2006). Overlaid on the dichotomized view of Maya and indigenous, there are also bipolarities in images about eastern and western Guatemala. Michelle

Moran-Taylor (2008) notes that although these two regions often are contrasted due to the differences they exhibit in ethnicities, landscape, and land tenure systems, researchers rarely focus on ladinos (in eastern Guatemala) because they lack the exoticism of the Altiplano. Ladinos, however, have not been completely erased from scholarship on Guatemala (beyond the study of racial and ethnic relations); they were the subject of research in classical historical and anthropological studies of Guatemala, several of which focused on comparing and contrasting the customs, social organization, and lifestyles of Mayas and ladinos (cf. Goldín 1987; Maynard 1975 [1963]), as well as the systematic social inequalities and hierarchical relations between and among Mayas and ladinos (Adams 1964; Bossen 1983, 1984; Reina 1973; Tax 1942). But in current scholarship on Guatemala there is an undisputed focus on the Maya. Hale's (2006) recent work stands as an exception in contemporary examinations.

Following in the tradition of recent scholarship on Guatemala, women in the Guatemalan Altiplano, mostly Maya, have been the subject of research (e.g., Carey 2006; Ehlers 2000), though a considerable portion of this work has not engaged with issues of violence. Only a few scholars interested in unearthing the brutality of state terror have focused on its gendered expressions among Maya women (see Green 1999; Zur 1998). However, research on Maya women in the Altiplano has highlighted important gender inequalities and its consequences for their lives (see Ehlers 2000). My own work on the lives of ladinas in Oriente is substantively informed by this research and in many ways complements the work that has been conducted in the Altiplano.

DEVELOPMENT OF THE THEME

At this point it is helpful to give a brief account of how I arrived at the study of violence in women's lives. I must clarify, for instance, that I did not set out to do research on violence in Guatemala, as has been the case for many other scholars who have documented it in their writings. In fact, during my first several visits and interviews, beginning in late 1994, I did not ask the women in the town in Oriente I call "San Alejo" any questions about manifestations or expressions of violence in their lives. It was not my aim to look for violence; instead, the women pointed it out to me. It was their own narratives and my close listening to what they were telling me that eventually led me to an examination of violence in their lives.

I was participating in a project whose objective was to study how women's informal networks help them deal with pregnancy-related health care and with their children's illnesses, both in Maya and in ladino towns. I had been interested in immigrant informal networks and how individuals perceive their participation in them; joining a project in Guatemala offered me an opportunity to do a comparative study of networks in the home country with networks among immigrants from the same communities in the United States (I also did fieldwork among Guatemalan women in Los Angeles as part of this project). Thus my main task was to conduct in-depth interviews with Mayas and ladinas about the role of their informal ties in relation to medical treatments, which I did. But in an inductive fashion, the topic of violence evolved from my fieldwork. I had expected, to a degree, that the Maya women in the Altiplano would bring up the topic of violence (in particular, in its political forms) and its impact on their lives.[12] I had not anticipated, however, that the ladinas would also bring up violence (in its other manifestations) in our conversations. The ladinas would mention events and situations that were similar to those I had expected to find in the Altiplano, such as deaths and similar forms of direct violence. But their narratives also shed light on the suffering that comes from social exclusion and extreme poverty, as well as the injuries that come from gender inequality. Perhaps after spending a long enough time in Guatemala, violence in its multiple forms becomes a topic that is hard to ignore, not only as expressed through words in conversations, but also as seen palpably through observation of life in general. The ladinas would bring up topics that evinced suffering, fear, and pain in different spheres of their lives in a matter-of-fact way, as they would tell me, "Así es por aquí" (It's the way it is around here). Like pulling a thread, I followed their lead to eventually identify violence in their lives and to unearth multiple connections to weave the different parts into a story of violence that was specific to Oriente.

As I pored over sets of field notes and interview transcripts from the first visits to San Alejo, looking for patterns of usage of informal ties, I noticed at first that the women were preoccupied with the insecurity of life, with what I thought were issues of poverty and its consequences. Their words, however, conveyed much more than that. I also noticed that it was not only poor women who seemed anxious, as if they were in a permanent state of anxiety; women with more resources and relatively wealthy women in town also spoke in similar terms about the afflictions, humiliations, and indignities they experienced as women. I then started to take note of the words the women were using to describe their lives, words of urgency that conveyed much more than a general preoccupation with everyday events. One striking word that in itself may not be associated with violence as it is commonly understood but that came up repeatedly in the women's narratives was *aguantar,* "to endure," conjugated in various forms and referring to a wide variety of situations. For instance, women would say, "¿Y qué puedo hacer? Nomás aguantar me queda" (And what can I do? The only thing left for me to do is to endure), or "Aguanto, ¿y para dónde?" (I must endure, what else can I do ?). This verb conveyed an underlying, steady suffering in the women's lives but also resignation and acceptance; it also implied that everyone went through it, and thus it was nothing out of the ordinary. In subsequent visits I limited myself to listening more attentively to these topics as they came up during conversations, probing a little but not digging too much so as not to obtain responses that would simply confirm what I expected. I was not sure of my initial observations and needed to pay closer attention. In my last visits I did bring up the topic in very general terms with people who worked at a health post, with a pastor, and with other individuals in town, as well as with colleagues in Guatemala City. In typical fashion in qualitative research, therefore, key insights that would veer the course of my investigation in a different direction came from the women's own observations about their conditions, from conversations with many more people than the women I formally interviewed, and from reflections about life in general during discussions in encounters with others during the time I spent in the field. As such, it took me a long time to arrive at this examination of violence. To convey the women's own understandings, I use *endure* in the title of this book to mean an enduring, lasting condition but also in the sense of *aguantar* (to endure, to tolerate), as the women used it.

In one of my last visits to Guatemala, during dinner in Guatemala City with a Guatemalan physician friend, we discussed the topic of violence. Comparing life in Guatemala and El Salvador, where I had just visited, I mentioned that somehow I felt more insecure and wary in Guatemala than in El Salvador, when both countries were in "postwar" transitions and had similar rates of violence and common crime. She told me that many people felt that way and assured me it was irrelevant that I was a native of (and more familiar with) El Salvador and perhaps less familiar with Guatemala. "It's that Guatemala is violent," she added with a smile. "That's the truth, what can I tell you!" She went on to explain the many aspects in which she considered her country violent, a list that went far beyond robberies, kidnappings, or killings. We had a good discussion of the fear that not only comes from direct physical violence but also is embedded in institutions and practices. After listening to similar assessments from others, going back to San Alejo to corroborate my thoughts, and taking the time for reflection, I started to search the literature for a framework that would allow me to grasp the multisided violence I observed in the lives of ladinas in eastern Guatemala. The framework I have put together has helped me to make sense of how a context of multilayered violence shapes the lives of those who live in it and to understand the manifold ramifications of fear and terror in a society during "peacetime."

RESEARCH NOTES AND REFLECTIONS

This project started out as part of a larger comparative study of maternal and child health in Maya and ladino communities in Guatemala. From the initial stages, in late 1994, I started visiting and conducting fieldwork and in-depth interviews in a predominantly Maya town in the Guatemalan Altiplano and in an overwhelmingly ladino one in the eastern part of the country. My fieldwork consisted of relatively short visits that extended over five years, ending formally in 2000. In the initial stages of fieldwork, I conducted thirty in-depth interviews with ladinas in San Alejo and twenty-eight interviews with Maya women in the Altiplano. After asking the women for permission, I recorded all the initial interviews and at least one, but usually more, follow-up interviews. I found that carrying my tape recorder, even if I did not always record all conversations, was useful for establishing my presence as a researcher, and it allowed the women to signal whether a topic that came up was or was not to be part of the study. One woman in the Altiplano did not want to be tape-recorded but agreed to the interview. Two women in San Alejo asked me to turn off the tape recorder while we conversed about issues they did not want me to record (and thus are not part of this book).

I followed up my initial interviews with visits to the same women on average once a year in both towns. I went to their homes, walked in the streets where we would converse, attended church and temples, and spent time in the places where they conducted their daily lives. I lived in a room I rented in a house in the center of both towns, and in the Altiplano I developed a good friendship with the owner of the house.[13] The owner of this house rented rooms to people who came from Guatemala City to work in the town, such as a Maya dentist, a physician, and a justice of the peace, so I had the opportunity to have regular conversations with them. She also served lunch and dinner at her house as part of her business. One of the regulars was a well-respected Maya schoolteacher who lived in a large house in the center of town. He was a bachelor and preferred to take his meals at this woman's house. My conversations with him helped me to understand many aspects of life in Guatemala, including the effects of the political violence and the 1976 earthquake, among other topics. In addition, I met with officials in both towns, with council members (including the mayor of San Alejo), priests, pastors, neighbors, teachers, coworkers, nurses at the health posts, and physicians, often more than once. In San Alejo I had the opportunity to converse several times with an older, respected man from a well-to-do family who provided me with a great deal of information. In the text I refer to him as the self-appointed historian of San Alejo. This man and two nurses and a physician at the health post became good sounding boards for my thoughts and reflections about life in San Alejo in general.

An important aspect of the initial stages of my fieldwork, which I retained for the duration of the study, was alternating my research stints between the two towns.[14] I would stay one week in San Alejo, go to the Altiplano for one week, return to San Alejo for another week, and so on. This back-and-forth approach was key to helping me develop some of the most important points in this project. It allowed me to compare, contrast, reflect, and rethink what I heard from the ladinas in light of what the Maya women, who lived in the epicenter of direct, political violence, were telling me. I was not looking for the *same* or even *similar* kinds of violence in the ladinas' lives, or seeking to compare "rates" of violence, but the accounts of the Maya women helped me to retrieve the violence in the narratives of the ladinas.[15] Given their importance in the development of my argument and my overall framework, comparisons with the women in the Altiplano are mentioned throughout the book.

To ensure that the focus of this book would be the town in Oriente and to avoid the impression that this is a fully comparative study that devotes equal time and treatment to women in both contexts, I decided to give a specific (fictitious) name to the eastern town (San Alejo) and use the general name of the highland region, Altiplano, for the town that is not as salient in my analysis but that affords me a key comparative lens. I am fully aware that ladinas also live in the Altiplano and that Mayas also live in Oriente and that it is complicated to equate geographic regions with social groups so neatly. My references to the fieldwork in the Altiplano should serve as a reminder of the essential place of that region in how I approached the study of violence in Oriente. Just as the rich literature about the Altiplano has influenced my thinking about violence in Guatemala, my own observations there shaped my reflections on violence in women's lives in Oriente.

I follow the same logic in giving pseudonyms to my study participants; I assigned a fictitious name to each of the women I interviewed (and with whom I remained in contact throughout my study in both towns) to protect their confidentiality. But I did not give a name to others in their families (e.g., mothers, daughters, husbands, sons), unless I also interviewed them.[16] As in a photograph, this strategy helped me to include key figures in the women's lives in the analytic picture while keeping the focus on my study participants. And I use only first names for the women. Thus I do not use the customary honorific *doña,* which I did use throughout my fieldwork, regardless of the women's age or social position. In the field, but only when the women requested it, I later used only the more informal first names, as it sometimes became a bit awkward to continue to use the formal salutation in our conversations.

I was careful to include women from different socioeconomic backgrounds in San Alejo (and to some degree in the Altiplano, too). This approach allowed me an invaluable vantage point to examine how the combined effects of social class and gender inequalities operated in the women's lives, as well as to grasp the workings of orthodox gender ideologies that cut across social class. Thus both the comparisons by ethnicity between San Alejo and the Altiplano and the comparisons by class in San Alejo were key to helping me sharpen my analytic vision and the arguments I present here.

Why, several colleagues and friends have asked, if I collected data on the Altiplano did I not write about violence in the lives of women there. They gave compelling reasons for doing so, including the fact that the undisputed atrocities against the Maya deserve the attention of many more scholars. Others said that the Guatemalan Oriente is a place that does not offer much in terms of analysis. "It's boring over there," a Guatemalan colleague said with a touch of disappointment when I told her where I was going to do fieldwork. However, she added something that planted a seed of curiosity in my head: "It's crazy out there. No laws there, only *la ley del muy macho* [the law of the very macho]. Be careful, OK? It's our Wild West out there." "Yes, the Guatemalan

Wild West is in the east," she added with a chuckle. Another colleague explained that the Maya had an amazingly rich culture and that I should study their traditions instead.[17] "Besides," a friend noted, "it's too hot and dusty in Oriente." These perceptions about the Guatemalan Oriente sometimes have a base in reality. For instance, Moran-Taylor (2008: 80) describes the region in Oriente where she did fieldwork as hot, dry, and characterized by large estates, cattle ranches, and *machista* values. At the same time, images of Guatemala's Oriente as the polar opposite of the highlands might serve to perpetuate the indigenous-ladino bipolarity and to accept the differences between the two groups as natural and immutable and not as socially constructed (see Tarracena Arriola et al. 2002: 38). Arguments that Guatemala's political violence occurred in the Altiplano while the violence of "common" crime occurred in Oriente build on this geographic bipolarity to construct an image of these types of violence as different and independent of each other, obscuring the deep links that exist between the two. In the end, perhaps because only a couple of colleagues seemed encouraging about my fieldwork in eastern Guatemala, I decided to focus my energy on learning more about women's lives there.[18] Thus my work sometimes conforms to the often stereotypical notions of Oriente as chaotic and violent; but it also challenges these images by pointing to the complexity and diversity of social life in this understudied region. And though my focus is the lives of the ladinas, my work also illuminates important aspects of how Maya women live with and experience old and new forms of violence in their everyday lives.

The town of San Alejo has a largely homogeneous ladino population, but the southeastern department of Jalapa where it is located has sizable minorities of K'iche' and Pokomam Maya, among other Maya groups. My fieldwork in the Altiplano took place in the western department of Chimaltenango, a predominantly Maya region with ladino concentrations in some *municipios* (townships), but the town in which I did fieldwork was overwhelmingly Kaqchikel Maya. The towns were roughly equal in terms of population size, and agricultural production was the main form of employment. Indeed, they were selected for inclusion in the larger study based on their comparability. Since details of the women's lives are key to making my points, I did not alter their stories, unless they compromised the women's confidentiality. Instead, I give fewer details about the towns themselves, to make them (I trust) unrecognizable and therefore provide whatever protection I can to my study participants' privacy.

As it is customarily expected in research that involves in-depth interviews, field observations, and long-term interaction with study participants, I offer a brief account of how I think I was perceived and my position vis-à-vis my interlocutors. No doubt, my study participants' perceptions of me provided the contour for the nature and content of our conversations and my work.

The project in which I participated initially was housed in Guatemala at the Instituto de Nutrición de Centro América y Panamá (Central America and Panama Institute for Nutrition, INCAP). In the towns where I did the research for this project, my first visits were to the authorities (mayors and public officials) to ask for their permission to conduct fieldwork. I then met with the employees at the health post, since the project's objective was to look for women with children at home to see what they did when they or their children were ill. From that point, I started to contact individual women, whom I approached as part of the project. Although I explained that I was there to study what mothers did when they or their children were ill, some people knew me as someone who was interested in children (even as I would correct misperceptions). But in San Alejo I conveyed an additional image: because I concentrated on speaking with women and spoke with men only in the presence of women and because I also talked with pastors and priests and attended religious services, I came to be perceived as a "religious" worker. A woman told me that this was the case because I always walked around accompanied by my assistant, a Guatemalan, dressed "decently" (no pants, no jewelry, no makeup, long skirt) and was not interested in approaching men. Although I always corrected this impression, it persisted for some time.

Language and ethnicity also work in interesting ways. In the Altiplano, because I do not speak Kaqchikel, I was able to speak only with the women who could communicate in Spanish. My native fluency in Spanish obviously would not offset my lack of knowledge of Kaqchikel in the Altiplano, but in San Alejo it led to an interesting dynamic. There people would immediately detect that though I was a native speaker, I was not from the region. They would politely ask me if I was "Central American" or, more often, "de por aquí" (from around here), though a few correctly guessed my Salvadoran origin at first try. In my initial visits a couple of women told me that I should not, at least at first, be too open about my Salvadoran origin.[19] "Salvadoran women," one woman noted, "with my respect to you, because you are decent, do not have very good reputations around here." "You see," the woman who ran the health post explained, "this is embarrassing for me to tell you, but I have to. There have been many [female] compatriots of yours who have passed through here [on their way North] who have not behaved properly. Some have gotten involved with men, married men and like that, you know, and everybody now thinks that all Salvadoran women are prostitutes. It pains me to tell you, but don't feel bad. As the saying goes, 'De todo hay en la viña del Señor' [In God's vineyard one can find good and bad]." She went on to explain that two Salvadoran sex workers who were supposedly infected with AIDS had just passed through. "Even on the radio they were announcing that two Salvadoran prostitutes were going around infecting men with AIDS. So just try not to speak like a Salvadoran," she warned, "at least not at first."

Thus what I had thought would be my language advantage, at least initially, proved a challenge for me. As I got to know people and they got to know me, I began to disclose my origins little by little. To my surprise, however, I discovered that most had already figured out where I was from, quite easily actually, but had also decided that I had "no bad intentions" and that I was "respectable" and "decent" because no one ever saw me "behaving improperly" with men. This, of course, has to do with gendered expectations about how women should behave and also with how gendered ideologies restrict women's freedom of movement in social spaces.

I suppose I was an outsider/insider in San Alejo. I was perceived as an outsider because of my national origin, sometimes prompting people to explain certain things to me in detail, such as wedding customs or certain ways to cook a dish, or to tell me a joke about Salvadorans (women would invariably stop men from sharing jokes about Salvadoran women with me; "No, not to her," they would say). But I was viewed as an insider because of my ethnicity. I was identified as a ladina, perhaps as one of them, and the result of this identification could be noticed in some of the subtleties in the conversations we had but also sometimes more overtly. In fact, two women told me that because I "looked" Guatemalan and at times even "sounded" like one when I inadvertently spoke with a similar accent or used a Guatemalan colloquialism in my speech, I would probably be expected to behave in certain ways, like someone "from here, not from other [places], like a gringa; one knows that they behave more, like, more open, more libertine."[20] Dorinne Kondo (1990) noted similar experiences while doing fieldwork in Tokyo.

In the Altiplano, where I was seen as another outsider, people seemed more familiar with researchers and other types of foreign visitors, such as the Americans and Europeans who worked in the textile cooperatives or church missions or researchers doing work similar to what I was doing. I became close with two families, especially with Flor, a well-known woman who also worked at the health post, and her extended family. When my husband came to visit me, they had a small gathering and took the opportunity to feed us, joke, laugh, tease me, and even dress me in their *traje* (traditional clothing) for a photo with their entire family. When I had visitors I always took them to meet these families as a sign of respect but also so that these families could get a glimpse of who I was and meet my loved ones as well. In the end, I trust that in both towns I was able to converse easily with the women and others in a respectful, open manner.

ORGANIZATION OF THE BOOK

In chapter 2 I present my conceptual framework for studying violence and begin to introduce study participants as I lay out each component of the framework so as to illustrate the different forms of violence and the normalization of each form. This is the only chapter of the book in which I discuss each of the different forms of violence that I examine separately, and I do so only for analytic clarity. Starting with chapter 3 and continuing through chapter 7, I present different spheres of the women's everyday lives in which the diverse forms of violence coalesce and are normalized. But it is important to note that in real life these occur simultaneously. In order to dissect each sphere of life analytically, I unfurl each linearly in the chapters ahead. And I do so according to a certain order.

Chapter 3 begins with a consideration of the closest, most intimate sphere, the body. I examine how women experience in their bodies the violence that comes from structural inequalities and unequal access to health care and other resources, as well as from the gender ideologies that constrain their lives. This account includes various forms of illnesses and the ways in which the women deal with them. Chapter 3 also presents an examination of the social control of the body, exemplified in the strict control of women's movement that comes from orthodox gender ideologies. Chapters 4 and 5 deal with immediate aspects of the women's home lives, such as marriage and children. Chapter 4 presents a semichronological sequence of marriage, beginning with courtship, and includes an examination of alcoholism, infidelity, and interpersonal abuse, a tripartite source of violence that has become so bound up with constructs of maleness that it is seen as natural (Hume 2008). Chapter 5 is devoted to children, also following a semichronological progression that starts out with pregnancy, continues with childbirth and the care of children, and ends with child deaths. Each aspect traces the links between the individuals' actions and perceptions and the structures of violence that shape lives. Chapters 6 and 7 discuss aspects of life outside the home, such as work, church, and religion. I do not mean to draw a strict division between what is private and what is public in women's lives; as we know well, productive and reproductive spheres are not so clearly demarcated. Indeed, it is in this light that I include two chapters on what some may see as public spheres but are not presented as such in my analysis. The private is very much part of life beyond the home and vice versa, and these chapters help to dissolve the perceived strict demarcations. Examining life in the areas of work and church and religion, away from the intimacy of the home, allows us to see how violence is embedded in structures and social relations and actively normalized beyond the home. Chapter 6 deals with meanings that women (and others in the family) attach to women's work outside the home and the opportunities that such work presents for sociability, but it also shows the workplace as a site that highlights the insecurity of life and sources of suffering. Chapter 7 discusses the place of religion and the church in the women's lives, presenting information not only on how the women perceive this area of life but also on how religious spaces end up normalizing the reality of their suffering, providing succor but through doing so maintaining structures the way they are. In chapter 8 I place my observations about violence in Guatemala in a broader context, linking them to more open, recognizable forms, such as the current wave of feminicide in the country.

CHAPTER 2

A Framework for Examining Violence

People say that before the fighting we had peace. But what do you call peace? The war begins at the psychological level, in the plantations, where every day we were dying a little bit, every day we were consuming ourselves.

—Guatemalan peasant, quoted in Daniel Wilkinson, *Silence on the Mountain*

Es que la vida de una mujer es dura, Usted. Los hijos sirven de consuelo. A veces uno dice, "Ay Diosito, no me olvides, por favor ten piedad!" Pero es que así es la vida de uno, no?

[A woman's life is tough. Children are the consolation. Sometimes one says, "Oh, my little God, don't forget me, please have mercy!" But that's our life, no?]

—Woman in San Alejo

The first epigraph above points to the usefulness of opening up the analytic lens to examine instances of violence beyond those embodied in physical pain and injury, and the second brings up reflections on everyday violence in the world of the women I came to know. Both express the enduring reality of violence that crosses multiple spaces and spheres of life, and they elucidate the two aspects of violence I wish to examine in this book: the multifaceted character of violence and its expression in the quotidian lives of ladina women that contributes to its normalization.[1] Raka Ray and Seemin Qayum's (2009: 4) conceptualization of "normalized" as "legitimized ideologically such that domination, dependency, and inequality are not only tolerated but accepted" is useful here to convey what I mean by the normalization of violence. Although a neat compartmentalization of the multiple sources of suffering is rarely found in practice, here I disaggregate them for the purpose of presenting my analytic framework. Taken individually, the structural, symbolic, or gender forms of violence can be so general as to be visible anywhere, and they can be interpreted differently (e.g., structural violence can be taken as poverty); and each can arise in any number of situations. However, taking these forms of violence *as a whole,* in this context and from the angle I propose, allows us to see that they are mutually constituted. Paraphrasing James Gilligan (1996), the question of whether to disentangle the different forms to see which one is more dangerous is moot, as they are all related to one another. The approach I lay out also permits me to unveil a context of violence that shapes the lives of women in gender-specific ways and in a manner that exposes deep power inequalities. This approach reveals the systematic patterns of disadvantage that are neither natural nor necessary (cf. Kent 2006); or in Gilligan's (1996: 196) words, "not acts of God."

In establishing the links between violence at the interpersonal level with that which originates in broader structures, I seek analytic distance from individual-focused explanations or those that focus on "tradition" to elucidate the roots of violence in structures of power, away from personal circumstances.[2] Farmer (2003, 2004) warns against conflating poverty and cultural difference, for example; in his view, the linkage of assaults on human dignity to the cultural institutions of a particular society constitutes an abuse of cultural concepts. He (2004) then cautions that such an approach is especially insidious because cultural difference as a form of essentialism is used to explain suffering and assaults on dignity. Thus although it is important to interpret particular situations as forms of violence, it is equally significant to trace links to broader structures, lest we inflict even more harm on the vulnerable.

There are three considerations regarding my discussion of violence. First, the political economy of violence does not affect everyone in the same manner; violence weighs differently for those in dissimilar social positions. Women and men from different social classes and ethnic and racial backgrounds face dissimilar forms of violence and may experience the same violence in different ways. Thus class violence parallels sexual and ethnic violence, and these are often conflated in real life (Forster 1999: 59). Second, following the scholars on whose work I have built this framework, I argue that violence is not always an event, a palpable outcome that can be observed, reported, and measured. From the angle

I propose, violence constitutes a *process,* one that is embedded in the everyday lives of those who experience it. Third, as Torres-Rivas (1998: 48) observes, not all societies recognize the same things as violent, either in their origins or in their effects. Torres-Rivas's observation can be extended to researchers, for scholars often make use of different theoretical repertoires and frameworks to examine the same cases and thus do not assess them in the same manner. In Rashomonesque fashion, the same situation may be interpreted in a different light according to the lens used to examine it. In the rest of this chapter, I present one lens, one in which violence emerges as fundamental.[3] I present each of the components and end with a discussion of how they intertwine to affect life in a gender-specific fashion. As Martín-Baró (1991b: 334) noted, considering forms of social violence other than the political-military helps us to "arrive at a picture that is more complex but also more distressing." My portrayal of the lives of Guatemalan ladinas in this book, therefore, is not sanitized and should not be taken as culturally accusatory or as a careless characterization of an overly objectivized world.

STRUCTURAL VIOLENCE

Torres-Rivas (1998: 49) notes that structural violence (or structural repression) "is rooted in the uncertainty of everyday life caused by the insecurity of wages or income, a chronic deficit in food, dress, housing, and health care, and uncertainty about the future which is translated into hunger and delinquency, and a barely conscious feeling of failure. . . . It is often referred to as structural violence because it is reproduced in the context of the market, in exploitative labor relations, when income is precarious and it is concealed as underemployment, or is the result of educational segmentation and of multiple inequalities that block access to success." And for Farmer (2003: 40), "the term is apt because such suffering is 'structured' by historically given (and often economically driven) processes and forces that conspire . . . to constrain agency."

An important feature of structural violence, Kent (2006: 55) observes, is that "it is not visible in specific events." Structural violence is "exerted systematically, that is, indirectly by everyone who belongs to a certain social order" (Farmer 2004: 307). Indeed, in Johan Galtung's (1969) classic work, the differentiating aspect between direct and structural violence is that in the second there is no identifiable actor who does the harming, so that "violence is built into the structure and shows up as unequal power and consequently as unequal life chances" (171). For him, direct violence comes from harmful acts of individuals that leave physical scars, whereas structural violence is not observable and is the result of a process. Thus, in contrast to direct, physical violence, structural violence causes people to suffer harm indirectly, often through a slow and steady process. But it is easier to see direct violence (Kent 2006); and when violence is a by-product of our social and economic structure, and it is invisible, it is hard to care about it (Gilligan 1996). As Galtung (1990) observed, for some people, malnutrition and lack of access to goods and services do not amount to violence because they do not result in killings, but for the weakest in society, such shortfalls amount to a slow death. An examination of the ills that afflict the poor from this vantage point highlights how a political economy of inequality under neoliberal capitalism promotes social suffering. As Miguel Ángel Vite Pérez (2005) observes, when trying to understand how individuals become unemployed one must focus on how neoliberal economic regimes have led to labor instability, to the commodification of public services, and to a precarious situation that engenders poverty rather than focus just on someone's inability to keep a job.

Structural violence as expressed in unemployment, layoffs, unequal access to goods and services, and exploitation has an impact on a range of social relations in multiple forms, including those that lead to the formation of social capital, a point I developed in fieldwork among Salvadoran immigrants in San Francisco (Menjívar 2000). Kleinman (2000: 238) argues, "Through violence in social experience, as mediated by cultural representations, . . . the ordinary lives of individuals are also shaped, and all too often twisted, bent, even broken." And as Bourdieu (1998: 40) noted, "The structural violence exerted by financial markets, in the form of layoffs, loss of security, etc., is matched sooner or later in the form of suicides, crime and delinquency, drug addiction, alcoholism, a whole host of minor and major everyday acts of violence." The broader political economy does not *cause* violence directly, but one must understand the extent to which it conditions structures within which people suffer and end up inflicting harm on one another and distorting social relations (see also Bourgois 2004a).[4]

While it is crucial to acknowledge the devastating effects of neoliberal structural adjustment policies initiated by the International Monetary Fund (IMF) in Latin America that have resulted in sharp and unprecedented levels of poverty (see Auyero 2000; Auyero and Swistun 2009), it must be noted that what the region is experiencing is the cumulative effects of disadvantage in a much longer historical process. Economic vulnerability is a part of this process rather than a condition or state, and this process is cumulative, dynamic, and relational (see Auyero 2000). Thus Guatemalans' current living conditions are hardly the result of a few decades of neoliberal reforms.

Latin America historically has exhibited a high degree of income inequality relative to other regions; it has the most unbalanced distribution of resources of all regions in the world (Hoffman and Centeno 2003).[5] And Guatemala has consistently ranked among the most unequal, even by Latin American standards. The richest 10 percent of Guatemalans earn 43.5 percent of the country's total income, whereas the poorest 30 percent earn 3.8 percent (World Bank 2006). In 1998 Guatemala's Gini Index was 55.8, five years later it was 58, and in 2002 it was 55.1, which indicates that inequality rates remained stable over time. As an aggregate measure of inequality, the Gini Index does not detect levels of absolute poverty. For instance, between 1990 and 2001, 16 percent of Guatemalans lived on less than $1 per day and approximately 37.4 percent on less than $2 per day (UNDP 2003), meaning that about half of Guatemalans live under $2 a day. Guatemala also holds the dubious distinction of having one of the two most exploitative and coercive rural class structures in Central America (the other one is El Salvador), with high rural poverty and inequality and high levels of unequal landownership (Brockett 1991: 62–70). Whereas 3 percent of landholdings control 65 percent of the agricultural surface, close to 90 percent of the landholdings are too small for peasant subsistence (Manz 2004: 16). Such disparities vary by ethnicity and location. Thus 58 percent of Guatemalans nationally lived in poverty in 1989, while 72 percent did so in rural areas, a proportion that dropped to 56 percent nationally in 2002 but rose to 75 percent in rural areas the same year (World Bank 2006). And although the majority of ladinos are poor and lack access to basic services, the Maya are even poorer and disproportionately disadvantaged. And in spite of development programs aimed at reducing the poverty gap, inequality has increased in Guatemala.[6]

Structural violence also comes in the form of a sweatshop economy that exacerbates gendered vulnerabilities. In a careful examination of the effects of sweatshop *(maquila)* employment in Guatemala, María José Paz Antolín and Amaia Pérez Orozco (2001) discuss the psychological violence that takes place in the maquila, with serious consequences for the workers, including loss of self-esteem. According to the authors, this situation creates a belief among the women that it is their fault that they do not have more education, and thus they blame themselves for their precarious situation. Indeed, the women with whom I spoke in San Alejo were well aware of the benefits that education can bring, but due to the need for their labor in their families many had been forced to abandon school early or not to attend at all. However, they pointed to themselves or their families as culpable for their lack of education and diminished potential for success in life. The average years of schooling for adults in Guatemala is three and a half years, even though the duration of compulsory education is eleven years, and the literacy rate for men in 2002 was 75 percent and for women 63 percent (World Bank 2006). Education and level of poverty are related; by the Guatemalan government's own estimates, more than 95 percent of the poor have had no secondary education, and 44 percent have never attended school at all (Manz 2004: 16–17).[7]

Nine of the thirty women I interviewed in San Alejo had never attended school. Some had learned how to sign their names or to read simple words, a couple had attended adult literacy classes, and another nine had only attended elementary school. They cited their parents, other relatives, or themselves as the reason they had not acquired more schooling. It is only by tracing the links to the profoundly unequal access to education and resources that one can turn attention to the root of this lack of opportunities. Hortencia, the mother of five whom I mentioned in chapter 1, explained why she never attended school:

> Because my *papa* was a *mujeriego* [womanizer] and a drunk and my *mama* suffered a lot with him so they never sent me to school. I had to help her. I learned in the *alfabetización* [literacy classes] how to read and write, and now I have even written letters to the United States for other people who don't know how to write [she smiles and her eyes light up]! The other day my *compadre* [lit., "co-father"; co-parent] came by so I could help him calculate how old he is because he needed to go get his *cédula* [ID card]. Ay, the shame of having to learn how to read and write as an adult . . . one feels bad, ashamed. I was very embarrassed, but in time I learned.

While Hortencia saw her father as responsible for her illiteracy, one must recognize that access to education in rural Guatemala when she was growing up was a privilege, not a right, especially for poor women. Not everyone could attend school, and since the town had only a primary school, many who did attend stopped at the sixth grade; only the few with more means traveled to the city to continue beyond the sixth grade. Thus blocked educational opportunities and illiteracy are expressions of the structural violence that assaults the lives of the poor. However, some women of more means noted that the poor (or the children of the poor) do not attend school because they are "lured" to work, not forced to work, as women from poor backgrounds explained. Lucía, a teacher, said:

> The children work too much. People cultivate tomatoes in this area, and the kids go to harvest them and then don't go to school. Instead they go to a literacy course in the afternoons. You see lots of patojos, young ones, congregated outside those centers [for literacy classes]. Instead of wanting an education, they want to earn money. Oh yes, they are poor and need money, but they don't want the education. No, really, believe me, they just don't want to be educated, otherwise they would go to school, don't you think? As a teacher, it pains me to see how kids go for money and not their future. But it's all the parents' fault.

Other women were more elaborate in their assessments, but most explanations ended up blaming the poor for their predicament, adding insult to injury. Ofelia, a receptionist, explained, "You see, they [the poor] have many children, so their money is never enough. You know why? Because there is no family planning. Well, there is, but the *gente humilde* [lit. "humble people," meaning the poor] don't accept it, and they prefer to have as many children as God sends them. So it's because of their beliefs that they end up worsening their own situation, right?"

The majority of the women with whom I spoke in San Alejo mentioned situations they faced in their daily lives that highlight structural violence and the normalization of inequality. Several women talked about the effects of the unequal land distribution system, couching their reflections in a framework of the ordinary, explaining multiple forms of exploitation as the way things were. In San Alejo women do not work the land directly (they can participate in the harvest), but the men do, and they do so through an exploitative land tenure system. Many are landless and rent land from landowners through a contract called *medianía,* which implies "half and half" but is hardly that. As it was explained to me, the landowner provides the land and the renter tills it and supplies everything else—seeds, fertilizer, and workers to harvest the crop. Then the landowner and the renter supposedly share the crop. Such a system lends itself to multiple forms of abuse, and it is risky for the renter but not for the landowner.This system exemplifies what Galtung (1990) conceptualizes as the archetypal structure of violence.

Many women brought up the injurious consequences inherent in the system. Sometimes their partners were hired to work the land but were cheated and not paid after the harvest, losing money that was earmarked for other purposes, including medicine and food. Mirna, twenty-eight years old and the mother of five, complained that the landowner with whom her husband worked would deduct money for everything needed to work the land, leaving them with Q.100 (about $15 in 1997) per month in profits. She had to use some of this money to feed the twelve laborers who helped her husband, even when she was eight months' pregnant. In the case of Leticia, when her partner fell ill from HIV/AIDS they had to sell half of a tiny plot of land so that he could afford his checkups in the capital. After he died, she found out she also was infected, and she sold the other half of the plot to pay for her own checkups. In her last year of life she was tormented about being unable to leave any land, or even a small adobe structure, to her young daughters. When she was already ill, one of the few ways she could make a living was picking tomatoes in the fields, but even this became difficult toward the end because others in town knew of her illness and some potential employers did not want any contact with her. As the women recounted these stories, they presented them as the way things were, normalizing the relationship between those who own the land and those who till it, only occasionally insinuating how exploitative this "natural order of things" was.[8] Not surprisingly, when I spoke with the women whose families owned the land, their stories conveyed the other half of the picture, naturalizing the narratives of exploitation I heard from poor women.

POLITICAL VIOLENCE AND STATE TERROR

For thirty-six years, from 1960 to 1996, political violence and state terror were the order of the day in Guatemalan society. During this time politically motivated violence became an integral part of the functioning, governance, and maintenance of the state (Falla 1994; Jonas 2000; Nelson 1999). Violence and terror, epitomized in public assassinations, ruthless massacres, and unsolved disappearances, became the favored political tools for Guatemala's military and political elites (McCleary 1999, cited in Torres 2005). Politically motivated violence was so successful during Guatemala's reign of terror that it came to be known as a "cultural fact," as somehow "natural" and "cultural" (Nordstrom 1997; Sluka 2000; Torres 2005). The Guatemalan anthropologist M. Gabriela Torres (2005: 143–44) notes that "the naturalization of political violence into a cultural fact was produced, in part, through the creation and promotion of a language or pattern of political violence that—while it generated terror—at the same time obfuscated the political economy of its own production."

Until 1980 the targets of state terror were primarily ladinos—students, peasants, union organizers, politicians, and revolutionaries—and in the 1960s and 1970s the state-sponsored violence had an urban character (Godoy-Paiz 2008). But in 1981 the army launched its scorched earth campaign against Maya communities.[9] Throughout this period ladinos continued to be killed, but the atrocities committed against the Maya, described as ethnocide or genocide, targeted "Indians as Indians" (Grandin 2000: 16). The widespread and systematic nature of this slaughter arguably reached the threshold of crimes against humanity. As an intricate aspect of a regional political structure in which U.S. political interests have weighed heavily (Menjívar and Rodríguez 2005), in 1954 the U.S. government orchestrated the overthrow of democratically elected Jacob Arbenz Guzmán and installed a military regime that would govern the country, in various guises, for the next several decades. Successive U.S. administrations supported this regime as it engaged in widespread human rights violations, providing training and support for the Guatemalan army's counterinsurgency operations (Manz 2004; Menjívar and Rodríguez 2005). According to the 1999 report of the U.N.-sponsored Truth Commission, formally known as the Comisión para el Esclarecimiento Histórico (CEH; Historical Clarification Commission), the state responded to both the insurgency and the civil movements with unimaginable repression, repression that climaxed in 1981–82 with a bloodbath in which the army committed over six hundred massacres (Sanford 2008: 19). It tortured, murdered, and was responsible for the disappearance of more than 200,000 Guatemalans (mostly Mayas); it destroyed 626 villages, and hundreds of thousands were displaced internally and internationally (Parenti and Muñoz 2007; Sanford 2008).

Although ladino communities were not targeted in the scorched earth campaigns, there are ways in which the general political violence led to the normalization of violence, distorting social relations and affecting life in ladino communities as well. The breadth and depth of state-sponsored terror reached all Guatemalans in one way or another, for one of the most destructive aspects of state terror in Guatemala was the widespread reliance on civilians to kill other civilians (Ball, Kobrak, and Spirer 1999), as well as the strategic dissemination of gruesome killings in the media. Thus the political violence that claimed many lives and destroyed communities in the Altiplano was so pervasive that it engulfed the entire country. Writing about the insidious effects of the militarization of life in El Salvador, Martín-Baró (1991c: 311–12) stated, "The militarization of daily life in the main parts of the social world contributes to the omnipresence of overpowering control and repressive threats. . . . This is how an atmosphere of insecurity is fostered, unpredictable in its consequences, and demanding of people a complete submission to the dictates of power." He referred to this phenomenon as the "militarization of the human mind" (1991b: 341). In such contexts, to paraphrase Cynthia Enloe (2000), lives become militarized not only through direct means and exposure but also when militarized products, views, and attitudes are taken as natural and unproblematic (see also Green 1999). Even if concrete expressions of political violence differ in degree, tactics, and expression, the broad effects cannot be contained or isolated in one geographic area when the state iself is the chief perpetrator. As Galtung (1990: 294) observed, "A violent structure leaves marks not only on the human body but also on the mind and the spirit." It was this kind of political violence, created and spread through state structures, that reached, in one way or another, everyone in Guatemala.

Political violence is linked to other forms of violence, including interpersonal violence in the home (itself linked to symbolic violence) and what is referred to as "common crime." Douglas Hay (1992) notes the reciprocal relationship between violence from the state and violence in private spheres. And referring to a chain of political violence, Jennifer Turpin and Lester Kurtz (1997) note the interrelated causes of violence at the micro- and macrolevels, such that the violence that occurs in intimate relations is connected to the violence that occurs between ethnic groups, which in turn is linked to global patterns of interstate wars, because the same mechanisms sustain them. Understanding the links between the different manifestations of violence, they argue, is a key step toward addressing the causes.

Thus the cruelty with which certain assaults such as robberies and burglaries are sometimes committed in the context of common crime cannot be examined independently of the violence engendered by state terror, as Taussig (2005) has observed for the case of Colombia. Often, acts of common crime are characterized by the same brutality and professionalization with which acts associated with political violence are carried out. Torres-Rivas (1998: 49) notes that the criminogenic conditions of postwar violence can be examined in the context of power and state violence: "The bad example of the use of violence on the part of the state is then imitated by the citizens." "Common criminals" adopt strategies similar to those used by the state (the same individuals may be engaged in both), and, as posited by examinations using brutalization frameworks (see Kil and Menjívar 2006), individuals who commit common crimes mimic the state as it metes out punishments on enemies or dissidents. The violence of common crime therefore is not dissociated from state-sponsored political violence.[10] However, as Snodgrass Godoy (2006:25) notes, "The depoliticization of crime [is] among the hallmarks of neoliberal governance in our insecure world[,] . . . most starkly sketched in settings of extreme marginality."

The effects of political violence, then, are seldom contained in a specific geographic area, among the members of only a targeted group, or in only one aspect of life. It is not surprising therefore that the ladinas with whom I spoke did not openly question the taken-for-granted world of violence that surrounded them, conveyed daily in newspapers, on television, and along the roads. Regular images and stories of gruesome deaths created a climate of insecurity and continuous alert (the "nervous system," in Taussig's [1992] conceptualization) in eastern Guatemala as well, and it was "part of life." Moving the analytic lens from the Altiplano, where political violence has been well documented and acknowledged, to eastern Guatemala, where for the most part it has not, unearths the breadth and depth of the project of state terror that engulfed, with varying degrees of force and visibility, the entire country.

Torres (2005) argues that in the process of making violence quotidian, "natural," and "cultural," the Guatemalan Armed Forces relied on a discourse expressed in the patterned and continuous appearance of cadaver reports and articulated through both the signs of torture left on bodies and the strategy of displaying the reports. Mutilated bodies left on the sides of roads and the unidentifiable victims of torture were meant to send a message to the living. Victims of terror "disappeared" from their normal existence, making the disappearance itself a powerful message of what awaited those who contemplated sympathizing with the opposition (Menjívar and Rodríguez 2005). The innocent bystanders who witnessed abductions or discovered a tortured body on a road got the message, one that was carefully and strategically broadcast in the media (Torres 2005). Although such sightings are associated with the Altiplano, they were not uncommon in other parts of Guatemala.

These observations are not meant to suggest that the entire country experienced state terror in the same way or to lessen the atrocities committed against the Maya in the Altiplano; on the contrary, they underscore the reach of the political violence suffered in Guatemala. As scholars have documented for the Altiplano, relatives of the disappeared who never saw their loved ones again live with the torment of not knowing if these relatives were in fact killed. Rosita, whom I interviewed in the Altiplano, would cry whenever she tried to explain what it meant to have had her husband disappear fourteen years earlier. On one occasion she told me, "I live wondering, will he come back one day? How about for our daughter's fifteen-year celebration? Every Christmas, every New Year's, every birthday, I wonder if he will come back. Sometimes I almost go crazy. Why did they [government army] not return his body to me? Why such cruelty? I think my torture will last all my life." Filita, on the other hand, explained that her father was killed right in front of her and her siblings rather than having been disappeared and noted that this had been a consolation to the family because at least they could give him a proper burial. Only in the brutality of Guatemala's reign of terror could the killing of a father in front of his children serve as consolation. The women I interviewed in San Alejo did not have similar experiences, but this kind of violence often loomed in the background of their assessments and perspectives.

As the project of state violence reached all corners of the country in different ways, the militarization of life was evident beyond the Altiplano; it materialized in soldiers and military vehicles on roads even in areas that were supposed to be far from the "conflict" zones, such as in San Alejo. The military presence there served as an eerie reminder that violence was never far or contained in just one area, and thus everyone could be "at risk." Military violence was not separated in a black-and-white geographic mapping because the repressive state could reach anyone, anywhere, any time, and the reminders of this were ubiquitous. One day as my assistant, our driver, and I were on the main road leading to San Alejo, we saw there was commotion, and traffic was slow in a large town we were supposed to pass through. A crowd was lined up on the sides of a semipaved road; it looked as if they were waiting for a pageant to go by, and I did not want to miss it. To my surprise, I saw a convoy of U.S. military vehicles, Humvees too wide for the narrow roads of the town. People had come out of their homes to look at how these massive vehicles almost touched the houses on both sides of the road as they maneuvered their way through town. The military presence felt as huge as those vehicles in that narrow road, and I wondered about the need to establish such a presence even in this region of Guatemala. I was told that a military presence—both Guatemalan and U.S.—was in fact routine; the reason people were watching that day was out of curiosity. I asked a small group of people what this was all about, and a man said, "It's the gringos. They are on their way to fix the roads around here." "So they have come to help?" I ventured to ask. The man smiled, shrugged his shoulders, shook his head slightly, and simply responded, "Saber" (Who knows). As Linda Green (2004: 187) observes, civic actions mixed with counterinsurgency strategies do "not negate the essential fact that violence is intrinsic to the military's nature and logic. Coercion is the mechanism that the military uses to control citizens even in the absence of war." The scene was troubling to me, but for the town dwellers and everyone in the region, accustomed to such sightings, it was life as usual. As Green (2004: 187) continues, in Guatemala "language and symbols are utilized to normalize a continued army presence."

The end of the armed conflict has not resulted in an absence of violence, and in fact new modalities have emerged. Death threats, attacks, kidnappings, and acts of intimidation are a daily occurrence in "postwar" Guatemala.[11] Mutilated bodies are still found on the sides of roads, kidnappings occur regularly, people live in fear, and there are guns and security forces in places where people conduct their daily lives—challenging conventional assumptions about what it means to live in "peacetime." All this is exacerbated by the impunity that has been the hallmark of the postwar regime; many of those responsible for human rights violations have entered politics and have even been elected to public offices (Menjívar and Rodríguez 2005).

EVERYDAY VIOLENCE, INTERPERSONAL VIOLENCE, AND CRIME

Everyday violence refers to the daily practices and expressions of violence on a micro-interactional level, such as interpersonal, domestic, and delinquent (Bourgois 2004a: 428). I borrow the concept from Philippe Bourgois to focus on the routine practices and expressions of interpersonal aggression that serve to normalize violence at the micro-level.[12] This concept focuses attention on "the individual lived experience that normalizes petty brutalities and terror at the community level and creates a common sense or ethos of violence" (Bourgois 2004a: 426). Analytically, the concept helps to avoid explaining individual-level confrontations and expressions of violence, such as "common" crime and domestic violence, through psychological or individualistic frameworks. Instead, this prism links these acts to broader structures of inequality that promote interpersonal violence. As Alejandro Portes and Bryan Roberts (2005) note, increasing trends of inequality are very much associated with rising crime in Latin America (see also Torres 2008), even if precise causality cannot always be established. Indeed, Portes and Roberts (2005: 76) note, "from a sociological standpoint, the reaction of some of society's most vulnerable members in the form of unorthodox means to escape absolute and relative deprivation is predictable." From this angle one can trace the violence of common crime to structural and political violence, as well as to the creation of a "culture of terror" that normalizes violence in the private and public spheres, and can begin to understand how those who experience it end up directing their brutality against themselves rather than against the structures that oppress them (see Bourgois 2004a, 2004b).

Thus the most immediate threat in postwar Guatemala in the eyes of Guatemalan women and men is common crime, and today there is gang-related crime everywhere, from the capital to the countryside (see Manz 2004). Guatemala's homicide rate is one of the highest in the hemisphere, and it has escalated annually. In 2001 there were 3,230 homicides; in 2005, 5,338 (Procuraduría de Derechos Humanos [PDH], in Sanford 2008: 24). If the rate continues to increase, Sanford (2008) notes, there will be more deaths in the first twenty-five "postwar" years than in all the thirty-six years of "wartime." In an unsettling situation (also observed in other postconflict societies), street youth in Guatemala, the criminalized young women and men often referred to as *maras* (gangs) because their origins have been traced to a gang bearing that name, are often blamed for the high levels of crime. Public officials and the media offer these gangs as "explanations" for interpersonal violence and crime and make it seem necessary to "eliminate the maras," as a man in San Alejo once told me. Guatemala is not alone in this predicament. In his examination of the *"limpieza"* (cleansing) in Colombia, Michael Taussig (2005) notes the ease with which the seemingly random violence in postconflict societies is attributed to delinquent youth. My point here is that blaming poor young women and men for the postwar violence isolates the issue, a strategy that depoliticizes it (see Godoy-Paiz 2008) and muddles attempts to explain and understand it.

On a return visit three years after I first went to the Altiplano, I happened to see an extraordinary image: two girls, in their traditional traje, writing graffiti on a wall and then walking into a local arcade to play video games with their friends. In my conversations with people in town, I mentioned what I saw, and the talk quickly turned to crime. I was told that all the crime committed these days was the work of the maras, integrated by teenage boys and girls whose "parents don't know what the kids are doing." People were concerned because they used to hear about these activities in the capital but not in their town. Perhaps because of the military attacks this town suffered during the years of the violence, some of the town's residents were quick to link the militarization of life to the emergence of the maras. For example, Lita, a thirty-nine-year-old mother of three, observed, "Thanks to God, my husband didn't want to stay in the army any longer. Maybe he could have had a higher rank by now. But he wouldn't have been content with that and would have become a thief, because the more you have, the more you want. And the longer you stay in the army, the worse a person becomes. You learn how to pressure people to do what you want."

Paralleling Lita's assessment, the emergence of the maras in Guatemala, as well as in the rest of Central America, has been linked to the militarization of life during the years of political violence.[13] However, even if poverty and a recent political conflict are mentioned as factors behind the emergence and expansion of gangs in Central America (and of the violence we see today), it is interesting that it is the countries with a recent history of *state* violence (not just political conflict) that targeted their own people, such as Guatemala, El Salvador, and, to some degree, Honduras, where this seems to be the case. On the other hand, in Nicaragua, where there are similar conditions of poverty and recent political conflict but where the state was not involved in terrorizing its own citizens (in that conflict, the "Contra War," the government fought external aggression), youth gangs have not proliferated, and those that exist do not seem to be as violent as those in the other Central American countries.

Though I did not ask directly about violence in their lives, San Alejo women brought it up in our conversations, often in its direct, physical form, even when we were talking about aspects of their lives that seemed remote from the topic of violence. Sometimes they would mention instances of common crime that their friends and families had experienced; sometimes they would talk about how "easy it is to die" in their town. Yet at other times they would talk about additional sources of fear and suffering. It was surprising to me how easily and often this issue came up. In fact, the topic of direct violence made such an impression on me that in a field note entry in 1995 I wrote, "Almost everyone in this town seems to have had a relative killed. Everyone seems to own and use guns. Is it supposed to be this way here [in San Alejo]?" What I was trying to reconcile was that this was the region of Guatemala considered relatively peaceful, far from the Altiplano, where overt, direct forms of political violence were more likely to take place. Isabel mentioned that her brother had been shot and was recuperating. The incident reminded her of the time, two years earlier, when her uncle was shot and killed not far from where her brother had just been shot. She also mentioned a series of robberies and assaults on people close to her. She attributed such acts, like others did, to drunkenness, jealousy, and revenge. Similarly, when Teresa and I were talking about her family, she said, "These days my uncle is recuperating from a gunshot wound. Oh, he had a few drinks, you know how it is, then got his gun and shot himself in the leg." And Estrella, with a shrug of the shoulders, said, "There are always people being killed around here. Sometimes you walk around and see a crowd of people, and most of the time it's going to be someone killed in the street. Normally it's a *bolo* [drunk]." Isabel seemed a bit relieved when she said, "These days, it's only my brother"; no one else in her family had been assaulted recently. And Mirna was worried about a brother-in-law who drank too much; in the end, she said, anyone could be killed: "No one is safe. Such is life, one is here today and gone tomorrow, right?" Perhaps what seemed more startling to me was the element of ordinariness in the women's accounts. As Scheper-Hughes (1997: 483) notes, "The routinization of everyday violence against the poor leads them to accept their own violent deaths and those of their children as predictable, natural, cruel, but all too usual."

The topic of direct physical violence came up even when speaking with Lucrecia about the town's fiesta. We were having a lively conversation in the living room of her house about the music, the queens, the three days of festivities, the *bailes* (dances), when suddenly she said:

> Oh yes, for the fiestas *siempre hay muertos* [there are always dead people]. People drink too much. Oh God, there is always a *matazón* [widespread killings] during the fiestas. They kill each other. Well, this time, I don't know, I think there were only three or four dead. Not too many this year. In other years there are more, sometimes eight or nine. There will be at least some dead people during the fiestas. It's what happens during a fiesta, right?

During my last visits to San Alejo in 1999 and 2000, I heard gunshots almost every night. One evening a man brandishing a gun, chasing another man, ran past our street, and I was told to stay inside. I was left shaken, but my reaction made everyone laugh and tease me because I had made a big deal out of a guy running around with a gun. This experience and others corroborated the women's normalized descriptions of direct violence in their town. Again, this was postwar, "nonconflict," eastern Guatemala.

SYMBOLIC VIOLENCE AND THE INTERNALIZATION OF INEQUALITY

Symbolic violence, according to Bourdieu (2004), refers to the internalized humiliations and legitimations of inequality and hierarchy that range from sexism and racism to intimate expressions of class power. As Bourdieu and Loïc Wacquant (2004: 273) put it, "It is the violence which is exercised upon a social agent with his or her complicity." And, according to Bourgois (2004b), this violence is exercised through cognition and misrecognition, with the unwitting consent of the dominated. In this conceptualization, "the dominated apply categories constructed from the point of view of the dominant to the relations of domination, thus making it appear as natural. This can lead to systematic self-depreciation, even self-denigration" (Bourdieu 2004: 339). A key point in Bourdieu's conceptualization that captures a fundamental aspect of the case I examine here is that the everyday, normalized familiarity with violence renders it invisible, power structures are misrecognized, and the mechanisms through which it is exerted do not lie in conscious knowing.[14] According to Bourdieu:

> Symbolic violence is exercised only through an act of knowledge and practical recognition which takes place below the level of consciousness and will and which gives all its manifestations—injunctions, suggestions, seduction, threats, reproaches, orders, or calls to order—their "hypnotic power." But a relation of domination that functions only through the complicity of dispositions depends profoundly, *for its perpetuation or transformation*, on the perpetuation or transformation of the structures of which those dispositions are the product. (2004: 342; original emphasis)

Significantly, symbolic violence in the form of feelings of inadequacy, mutual recrimination, and exploitation of fellow victims diverts attention away from those responsible (e.g., the state and classes in power) for the conditions of violence in the first place (see Bourgois 2004a, 2004b). This theoretical angle allows us to capture how multiple inequalities, power structures, and denigrating social relations become internalized dispositions (Bourdieu's "habitus" [1984]) that organize practices and are unquestioned, misrecognized, accepted, and ultimately reproduced in everyday life. Bourdieu's key conceptualizatization, as it focuses on gender violence, constitutes my main framework for examining the different aspects of life of the women in San Alejo.

Symbolic violence is exerted in multiple forms of stratification, social exclusion, and oppression in Guatemala; as such, it is constitutive of other forms. I began to reflect on the insidiousness of structural violence and its links to the hidden injuries of symbolic violence when a female street vendor outside the city hall in San Alejo shooed away a barefoot blond boy (his blond hair was the result of extreme malnutrition) wearing a tattered Harvard Alumni T-shirt of undescribable color, because she thought he was bothering me when he asked me for food. He took a couple of steps back and looked afraid. The expression on my face led the woman to explain her actions and she assured me that it was okay to shoo him away, saying, "Ay, estos patojos son peor que animales, son como moscas, Usted" (Ah, these kids are worse than animals; they are like flies). At first I wondered why this woman, who did not look much better off than the patojo in question and had probably experienced hunger herself, could not feel compassion for him. As I thought about the incident I realized that it had more to do with the context of multifaceted violence in which both she and the boy lived than with the woman's lack of compassion. I had mistakingly interpreted this act. In a fashion similar to the initial reaction of Scheper-Hughes (1992) to the seeming indifference of the mothers to their infants' deaths and life chances in Bom Jesus do Alto, I was not initially aware of the inadequacy of my reading. To link this moment to the ravages of violence in the lives of this woman and this child required shifting from a focus on the individual interaction to the structures that give rise to and facilitate these forms of violent relations, and it parallels other examinations of dehumanization and objectification, such as Douglas Massey's (2007) discussion of the dehumanization of undocumented immigrants in the United States that opens up the way for inhumane treatment.

The women I met in the Altiplano had countless stories, many dealing with racism, about their experiences of symbolic violence in its overt forms. For instance, Lita's teenage daughter spoke about her life as a worker in Guatemala City, where ladinos often stare at her, scold her *(regañan),* and speak roughly to her, calling her *india,* just because she is a "*natural*" (the term Maya often use to refer to themselves).

Equally important to note is how such expressions of violence are internalized by the dominated and how the self is wounded under these conditions. Ivette, a thirty-year-old ladina in San Alejo, was married to a Maya man from the town in the Altiplano where I did research. Ivette wore fashionable clothes, always had her nails manicured, and had dyed her hair blond. We were talking about what life was like for her, as a ladina, in the Altiplano, and she said:

> Well, I live well here. Everyone speaks Kaqchikel around here and all the women wear traje. But my husband says that that's why he married me; he didn't want a woman with traje. In fact, he never had a girlfriend who wore traje. Yes, on purpose, he didn't want *una de traje* [a woman who wore traje, meaning a Maya]. And he doesn't want me to dress our daughter with traje. My sisters-in-law tell him to, but my husband doesn't like it; he thinks it's not in good taste.

The stories I heard in the Altiplano were disturbing and provided me with a small window onto how racism in Guatemala is experienced. In the Oriente I heard stories that show the other side of racism and support those I heard in the Altiplano. Comments in San Alejo usually came in the form of an outright racist statement about the Maya, or in the form of a joke (see Nelson 1999), or in a naturalized, normalized assertion (I return to this in chapter 7). On one occasion I was chatting with a couple of women in San Alejo on the steps of one of their homes, and the life and accomplishments of Rigoberta Menchú came up. With surprise, one of them explained what she thought about the Nobel Prize winner: "Right, she is not dumb. Because, you know, one thinks that the Indians are dumb, well, that's what one believes, right? But you'd be surprised. Many are not. Look at La Rigo [Rigoberta], *que chispuda salió* [how smart she turned out]."

However, in San Alejo I was stunned by stories of another form of symbolic violence that is also naturalized and misrecognized. I often heard the ladinas talk about their perceived inadequacies, their understanding of being "naturally" unequal to men, and how "as women" they knew "their place." Such expressions were so common that one hardly noticed them. These powerful and insidious forms of symbolic violence encapsulate Bourdieu and Wacquant's (2004: 272) conceptualization that, "being born in a social world, we accept a whole range of postulates, axioms, which go without saying and require no inculcating. . . . Of all the forms of 'hidden persuasion,' the most implacable is the one exerted, quite simply, by the *order of things*" (original emphasis). I discuss this form of violence under gender violence below, because for Bourdieu and Wacquant (2004) gender domination is the paradigmatic form of symbolic violence.

GENDER AND GENDERED VIOLENCE

I examine the different forms of gender violence that assault women's lives in San Alejo by borrowing from Lawrence Hammar (1999), from a Guatemalan team of social scientists who conducted a thorough study of gender and gendered violence in Guatemala (UNICEF-UNIFEM-OPS/OMS-FNUAP 1993), and from Bourdieu's work on gender violence. According to Hammar's (1999: 91) conceptualization, gender differences in a gender-imbalanced political economy that disadvantage women represent *gender* violence, whereas acts of violence, including physical, psychological, and linguistic violence, constitute *gendered* violence. The Guatemalan team differentiates public from domestic violence and notes that the two cannot be isolated from each another; they define violence as "intentional maltreatment of a physical, sexual, or emotional nature, which leads to an environment of fear, miscommunication and silence" (UNICEF-UNIFEM-OPS/OMS-FNUAP 1993: 22). The team notes that all forms of violence are the product of unequal power relations; among these the greatest inequality is that between men and women. And, according to Bourdieu and Wacquant (2004: 273), "the male order is so deeply grounded as to need no justification[,] . . . leading to [a] construct [of relations] from the standpoint of the dominant, i.e., as natural." They argue further: "The case of gender domination shows better than any other that *symbolic violence accomplishes itself through an act of cognition and of misrecognition that lies beyond—or beneath—the controls of consciousness and will,* in the obscurities of the schemata of habitus that are at once gendered and gendering" (original emphasis). Similarly, as Laurel Bossen (1983) observed in her research on Guatemala, an added dimension of systems of gender stratification is the development of ideologies that reinforce and rationalize sexual differentiation and inequality.[15]

Gender and gendered violence and public and domestic violence work in conjunction, and the interlocking of gender violence and gendered violence increasingly hurts women, as new arenas in which gender is a significant axis of stratification multiply. Guatemala's Gender Development Index is 0.63, which places it 119th of 175 ranked countries, below the 0.71 overall rate for Latin America and the Caribbean (UNDP

2003). Education at different levels is unequal by gender, and access to land is equally lopsided. Already 40 percent of rural families do not have access to land, and within this hierarchy women have a much lower rate of direct ownership. A survey found that only 28 percent of 99,000 female agriculturalists in Guatemala had permanent salaried employment; the rest were employed temporarily (Escoto et al. 1993). Disparities by ethnicity further exacerbate gender inequality, as indigenous Maya women fare far worse than ladinas in human development indicators.

The study by the Guatemalan team mentioned above presents a number of insights that show the institutionalization of gender hierarchies and violence, as authorities in the medical and judicial fields frame their actions and decisions in the same "social order of things" that shapes gender and gendered violence. The team interviewed sixteen professionals, including physicians, nurses, policemen, lawyers, gynecologists, a journalist, and a social worker, working in the public and private sectors who, in one way or another, dealt with instances of domestic violence. They were asked about their views of men and women, and overwhelmingly all agreed that "women are weaker," that "women are dependent on men," that "women must obey men," that "men are the ones who hold authority," and that "women are loving and caring." When they were asked under what conditions a man is justified in assaulting a woman, five of the professionals pointed to jealousy, alcoholism, or infidelity on the part of the woman. When they were asked if violence against women affected society in general, they responded negatively, indicating that these are isolated cases that do not have a wider effect. Some of the professionals did say that violent acts against women can have a broad effect when the children imitate the actions of the fathers and become aggressors themselves, when families disintegrate, when women become a public charge if they are left physically unable to work, and when society in general becomes more violent (UNICEF-UNIFEM-OPS/OMS-FNUAP 1993). Therefore, institutions such as the criminal justice system reinforce and formalize violent structures, causing more injury and suffering (often though not solely through neglect).

Gender and gendered violence in Guatemala emerge in quotidian events, and it is precisely these everyday forms, sometimes expressed in seemingly innocuous acts, that contribute to their normalization. Gender idologies create spheres of social action that contribute not only to normalizing expressions of violence but also to justifying "punishments" for deviations from normative gender role expectations. This is manifested in imposed demarcations of public and private spaces and in the resulting restriction of women's movement in public, as well as in practices that are more directly physically violent, such as abductions of women before they marry *(robadas),* a point to which I return in chapter 4.

Often the women I spoke with found their self-perceptions corroborated by their partners' threats, assaults, reproaches, and orders, but in some cases it was other women who did the reproaching or contributed to the assault. For instance, Delfina told me that her husband insulted her in front of friends and family, threw food at her when it was not prepared to his taste, and often threatened to leave her for a younger woman. This treatment was routine, though in a moment of reflection that epitomized the normalization of gender violence and gendered violence in San Alejo she somehow considered herself a bit fortunate. In her words, "He's never touched me. Can you believe he's never hit me? Yes, I'm serious. It's true. You'd think, with his character, it could be awful. But he's not like others who hit their wives." Delfina's reflection about physical violence in the lives of women and its absence in her life casts it as normalized for others. Nonetheless, Delfina mentioned that she felt depressed, tense, and unloved; the perverse effects of her husband's behavior also led her to accept her situation as ordinary. So many other women she knew suffered similar (or worse) assaults routinely that she did not find her own condition "that bad." I am not recounting these comments in an accusatory manner; rather, I want to call attention to the connection between extrapersonal, macrostructures of inequality and the microlevel, everyday world, as it is here that gender-based symbolic violence, the violence found in the social order, is instantiated.

To be sure, gender violence and gendered violence, and their normalization, are not new in Guatemala. In an examination of gender and justice in rural Guatemala, Cindy Forster (1999) notes that between 1936 and 1956 there were several recorded cases involving harmful acts against women (one had been killed) that failed to generate criminal proceedings. Authorities noted "nothing strange" in criminal acts against women; the "business as usual" attitude was especially noticeable in cases in which the women were poor and/or Maya. A justice system that carries inconsequential punishments for crimes against women, Carey and Torres (forthcoming) note, offers no legal sanction against gender-based violence. Carey and Torres, as well as Forster, link all these forms of violence against women. Forster writes:

> In Guatemala as elsewhere, dominant ideologies that justify coercion have shared a common purpose in the routinization of human inequality. Closely linked behaviors and social philosophies have legitimized the extraction of labor and obedience from masses of people across culture, class, or sex divides, sometimes through the use of terror. Abstractions that separate the political from the personal and gender from race or class, often damage the real-life permeability of these various oppressions. . . . Like violence against women, violence against the poor and nonwhite exists as a persistent threat. . . . In Guatemala . . . these oppressions were not necessarily parallel or dual systems. Rather, each was intimately bound up with the others, resting on the same scaffolding of structural inferiority and manifested in daily violence that enforced domination and submission. (1999: 57–58)

Gender violence and gendered violence in Guatemala today have roots in gender ideologies and in the country's history of political violence. Though only one quarter of the 200,000 disappeared and those executed extrajudicially during Guatemala's internal armed conflict were women (CEH 1999; REHMI 1998), Torres (2005: 163) notes that "when women were killed, their cadavers showed evidence of overkill and rape." This point, Torres (2005) argues, suggests that women more often than men were punished for divergence from expected behavioral norms. Indeed, in her meticulous analysis of published records, Torres finds that the victim's gender played a crucial role in determining the type of torture, the way bodies were disposed of, and the extent and type of reporting made on violated cadavers. Thus, Torres (2005) argues, the gender-specific necrographic maps and the significance of their signs point to the role of women in the restructuring of the Guatemalan nation through violence.

As in other politically conflictive societies, therefore, women in Guatemala have been murdered, disappeared, terrorized, and stripped of their dignity, and rape and sexual violence against them have been an integral part of the counterinsurgency strategy (Amnesty International 2005). Susan Blackburn (1999) and Cynthia Enloe (2000) have argued that such treatment can be linked to more obvious forms of state violence against women, as strategies of state terror and as part of a process of intimidation of dissidents or minority groups.[16] In this generalized context of gendered violence, indigenous women were singularly violated (Torres 2005), for this violence was directed at them because they were women and because they were Mayas. As Nelson (1999:326) notes, the disdain for indigenous life, in particular, indigenous female life, was temporarily extended by the counterinsurgency, which treated all "probable insurgents" "like Indians—expendable, worthless, bereft of civil and human rights." But the real magnitude of the violence women suffered during Guatemala's civil conflict will never be known, in part because many cases were not documented, but also because many women, out of guilt or shame, remained too traumatized to come forward, and afraid of rejection by their communities (Amnesty International 2005).[17] The U.N. Truth Commission report states that rape, especially in indigenous areas, resulted in "breaking marriage and social ties[,] generating social isolation and communal shame[,] and provok[ing] abortions [and] infanticide and obstruct[ing] births and marriages within these groups, thus facilitating the destruction of indigenous groups" (CEH 1999: 14).

Thus Guatemala's regime and militarization of life has made possible multiple acts of gendered violence, reflected in direct political violence against Maya women but also by the encouragement of abduction, torture, rape, and murder of female workers as a lesson to other women who might think of asserting their rights. Direct and indirect forms of violence have coalesced so that Guatemalan women have lived "in a chronic state of emergency," Carey and Torres (forthcoming) note, which has been a *precursor* to the violence we see today. Direct physical violence against women has increased in postwar Guatemala in absolute and relative numbers. Police records indicate that in 2002 women accounted for 4.5 percent of all killings, in 2003 for 11.5 percent, and in 2004 for 12.1 percent; figures compiled by the Policía Nacional Civil (PNC) (cited in Amnesty International 2005) note that the number of women murdered rose from 163 in 2002 to 383 in 2003 to more than 527 in 2004, and according to Oxfam (Oxfam Novib n.d.), in the first half of 2005 there were 239 women killed, including 33 girls under the age of fifteen. The Guatemalan lawyer Claudia Paz y Paz Bailey (quoted in Preston 2009) noted that over 4,000 women had been killed violently in Guatemala in the previous decade, with only 2 percent of the cases solved. In fact, Torres (2008: 6) argues that impunity in Guatemala demonstrates tolerance to multiple forms of violence but also "the extent to which violence has become naturalized in Guatemalan society." In Ciudad Juárez, Mexico, a similar pattern of killings has drawn international attention and condemnation. Aside from reports by Amnesty International and the Inter-American Commission on Human Rights, however, the Guatemalan women's deaths have started to receive international attention only in recent years.

As with the killings during the years of overt political conflict, those in Guatemala today are reported in gruesome detail in the national media, sending a similar message of uncertainty and fear. Only this time the message is directed at women, at *all* women regardless of ethnic background but especially at those from poor backgrounds who work outside the home. And as Godoy-Paiz (2008) notes, not all women in Guatemala experience life and violence in the same ways; social position shapes how women live and how they die. The women in both San Alejo and the Altiplano pay attention to the news; the images and descriptions refresh memories of the insecurity of life, and they often make decisions about travel, study, and work based on this information. For instance, several women in San Alejo mentioned that it was dangerous for women to travel by bus to work or to study, or to walk at certain times, even during the daytime, along roads that were not frequently used. Linking the violence of the past and the dangers of the present, Rosita, in the Altiplano, said that when her daughter informed her that she wanted to go to Guatemala City to study to be a secretary Rosita just about died thinking of the many dangers her daughter might face: "I couldn't sleep that night, just thinking and thinking. How could I live without her by my side? And memories of all the ugly things come to my mind. My hands shake just to think what can happen to her. One hears so much—well, I have seen horrible things. My sister-in-law tells me not to put this fear into the girl's head, to let her do what she wants, go to school, but this is terrible [Rosita is in tears]. Tell me, what if I see her photo in the newspaper [meaning as the victim of a gruesome death]?"

In two instances during my last visits to Guatemala, I had the opportunity to glimpse the feelings of insecurity and fear that women in both San Alejo and the Altiplano experienced every day, though I would not equate my limited experiences with what the women go through. In May 1999, during a conversation with Hortencia in San Alejo, she told me that two women had been found killed, their bodies badly tortured, on a road not far from her house. Then she added a sentence that sent chills down my spine: "Right away, I thought about you two [my assistant and I], since you two walk around town and work, and the two women found were workers. I thought, could it be Cecilia and her friend?" I responded with a nervous laugh that no, thank God, it was not us. In December the same year, during a visit to the Altiplano, the husband of one of the women I was visiting told me he had heard that a young woman was kidnapped and found dead about 30 kilometers away. "She was an anthropologist," he said, "doing the same thing you're doing here." In an instant reaction, not thinking clearly and perhaps seeking distance from the woman found dead, I responded, "But I am not an anthropologist," as if disciplinary training would have mattered. In a fitting comment to my ridiculous response, he added with a shrug of his shoulder and a chuckle, "Oh, maybe she wasn't an anthropologist either, but in any case, she was asking a lot of questions of women just like you do, and she was found dead." Hortencia's and this man's words were unsettling to me and left me thinking not only about my own safety but also, especially, about what it must be like for many of the women I had met to live every day with the constant threat of a horrific death.

The presence of naked or partially naked bodies in public places, on roadsides and city streets, continues to be an everyday sight in *postwar* Guatemala. One of the most gruesome recent sightings was four human heads and two decapitated bodies found in separate public points of Guatemala City in June 2010 (*El Periódico* 2010). And to be sure, men also have been affected by the violence; in fact, many more men than women have been killed. But the brutality and evidence of sexual violence (in most cases amounting to torture) creates a different context for the deaths of women. Amnesty International (2005) reported that although the murders may be attributed to different motives and may have been committed in different areas of the country, the violence today is overwhelmingly gender based. The murders of students, housewives, professionals, domestic employees, unskilled workers, members or former members of street youth gangs, and sex workers in both urban and rural areas, the overwhelming majority of them uninvestigated, are often attributed to "common" or "organized" crime, drug and arms trafficking, maras, or a jealous boyfriend or husband.[18] In response to increasing demands for action, in 2008 the Guatemalan government enacted a law stipulating special sanctions for these crimes against women (Preston 2009), but only a tiny percentage of cases have been prosecuted.[19]

Many of the women who have been killed in recent years come from poor backgrounds, which signals discrimation on the basis of both class and gender. Whereas the majority of women who were victims of violence during Guatemala's overt civil conflict were indigenous Mayas living in rural areas, the reported murder victims today are both Mayas and ladinas living in urban or semiurban areas. This new violence against women is all-encompassing. However, the brutality of the killings and the signs of sexual violence on women's mutilated bodies today bear many of the hallmarks of the atrocities committed during the political conflict, making the differences between "wartime" and "peacetime" Guatemala imperceptible.

MULTISIDED VIOLENCE IN THE LIVES OF WOMEN IN SAN ALEJO

Two examples from San Alejo demonstrate how multiple forms of violence can coalesce in a normalized fashion. They do not deal with direct physical violence and do not represent the kind of violence that attracts attention in the media or from activist groups. On close inspection, however, links and expressions of the different forms of violence outlined above begin to emerge in these examples. The first example involves men's emigration from San Alejo to the United States, and the second has to do with moneylending; often the two are related. Neither example is "abnormal" or extraordinary in this context, though both can perpetuate and exacerbate existing forms of suffering and even create new forms.

I cannot provide an extensive account of Guatemalan migration to the United States here, but suffice it to say that migration within and from Guatemala has a long history, linked to structural and political forms of violence. Since at least a century ago, indigenous Guatemalans have been participating in several patterns of labor migration, both to plantations in Guatemala's lowlands and to the Soconusco, in southern Mexico. As the political conflict intensified, thousands of Guatemalans, mostly Mayas from the Altiplano, fled their homes to refugee camps in southern Mexico and to the United States. Today migration has become a central aspect of life in San Alejo (as well as in most of the country); it is a normalized strategy to endure the consequences of deep socioeconomic inequalities exacerbated by neoliberal economic reforms and direct forms of violence. But far from addressing economic stagnation and inequality, migration can actually perpetuate them (see Portes 2009).[20]

At the beginning of my fieldwork in 1995, some women in San Alejo talked about their husbands, partners, brothers, or other (mostly) male relatives who were working in the United States. With every visit to the town, signs of migration became more visible and omnipresent. There were more cars with U.S. license plates circulating in the town and more conversations about life in the two U.S. towns to which the majority of men from San Alejo migrated. When I first met Nena, we sat in the living room adjacent to the small bookstore/school supply store that she owned and operated from her home. She always spoke with pride about how she stocked her business with the best products and was careful to select the merchandise she sold. Five years later the store was no longer there. The "Librería El Recuerdo" sign had been replaced by one advertising a travel agency. Surprised, I asked Nena what that was, and she explained that it was not a travel agency, "the way you and I understand what a travel agency is" but a travel agency "for everyone in town," that is, for organized groups of people traveling to the United States together by land. "Traveling . . . without a visa?" I inquired. "Yes, of course," Nena replied, "*mojados*" (a pejorative term imported from the United States). She explained that the owner of the "agency" had a booming business because he served the town and the surrounding villages and had asked her if he could rent her store due to its central location in town. During the time I was there in 2000, he took groups of about one hundred individuals approximately twice a month, Nena explained. And the local branch of a money transfer business had a long list of names of recipients, almost double what it had been just a few years earlier. By then, it appeared, the mechanisms by which people migrated seemed commonplace and "part of life."

I also noticed the increasing centrality of U.S.-bound migration in the Altiplano as a way to deal with everyday challenges. At the beginning of fieldwork there I came across only two families with relatives in the United States (confirmed later by the owner of a new branch of a money transfer business), but with each ensuing visit more people pointed out to me the houses that migrants' dollars had contributed to building, and in 2000, for the first time, I saw a "travel agency" similar to the one operating out of Nena's old store in San Alejo. Toñita explained why her husband had migrated and her views of the process: "He used to work here as a driver, but because we have so many children [ten], and they are all in school, we need money, so he left for the United States two years ago. . . . He's in Florida, Miami, I think. No, I don't know what he does. I think he works at a packing plant. Yes, he sends us money, but it's not enough. I have to invest it wisely, in daily expenses, the children's school, and for the corn that we have to plant."

Like Toñita, many of the women in San Alejo spoke of men from their town migrating to the United States. Lila explained that when she and her husband married, they had nothing, not even dishes in the house, so after their twins were born he had no other way to provide for the babies' medicines, food, and clothing than to migrate. Also in San Alejo, Mercedes, all but two of whose eight children lived in Chicago, said that most people migrate from San Alejo because there is "no employment." Estrella explained how scarcity and the worsening economic situation had created conditions for people to migrate: "If you don't work in this place, you don't eat. And you know what I do? I save my cents, so that when I am in need, I have my own money. The rest, they have their children in the States, they send them money, and that's how they live. So anyone you see here living more or less well, it's because they have a son or a daughter working over there." In the eyes of the women, migration was a "cure" for their afflictions. Ofelia, who worked at the health post, noted, "Why deny it? I think that [migration] has been a great help for Guatemala, here [San Alejo] and for the entire country. Before migration people didn't have houses, food, clothing. Now they do. It's the only way to improve your situation."

Financial difficulties (and direct political violence, especially in the highlands) were not the only problems that migration helped to solve; there were other kinds of personal worries, linked to gender-specific violence, for which the women thought migration was a solution. Lucrecia, a twenty-seven-year-old single mother in San Alejo, had never been married. People in town considered her "loose," and she intimated that she did not think she had a "good reputation." She thought the best way to resolve this situation would be to migrate. Lost in her thoughts, Lucrecia looked out the window and reflected, "I don't know, but I want to go to the United States. Yes, one dreams and dreams. I want to go there, but alone. I want to go there to work. I don't want to think about tomorrow, I won't have a husband here. Who's going to marry me? What man will want something serious with me? So I would like to go. It's better over there for women, well, for someone like me, without a husband, just alone with my kids."

As these brief examples demonstrate, migration from Guatemala is intertwined with the context of violence I have discussed, both in how this context creates conditions for people to seek options for a better life elsewhere but also in the consequences migration has for women. Despite the general praise for migration as a panacea for all problems, most of the women also spoke of its painful consequences. This is similar to the views of immigrants in the United States whom I interviewed (Menjívar 2006a, 2006b); many of them mentioned the pain and emotional and personal costs of living separated from their families and the lengths they went to to remain connected.

The women in San Alejo would say, "Me resigno" (I resign myself) or "¿Y uno qué puede hacer?" (And what can one do?) when asked about what they thought of their partners' migration. Indeed, even the phone calls that have come to symbolize migrants' efforts to remain connected with loved ones back home were painful for the women. If their partners called (and it was the men who initiated a phone call, as phone cards are cheaper and more readily available in the United States) and the women noticed just a minor change in the tone of their voices, or if the men forgot to ask about something the women considered important, the women would be left worrying about possible affairs the men could be having in the United States and thus about potential abandonment. And if the men did not call it was worse (see Menjívar and Agadjanian 2007). Vera referred to these phone calls as painful; she explained that every time she received a call from her husband in the United States she was left crying. "Of course, it's nice to get a phone call and hear his voice, but that reminds me that he's not here, that he's not seeing his daughter grow up. And who knows? He's alone over there, and men are men; they sometimes fall to temptation when they are alone."

Mercedes spoke in general terms about how people (mostly men) initially send money and remember their families, but over time "homes disintegrate."[21] And for Gracia María, whose five brothers were in the United States, her brothers' absence was quite difficult because she felt "alone," even though her parents lived in town: "With them here I feel their support as men, you know? I feel protected, I don't know, like stronger, with more backing. It's different when I'm here alone. As a woman, it's different not to have your brothers by your side. But I'm happy they left because life here is too difficult and I know that they'll improve their lives there [her eyes become watery]." As Gracia María's words indicate, it is not only the absence of the men but also what it means in this context for the nonmigrant women that is worth noting and linking to structures of violence. Thus Lucía spoke of what the absence of a male member in the family means for a woman in San Alejo. Her husband had been migrating seasonally to the United States, and she missed him very much.

> Yes, sometimes I get melancholic. Why lie to you? I get sad, and wonder why my life has to be this way. Why me, I wonder? And I ask God, Diosito, why me? And it's very hard when he's gone for a long time. It's not only the sex [she laughs], no, there are many other things. When he's here he can deal with a lot of things better. Having a husband around is helpful; when one has their support one feels more secure. It's how life is here.

Emilia added a historical angle:

> I miss my husband. My consolation is that at least I have the children with me. But I do feel lonely. You know, it wasn't like this before. People didn't leave town like they do now. Those people who had relatives in the States were so few that everyone knew them. Now it's the contrary. Those who don't have relatives there are the rare ones.

And Elvira, a nurse whose family has been migrating and has experienced the pain of these separations, explained how it felt:

> Let me give you an example. Once I read that Sergio Ramírez [the Nicaraguan writer] asked Julio Cortázar [the Argentine writer] what it feels like to have lost his wife, and Cortázar responds, "Like always having a grain of sand in one's eye; the pain, seemingly small and insignificant is huge, constant, it doesn't go away." I feel that this is how it feels to be separated from your parents, your husband, or your children, especially when you don't know how they are over there. This uncertainty is the part that's *insoportable* [unbearable].

However painful for the nonmigrants, it is not only the act of migration and the physical separations that matter here. Migration also interrupts celebrations, rituals, and the rhythm of life. Often I heard of baptisms and marriages being postponed. For instance, Mirna worried that only two of her five children had been baptized because her cousin, who was in Connecticut, wanted to be the godfather of the other three and could not travel back to Guatemala easily: "Well, the problem is that he left as a mojado, you know, without a visa, so he cannot come back for just a baptism. I worry because it's not good not to have your children baptized. What if something happens to the children, God forbid, and they are not baptized? And who knows when he'll be able to come for their baptisms; people say that it has become very difficult to travel." And Vera's daughter was supposed to have been baptized on the day she turned one year old, but both the girl's father and the chosen godparents could not make it back for the baptism. Vera searched for words to explain that she did not know when they would return. In the end, she only said, "I am not sure, really not sure. Our lives are pending, one can say."

Migration, given its context, characteristics, and historical moment, results in significant pain for those involved and increased power inequality in couples. Although the physical separation was a source of the women's insecurities and worries, the indefinite and uncertain nature of these separations presented a serious burden in their lives. And one must note that the nature of these separations is itself related to multiple forms of exclusion and violence that immigrants, especially those without documents or with uncertain legal statuses, face in the United States. With the militarization of the southern U.S. border and stiffer immigration laws, seasonal visits and regular physical encounters have become elusive, creating and exacerbating conditions of distress for the migrants and their nonmigrant relatives (Menjívar 2006a, 2006b).

Furthermore, in contrast to most of the literature examining the effects of male migration on the lives of women who stay, the women with whom I spoke in San Alejo did not seem to have "gained" much in terms of equality, power, or their roles. Often their movements were more closely monitored, and they did not appear to have expanded their areas of control (see chapter 3). The women still lived in a context in which orthodox patriarchal norms and few opportunities for paid employment existed, and men found themselves in contexts in which they had relatively more access to resources. As such, geographic location intensified gendered power asymmetries; men's position as breadwinners and primary decision makers was amplified and women's subordinate position exacerbated (see Menjívar and Agadjanian 2007). Thus structural violence curtailed the ability of many to find well-paid jobs, and political violence, bound up with structural violence, was the motivation for the emigration of many others. Symbolic and gender violence coalesced to create conditions in which migration emerged as a "natural" response that normalized women's pain and sacrifices and power inequalities. In turn, the consequences of migration exacerbated and created new forms of suffering that often left those involved ambivalent and wondering about the benefits that migration was supposed to bring.

My second example, moneylending, further demonstrates how multiple forms of violence come together in women's lives. Often I heard the women (and the men) complain about the poverty in San Alejo, about their inability to make ends meet, causing the women to borrow money to cover a variety of household expenses, most of them associated with their children. Given my general interest in reciprocal exchanges in different structural contexts, I asked women if under such difficult economic conditions others were likely to lend a hand, if friends, family, and neighbors would assist those in need. Similar to what I observed in the United States (see Menjívar 2000), this was not the case in Guatemala. As in the United States, I would hear of people not having enough to help others in need, as in the case of Gracia María. "No, how can people help one another if we don't even have for themselves?" she noted with a chuckle. "Imagine, people come to borrow money from me! Look at my situation! I tell them I can help with other things but not with things that involve money because I don't have any. I think many people in this town, even if they appear to have something, are in my situation." The amounts women borrowed were very small, usually around Q.50 (about U.S.$10 in the late 1990s). Also, the life of the loans was often very short—one week, one month—highlighting the urgency of the situation. So, I asked the women, do people lend money to one another as a form of help? Gracia María laughed and said, "Oh no, not to help others, but to help themselves! Cecilia, look, the only way to borrow money is to go through someone who does that for a living. You don't believe me [she laughs]! You'll be even more surprised when you find out who they are, who lends money for a living. You'll realize that it's unscrupulous people lending at high rates and taking advantage of those in need. Around here, it's the great majority who are in need, so those people take advantage." As I learned more about moneylending, it seemed that the interest rate varied in direct relation to the urgency of need. Although Estrella recognized that the interest rates were a function of how desperate people were, in contrast to Gracia María's view, she did not view moneylending as exploitation. "Well, it is a form of help, no?" she said. "Even if it's with a high interest, it's help. Well, that's how I see it."

As I began to pay attention to the issue of moneylending, I noticed that indeed there was quite a bit of it going on, but one had to dig a little deeper. An entry in my field notes reads, "Moneylending. Note it. It's very common here. High interests in moneylending are common." However, as Gracia María indicates, what needs to be noted is not just the moneylending but the high interest rates and the exploitative nature of the enterprise in which the vulnerable hurt one another, for that is what encapsulates the multiple forms of violence. Gracia María continued: "Those people that you've been talking to, yes, those. They seem so nice and kind, right? You should see, they lend money at such high rates, they're like leeches. Yes, the polite ones, those. They live off desperate people who need to take a kid to the clinic, or who need to pay rent; people feel like they're suffocating so they turn to moneylenders. Sure, they go to mass and church, you have seen them, and they beat their chests and all that, but behind all that they are the worst sinners because they are merciless." Like migration, moneylending too generated and exacerbated different forms of suffering; both practices were normalized responses to the conditions women (and men) faced. And both were nonphysical forms of violence.

I decided to pay a visit to the women in town who were known for lending money at high interest rates to hear their perspective. I was surprised to find that these women were not members of the well-off families in town and that in fact they were not much better off than those to whom they were lending. When I inquired about this, a nurse and a physician in San Alejo mentioned that the better-off families were less likely to lend money because renting their land remained more profitable (though equally exploitative). When I brought up the topic of moneylending with the women known for engaging in this business, they limited themselves to commenting that they had heard that some people in town *"alquilan dinero"* (rent money). But I had heard enough from others, including those who had borrowed money, about how it worked. One of the lenders, Isabel, owned a small store in the living room of her house, which was near the center of town and was not as well appointed as those of her relatives. Her husband worked in the United States and sent remittances regularly. Isabel would put the money to work by lending it to others in small amounts, sometimes at an interest rate of 25 percent. One of the women who had "hired money" from Isabel commented that it made more sense for Isabel to lend the remitted money than to put it to other uses, because "the profits are higher when people do business at the expense of those who are desperate." Two other women echoed this view in a slightly different fashion. Mirna said that it seemed "natural" that the poorer people would fare worse in these monetary transactions, for they would "normally be taken advantage of." "If you look poor, humble, then it's worse. Sometimes you really need money because a child is sick and you need to buy medicine, and because men are not there to help, you need to borrow money. But the poor are unlucky, the unluckiest people on earth, I tell you. 'Al perro más flaco se le pegan las pulgas' [The skinniest dog gets all the fleas]."

Like some of the other women, Hortencia added a specific gendered angle: "Well, for one, as a woman, the disadvantage is worse because if you borrow from men, then they expect you to pay back through other means, you know, like doing things with them. Respect is lost, so it's better not to have any money dealings with some men." Moneylending can be, as in Estrella's view, a form of help, but often it turns into outright exploitation and thus reflects the structural and symbolic violence in which the vulnerable exploit one another. I heard similar stories in the

Altiplano. Some women there said that the only help from others came in the form of loans, which, as in San Alejo, were for small amounts and for short periods. For instance, Lita lamented how difficult it was for her to survive, and she described the kind of help she sought from those close to her. When two of her children were sick and she had not received any money from her husband who was working in Guatemala City, she turned to her brother for help.

> He said that if I gave him the small plot of land that my father left me [as an inheritance] he could help me, he could give me Q.100 [about $20] a month, but he only gave me Q.100 once, and then nothing. Ah, the land? When the boy got out of the hospital I told him that I would give him back his Q.100. I told him that I would even give him the interest. But he said no, that I had already transferred the land to him, and he didn't accept the Q.100 back, and he didn't want to give me the land back. So I lost the land, and all I got was the Q.100. Yes, this is my own brother!

Amelia added that borrowing money had made matters worse and, demonstrating the internalized symbolic violence she had experienced, placed some of the blame on those in need:

> There are people who lend money at a high interest, but if we are in need, we pay the interest, right? Sometimes we just make enough money to pay for the interest because the lady [lender] comes by the house and she wants her money. So we work only to pay our debt, to pay the interest because we pay Q.60 a month. We ask her to wait a day or two, but she wants her money right there and then. My husband gives his merchandise on credit, so we get money to pay for the interest. But you know what? It's our fault because we are the ones who borrow this money; the lady doesn't come to our house to offer it to us. So it's no one's fault but our own.

Although the reasons for borrowing money, the consequences, and the self-blaming seemed similar in San Alejo and in the Altiplano, in the Altiplano I heard an additional angle on moneylending. Julia said that when she needs money she asks people whom she trusts, someone "*de confianza.*" Once she needed money to pay the men who were helping her with the harvest, for her husband was disappeared during the years of violence, and as an only daughter she did not have any men in her family to turn to for help with working the land. She said:

> Remember that man that you met at Doña Diana's house? [She is referring to the teacher who used to take his meals in the house in which I lived.] The one who used to work at the city hall? Well, I borrowed from him because he was someone I could trust. He is a man of integrity, trustworthy. Interest? No, he didn't charge me interest for the loan. He said that that's

> because I am a widow of the violence and a single mother, so this is why he didn't charge me any interest. I used to ask him, how much do you want for the favor, and he would always say, "God says that we need to help the widows," so he would never charge me.

This does not mean that all widows of the violence were treated with deference; it only highlights some differences, related to the political violence in the Altiplano, between the two contexts.

CONCLUSION

I have laid out a conceptual framework that includes structural, political, symbolic, everyday, and gender and gendered violence to examine the lives of the women I came to know in Guatemala. Three points need to be kept in mind. First, the multiple forms of violence I have presented never occur in isolation, though sometimes one form appears to be more salient. Thus in the chapters that follow they appear intertwined in different spheres of the women's lives. Second, violence is normalized in the women's everyday lives. Only when discussed or pointed to do routine practices (sometimes attributed to tradition) become obvious and disturb the normalized gaze. Indeed, it is the insidiousness of this routinized violence in regions that are perceived as "calm" or "peaceful," or in practices that are taken as "part of tradition," to which I call attention. It is through this normalization and misrecognition that dehumanization becomes possible and suffering becomes a part of life. Once violence is unleashed, whether in the form of state violence, domestic abuse, or exploitation, it emerges in different forms and shapes the lives and minds of individuals. In the chapters that follow I examine the women's "private terrors" that encapsulate the multilayered violence I have presented here.

CHAPTER 3

Corporeal Dimensions of Gender Violence

Woman's Self and Body

Es que yo pienso que para ser felíz, uno tiene que sufrir primero, y yo no sé como Usted va a interpretar esto, pero yo estoy bien consciente de que así es. La gente me ha criticado porque salí embarazada y él está casado con otra; la gente ha hablado mucho. Pero a lo mejor todavía no he sufrido lo suficiente como para poder entender la vida.

[I think that in order to be happy, first one has to suffer, and I don't know how you'll interpret this, but I'm very conscious that this is how it is. People have criticized me because I became pregnant and he [the father of the child] is married to another woman; people have talked a lot. But maybe I still haven't suffered enough to understand life.]

—Teresa, twenty-one years old

Yo no le puedo decir con exactitud, vaya, por ejemplo, con números y estadísticas, pero con excepción de quizás uno o dos casos, yo diría que todas las mujeres en este pueblo son maltratadas de una u otra forma.

[I really can't tell you exactly, with for example, numbers and statistics, but with the exception of maybe one or two cases I would say that every woman in this town is mistreated in one way or another.]

—Emilia, health care worker

Both gendered and symbolic violence are central to an examination of the embodiment of suffering, not only in the personal, individual dimensions of the physical body, but in its social dimensions as well. In social science theory there have been multiple approaches to the examination of bodily themes and questions surrounding the body, from postmodernist to poststructuralist (see Williams 1999). Green (1998) calls for attention to concrete manifestations of suffering in theorizing about how suffering is embodied, as violence inscribes the body with message and significance.

Heeding Green's call, I focus here on concrete corporeal manifestations of different forms of violence among ladinas in eastern Guatemala, using a sociologically (and anthropologically) informed approach that is substantively grounded. This approach situates corporeal questions within unequal social structures and thus contributes to debates about the relationship between body and society. However, in contrast to examining issues of representation or sexuality, I follow Farmer (2003, 2004) and others (e.g., Martín-Baró 1991a, 1991b, 1991c; Torres-Rivas 1998) to focus on concrete expressions of social suffering, on how multiple forms of violence and macro forces coalesce on the body. Similar to Barbara Sutton's (2010: 2) focus on the body as a way to capture multiple social and material crises in Argentina, my angle here also illuminates how forces beyond individuals' control "reach . . . lives and bodies in deeply personal ways." This examination therefore highlights how "power, history, and gender operate through embodied subjectivity and concrete bodily activity" (Green 1998: 4); how the body connects women to extralocal, even global, realms (Sutton 2004, 2010), and how suffering is normalized in small, routine moments. In Martín-Baró's (1994: 13) conceptualization, this examination exposes the "normal abnormality" that the vulnerable endure.

I first examine the physical expressions of violence as they are manifested in the women's bodies, such as common health ailments that result from emotional distress or from the structural violence that shapes their lives. I underscore the normalization of deeply entrenched gender inequality and domination on the more immediate, physical sphere of body ailments and then discuss how the embodiment of violence is expressed in the control of the body in the social milieu, such as women's socializing and visiting. This approach sheds light on visible *and* invisible, yet still pervasive, forms of violence manifested in the lives of women. Although direct physical harm is usually accompanied by mental and emotional pain, the latter is sometimes inflicted alone, leaving no physical marks and no possibility for tracking in tables or statistics. As Emilia noted in the quotation above, these forms of violence are equally damaging, as women are just as maltratadas in both cases.

I want to repeat here that even though violence is often concretized in individual acts, my project is to call attention to the structures, cognitive frameworks, internalized dispositions, and ideologies that make these individual acts possible, tolerated, and accepted. Men are of course affected by the same structures that make the women's pain possible. And I do not wish to negate the heterogeneity and complexity of men's identities and understandings of themselves that Matthew C. Gutmann (1996, 2007) documents so well.Thus, while violence can come from acts by those close to the women, my analysis refocuses attention away from purely individual acts to the structures that shape the context in which women's and men's views and actions are shaped.

HEALTH AND THE SOMATIZATION OF SOCIAL SUFFERING

The violence in the lives of the women I met in San Alejo was often embodied in illnesses (see also Green 1998, 1999), in the injuries inflicted by a brutal political regime, and in a castelike social structure that produces everyday forms of suffering, pain, and humiliation. The overwhelming majority of the women with whom I spoke had some form of ailment about which they wanted to talk. Sometimes their complaints appeared to be of a physical nature, sometimes of a psychological character, but the two were so closely linked that it was difficult to categorize them as one or the other.[1] I avoid such a classification and instead examine two dimensions that reflect the embodiment of multisided violence. The first focuses on treatments that address the physical manifestations of social suffering resulting from the intertwined effects of unequal access to health care and medicine along class and gender lines and from the naturalized view that the health of others in the family comes before the women's own, which places women of different social classes and ethnic backgrounds in a similarly disadvantaged position in relation to men.[2] The second dimension reveals embodied manifestations of distress, such as headaches, stomachaches, and *nervios* (nerves), conditions that may appear to be "psychological" or even "part of tradition" but that on close examination reflect how deeply linked they are to the sources of violence I identify here.

These two dimensions illustrate how violence is "misrecognized" and express the somatization of socially instituted gender differences (see Bourdieu 1996–97).

Guatemala is among the worst performers in terms of health care outcomes in all of Latin America. With 34 infant deaths per 1,000 live births and a life expectancy of 70 years (66 for men, 73 for women),[3] it has had one of the highest infant mortality rates and one of the lowest life expectancies at birth in Latin America (Gragnolati and Marini 2003). Although supply-and-demand-side constraints play a role, it has been found that supply has a more central role in rural areas (Gragnolati and Marini 2003). The total expenditure on health as a percentage of the GDP in 2003 was 5.4 percent, and health expenditure represented 15.3 of the total government expenditure (WHO 2006). There are 0.9 physicians and 4 nurses per 1,000 persons and 5 hospital beds per 10,000 persons (WHO 2006). Overall, spending for public health needs benefits disproportionately the highest quintiles of the income distribution of the population (Gragnolati and Marini 2003). Thus poverty emerges as a serious constraint on a family's choices about how to treat illnesses, and the availability of modern health facilities in a community has a substantial impact on the type of providers sought for treatment (Goldman, Pebley, and Gragnolati 2002). Although research has shown that Guatemalans often resort to multiple and simultaneous uses of home remedies, *curanderos* (folk healers), herbalists, midwives, pharmacists, physicians, and public and private health clinics and hospitals (Cosminsky and Scrimshaw 1987), recent research shows that modern medical care plays a key role in the treatment of infectious illnesses in rural Guatemala (Goldman and Heuveline 2000). In this general scenario, social position, dictated by social class, ethnicity, and gender, shapes who receives medical treatment and who does not; the Maya, notably poor Maya women, fare much worse than the rest of the population.

Limited access to health care based on class position and ethnicity is often compounded by the naturalized expectation that women fulfill their role by putting the well-being of others before their own. Thus the embodiment of structural, symbolic, and everyday violence in San Alejo is expressed in malnutrition and its multiple manifestations among women, in particular, poor women. To be sure, malnutrition as an expression of structural violence affects poor men as well, and poor ladino and Maya men also suffer from lack of access to good-quality medical care. Guatemala had the highest prevalence of chronic malnutrition in Latin America in 2000 (Marini and Gragnolati 2003), and the U.N. World Food Programme (n.d.) categorized it as having the fourth highest malnutrition level in the world, with 49.3 percent of children under the age of five (7 in 10 in rural areas) malnourished. Scholars attribute these poor outcomes to the country's deep socioeconomic inequalities (see Marini and Gragnolati 2003), which influence access to health and social services. However, how lack of access is perceived and naturalized differs for men and women, as it is compounded by gender ideologies that position women as sacrificing themselves for others. From the angle I use here, leaving reproductive and personal decisions to the women's partners even when the women's lives are in danger, putting the health of others before their own, and the normalization of being the last in the family to get treatment are expressions of the combination of gender and gendered, symbolic, and structural violence.

Gracia María, a mother of five I introduced in chapter two, often felt ill. Her family was not poor by local standards, but they were not wealthy either. They lived in the center of San Alejo in a large house, and she described herself as a housewife. Her husband owned land that he cultivated once a year, but he had resorted to migrating seasonally to Stamford, Connecticut, to complement through gardening work in the United States his declining income from agriculture. Like the other women I met, Gracia María told me that her health complaints were not important, that she could not see why they should be the topic of our conversation. Even when she did not feel well, she did not complain, she remarked with pride: "I can be feeling very, very ill, but I don't complain because it is normal for a woman to have *achaques* [health issues], right? As long as my husband and children are well, I am well." A couple of years after that conversation, I visited Gracia María again and found that she was pregnant for the seventh time with her sixth child (one pregnancy resulted in a miscarriage). She was concerned about this pregnancy because she felt tired; each pregnancy took a greater toll on her body, she said. Her penultimate child had multiple sclerosis and was less than two years older than her youngest child, who was just one year old when we first talked. She was visibly worried about this pregnancy because it had taken her months to recuperate from the previous two; she could not even sit up straight for a couple of months after the last birth. But she said that she had to "accept" it because she was married and her husband was happy with their large family. From her point of view, as was the case with many other women, she did not question her husband's (and her husband's family or even friends) controlling her reproductive and sexual life, even if she was well aware that his decisions put her health at risk.

Women in the Altiplano also noted in a straightforward manner that the health of others came first. Asunción, a thirty-four-year-old Maya with eight living children and three years of schooling, who had earlier suffered one miscarriage, told me that after the last few pregnancies she did not feel well. She explained, "Everything hurts, and I'm sick all the time. I get headaches, stomachaches, everything. I used to go to the doctor, but I wouldn't finish the treatment because we would run out of money. If a child got sick or another one needed school supplies, I had to interrupt my treatment. You know how that is." This "choice" between paying for her medicine or her children's should not be construed within "traditional" frames that paint a mother's altruism or self-sacrifice solely in a positive light but examined through a lens that reveals the harmful consequences of poverty, exclusion, and deeply entrenched gender inequality.

The women with whom I spoke in San Alejo often mentioned *debilidad* (weakness) as an illness that affected their partners, children, and themselves (this was also the case in the Altiplano). Women sometimes bought pills or tonics over the counter at a pharmacy or from vendors on market day to lessen the symptoms. Occasionally, the physician at the local health post would prescribe something for them to alleviate their debilidad. Mirna talked about what it was like for her and her family to try to get by while lacking what she considered important components of their daily diet: "Sometimes my mama comes by to see if I have a little bit of coffee left over because she gets headaches if she doesn't drink coffee every day. Me too, if I don't have a cup of coffee in the morning and at night, I have a terrible headache the next day, from debilidad. The thing is that we almost never have enough [money] to drink coffee every day. Also, my husband needs to eat so that he can work. So then [laughing] I often wake up with a headache." A San Alejo health worker told me that such headaches among women (and among some men too) were routine and explained that they were not the result of not having had coffee but of serious malnutrition that resulted from the women's *descuido* (disregard) for their own health. Although the health care worker rightly linked the headaches to malnutrition, she considered the problem the women's fault and not, as she could have, the inequality that is its root cause.

The case of Susana further illustrates how multilayered violence coalesces in the San Alejo women's bodies. Susana was twenty-six years old when we first met and had quit school in the second grade. She was the mother of four children (a fifth had died as a newborn). When I saw her a year later she was pregnant for the sixth time (she eventually had a miscarriage). Susana often ran out of money to buy medicine; often others in the family were ill or had other needs that apparently required more attention. However, she said that her husband had something to do with her ill health. She suffered interpersonal violence in the home, physical and psychological, and in our conversations articulated that this was the reason for her poor health. The owner of a nearby pharmacy knew of Susana's situation and often gave her medicine on credit or sometimes even gratis, especially when it was for the children. Susana said, "The owner of the pharmacy knows me; she knows my husband and our situation. She knows that he takes money from food and spends it on alcohol. The other day I had to buy my pills because this headache leaves me unable to do anything. I went to the pharmacy and she [the owner] gave me three pills, so that at least I could go to sleep. She has mercy on me."[4] It is important to note that Susana's husband often felt unable to provide for his family and in his frustration turned to the consolation that alcohol offered him. Susana seemed to have internalized the effects of structural and gender violence that contributed to her humiliation and thus accepted people's mercy in a normalized fashion. This view of herself as inspiring compassion in others allowed her to turn to the owner of the pharmacy to alleviate her pain.

Like Susana, other women in San Alejo mentioned people "having mercy" on them; however, "mercy" from others depended on many factors, including the woman's reputation. A striking case is that of Leticia. I met her one afternoon in the dark, damp, one-room structure with dirt floor that she shared with her two young girls. It took a few minutes for my eyes to get used to the darkness of the room, and then I began to discern Leticia's emaciated facial features. She was twenty-seven years old and had never attended school. A couple of years after we first met she died of complications from HIV/AIDS, two and a half years after her husband died from the same causes. According to people who knew her, "She left this world very sad; she worried so much about her girls because she knew they would be left orphans. Her last three months of life were so sad for her that she even lost her mind a little." Leticia knew that she was dying and that her girls would be separated, as neither set of grandparents had the resources to take care of both girls. During Leticia's last year of life no one would mention the name of her illness, but everyone seemed to know what ailed her. Some people would "take pity" and help her; others tried to avoid her. However, in Leticia's eyes those who helped her did so because she was a single mother and a widow and, most of all, respectable: "Because people see me alone and that I'm responsible for everything in the home, they help me. They allow me to pick tomatoes, to sell them, and that's help. Sometimes I would like to go to visit my family, but that costs Q.10 for the bus fare, and it's difficult for me to save that. Once in a while people help me with that too." But not everyone "took pity" on Leticia. I also heard from her sister and a health care worker that several people did not want anything to do with her and in fact had been cruel to her. Such attitudes are related to the symbolic violence that persons infected with HIV/AIDS experience (see also Gutmann 2007; Smith, Lucas, and Latkin 1999). They are also linked to women's image of propriety and to normative expectations of behavior that constrain their lives to the point of suffering.

Nervios, Headaches, and the Everyday Embodiment of Distress

Nervios is a "folk" ailment that refers to multiple symptoms associated with the loss of emotional control. Some researchers have linked this ailment to cultural, demographic, environmental, and personality factors. Guarnaccia, Lewis-Fernández, and Rivera Marano (2003) argue that there are different categories and experiences of nervios and that these provide insights into how suffering is experienced and expressed, pointing to different social sources of distress. Other scholars have noted that nervios is a culture-specific syndrome of brief duration common among Spanish-speaking people of the Caribbean (Oquendo, Horwath, and Martinez 1992). Perhaps there is a relationship between geographic location (e.g., Latin America and the Caribbean) and nervios, but instead of looking for its roots in an assumed common culture I would point to the region's high levels of inequality, the highest in the world, which generates insecurity and fear and aggravates physical ailments. And nervios is a condition that typically ails women. Situating this phenomenon, as well as headaches and other embodiments of suffering, within a social and structural framework that underscores the injuries of inequality calls for a shift in focus away from an individualistic or purely "cultural" (in the sense of looking at beliefs, practices, and rituals independent of social milieu or power dynamics) approach to the study of these illnesses.

Several San Alejo women explained that some of their ailments, including nervios, were related to the conditions in which they lived. Indeed, James Quesada (2004) and Scheper-Hughes (1992) have observed that nervios is an expression of embodied distress. For example, as Ivette, a ladina from San Alejo who married a man in the Altiplano, kept reiterating what a good life she had, her eyes shifted nervously and blinked constantly during our conversation. She later confessed that her nervios made her gastritis flare up, and she needed to take Maalox regularly because she was rarely without pain. And Isabel, a forty-one-year-old mother of two with five years of schooling, told me that years before we met her nervios were "killing" her. "I was very thin, like this [lifting her pinky finger]; I didn't want to eat anything. People gave me thousands of recommendations, of advice, 'here, take this or that herb,' teas, injections, pills, eesh, you name it. I got to a point where I didn't even care about my girls. I didn't want anyone to talk to me. It was at a time when I was suffering from a great *pena* [grief] and couldn't find consolation in anything. An evangelical lady started praying for me, and I started to feel better." At first I asked Isabel if her great pena had been of an economic nature, and she said it was. But months later she explained that she had been worried about her husband and an affair he was having, which would also have financial consequences for her, she confessed, because there was the possibility that he would abandon her. Some women in town mentioned that Isabel suffered greatly in those days, because her husband would parade himself with his mistress in front of the house he shared with Isabel; he would go to parties with his mistress and did not seem to care who saw him or when. According to Isabel's neighbors, this humiliation was killing her. They agreed that these kinds of penas could kill anyone, because "your nervios get destroyed from thinking." One woman said that this kind of suffering, which many women "always" experienced, was so painful psychologically and even physically that, in her view, it amounted to torture. Even though Isabel's suffering was talked about in a way that might seem as if it was unusual, the discussions (and Isabel's own reflections) demonstrated the normalization of this form of suffering among women.

Symbolic, structural, and gender forms of violence are also expressed in illnesses that are associated with nervios, such as insomnia, high blood pressure, and headaches. Any of these symptoms may be caused by poor diet or malnutrition (themselves expressions of structural and symbolic violence) or a range of other ailments. However, in the *women's* view these were caused by situations linked to the context (of multifaceted violence) in which they lived. Andrea, a mother of two, was twenty-three when we first met, though she looked much older because all but three of her teeth were missing and she always had an afflicted expression on her face. She was one of the women who had no schooling and had never been able to attend any literacy courses either. Looking nervous and a bit agitated, Andrea said that she felt "desperation" and a headache when people gossiped about her, and she felt her nerves being altered as a result. She also got colic when she was upset and cried when she knew people questioned her "decency." As in the case of Isabel, Andrea mentioned that prayer helped, especially if it was someone close to her who prayed: "When my brother Chusito prays, I get better. I think that God, the Holy Spirit, conquers all these demons around me, and I feel better." And Hortencia, with the wide-eyed, perennially worried expression I came to associate with her, mentioned that she almost had a nervous breakdown because of her problems. After Hortencia became a widow people had gossiped about her, and because she thought of herself as a decent woman gossip affected her physically, especially because she was trying to make an honest living to provide for her children.

> People were talking about me, saying that I had a man in my house and maybe I was even pregnant. I didn't get upset, but I got very sad. I felt a knot in my throat because the person who told me about this gossip is someone very close to my heart, and it hurt me a lot. She turned around and left, but I felt awful. I felt like crying. And I couldn't tell this person anything because she's very close and dear to me. I went to get a drink of water, but from then on I don't remember anything. I fell on the floor. My neighbors came, and they say that I had—my heart was beating so loud they could hear it. I don't know what they did, but I came to later on. The next day I went to work, but I felt very tired; just from walking to the market I was out of breath. I got to the place where I work, and I fainted in the kitchen. My *patrona* [boss] called the doctor, and then I went to his clinic. He gave me medicines and a diet, but most of all he told me that I needed to learn how to control my emotions. But this is hard. When you're alone [without a husband] people can destroy you.

Hortencia said that she was lucky her patrona had called the doctor; otherwise she could have died. However, this kindness left Hortencia in huge financial debt. The patrona paid for the doctor and the medicine but expected Hortencia to repay the entire amount. Hortencia then worried about being *enjaranada* (indebted). Hortencia's situation was not unlike that of many other women, and her words indicated that her distress was related to the conditions in which she lived, to social suffering, and was shaped by class and gender inequalities.

These expressions of nervios were not confined to poor women. Delfina, a thirty-five-year-old teacher whose family and husband's family were landowners and well off, is a case in point. Sitting in a well-appointed living room with a chandelier and ornate furniture, she said that she often felt that her "nervous system was altered," that her "nerves were destroyed," and that she was always living on the verge of a breakdown (Taussig's [1992] " nervous system" and perpetual state of emergency come to mind here). She took medicine for her nervios, but nothing helped, and she realized it was her husband who was the cause, not her. Her mother-in-law and others had suggested that she see a neurologist in Guatemala City and perhaps seek therapy there. But she felt she was in a catch-22 situation.

> I can't go to get treatment in Guate[mala] because I work all the time. Well, I *like* to go to work because I forget my situation. But if I want to go to Guate, who's going to make my husband his meals? Who's going to take care of him? He doesn't let me go. I wish I could go because I really feel like I need to be treated by a specialist. Oh no, he doesn't let any of our servants serve him; it always has to be me. God forbid I'm not home and available to serve him his meals exactly how he likes them! It turns into a scandal. Not even his mother can substitute for me. I truly live *esclavizada* [enslaved].

Delfina later reiterated that perhaps not even therapy and medicine would help, and she was convinced that she was not solely to blame for her condition.

Gloria also linked her headaches and nervios to her "situation" at home, and she had resorted to taking medication regularly. She explained that sometimes she even had convulsions, which she had suffered since she was a little girl but which had worsened in the last years of her marriage. "[My husband] won't change," she said, "so I have to do something. And what I can do is take my medicine and make sure that I see the doctor. That's all. I have to find treatment for myself if I don't want to lose my mind." Although both Delfina and Gloria said their husbands were to blame for their ailments, what I want to focus on is that their husbands' frames of reference, their cognitive repertoires, and views of how they should behave arise from the "social order of things" in San Alejo.

Women in the Altiplano were not much different in this respect. Many mentioned the same symptoms and sometimes blamed their husbands for their ill health. Alberta, a forty-four-year-old weaver and the mother of five, said that she got colic because of her husband's *carácter* (personality, nature); he got angry at her and the children for no reason at all and beat them. He claimed that he was the one who suffered from nervios, but for Alberta it hurt all the same. "One day he explodes and hits us, and the next day, for sure, I'll have my colic and my nervios. My stomach hurts, and I feel my heart aching too. Have you ever felt your heart aching? It's really painful. I don't go to the doctor because they charge too much and I don't earn enough. So I take rue, Alka-Seltzer, or Tabcin." Azucena, a twenty-three-year-old tortilla maker and part-time domestic worker and the mother of two toddler girls, explained that her nervios had resulted in something akin to cancer on her face. I found this intriguing and asked her what she meant. Azucena explained:

> After I had my second daughter my husband didn't bother to come from Xela [Quetzaltenango], even though I sent him, like, three telegrams. We had run out of corn, sugar, tomatoes. Poor doña Diana [one of the few ladinas in town] gave us tortillas but only for the children. Susi [Azucena's eldest daughter] was crying because she wanted to have some bread and coffee, and I had nothing to give her. From all that [tension] my face turned awful; it was like cancer. A neighbor gave me some sugar and a bag of bread. Finally my husband came by with some money. He was asking why I had to call him. "Can't you see, I told him, I don't have money even for wood for the stove or to buy corn?" And he still asked me why I wanted him to come by! So here I am with the girls suffering, and he's over there in Xela eating well. Tell me, is this just? And people fill my head with things. They ask me, "Are you sure he doesn't have another [woman] in Xela?"

Often the women in both towns were unable to obtain treatment for their various conditions. Either other family members' illnesses or needs came first or their husbands stood in the way. Susana had a permanent headache; it just never went away. It was difficult to describe to others, she said, because not many people knew what it was like to have a permanent headache.[5] Her nervios were bad too, or as she put it, "My nerves betray me often." The pharmacist she knew could not help her, and every time she wanted to go to the health post one of her children fell ill, and she had no money for both of them to have consultations and medicines. The fact that the women perennially suffered from these ailments did not seem to be a cause for alarm to anyone in their families. The women would say, "This is how it is around here," but they also pointed to the sources of their suffering in structures around them, sometimes to their husbands but often to the general conditions in which they lived, such as lack of access to medical care.

In the Altiplano I came across one of the most dramatic cases of nervios. Antonia was a devout Catholic and member of several church committees, and she often hosted church activities at her house. There was usually a big altar displayed in the main room of the house, and there were always pine needles on the floor, signs that there had been or was going to be a religious celebration there. She and her husband were held in high regard, and Antonia enjoyed the social recognition she commanded. She was a weaver and her husband an agriculturalist, but he also was in the army, which required that he be away from their home for months at a time. It seemed at first that Antonia lived in relative comfort, without much to worry about. She used to say that she almost never got sick, except that her nervios bothered her. She went to the departmental capital for treatment (an indication of her higher socioeconomic standing in town) but had to stop because she did not want to leave her children alone; besides, it was getting too expensive. The pharmacist examined her and told her to try to be calm because her nervios were altered: "The pharmacist told me, 'Look, you need to forget your worries, you think too much. You are alone, and you need not to worry so much.'" On another one of my visits, Antonia complained about a pain in her abdomen, which was related to nervios, she said. She thought her nervios had given her an ulcer, but she was confident that it would go away. However, two years later I visited her house once again and found her husband and the children alone. Her husband told me Antonia had died two months earlier, from complications from the pain in her abdomen. I was stunned by the news and told him that she had mentioned it to me on a few occasions but had assured me it was nothing to worry about. "But she worried too much about everything without telling people, you know how women are; they suffer in secret a lot, to not add troubles to others," he explained. "She worried about me, my job, and how far away I was, and the military and the *violencia* that can come back and all that. Los nervios se la llevaron [Her nerves took her life]."

In San Alejo I met Hortencia's neighbor, an affable woman with an easy smile. One afternoon I went to visit Hortencia and brought some cookies for her and her children. The neighbor met me outside and told me they were not home, so the neighbor invited me into her own house for a visit. Over chilled grape soda and the cookies I had brought, she recounted stories about her life, her preoccupations, and her plans but also her nervios and headaches. She pointed to a different immediate cause for her suffering, but a closer look revealed similar instances of pain linked to the context in which she lived. She was thirty-four and separated from her husband and had three living children (one child had died). She worried a great deal because her sixteen-year-old daughter had begun to "speak to boys," and she was afraid her daughter might start a relationship and go to live with the boy. I asked her if she worried because the girl was young. Although this concerned her, it was not the focus of her worries: "Well, yes, she's young, but I got married even younger. So, yes, I worry about that because one suffers in marriage [her eyes become teary]. But I worry more about the fact that she doesn't have a father. Who's going to be responsible for the expenses? Without a father who is responsible this is going to be difficult. If there's no father at home, people will think there's no respect at home. She will suffer afterward, and this worries me every night." What this woman meant was not that her daughter's father had died but that he had not been responsible for her and had stopped giving her money or even asking about her.

To be sure, women were not alone in lacking access to treatment, for poor men in San Alejo and most men in the Altiplano also had to make tough choices between paying for consultations and medicines for themselves or spending the money on food and clothing for their children. Poor men also suffered the effects of structural and symbolic violence, and some of them, like women, seemed to put the health of others before their own. However, for women it was natural to endure, and it seemed that others either did not notice what women went through or saw the suffering as an expected condition, just an aspect of being a woman. Either way, their suffering was so present that it went misrecognized and normalized.

In spite of the scarcity and its complexities in the women's lives, when they were ill they were seldom alone. Invariably, they would talk about good neighbors, friendly coreligionists, coworkers, and compassionate *patrones* who had come to their aid during an illness or a difficult moment. In San Alejo Mirna made it a point to tell me that whenever she fell ill or had given birth, her *vecinas* (female neighbors), not *vecinos* (male neighbors), always dropped by with sugar, soap, and money. One of them, who knew that Mirna loved to suck on lemons during her pregnancies, always brought her lemons in the last trimester of her pregnancy. The women in the Altiplano were no different.

Alberta always found refuge with her neighbors when her husband beat her, even though her husband argued with the neighbors for interfering. However, in both San Alejo and the Altiplano the women always qualified these instances of assistance. Mirna explained, "My neighbors will help, but it all depends on one's behavior. If I am helped, they also expect me to help them back. As the saying goes, *agrado quiere agrado* [roughly, if you are good to others, others will be good to you]. And Hortencia mentioned that if it had not been for her neighbors she would be in even worse shape, but she felt they had helped her because they saw that she was a struggling and *decent* single mother. These perceptions are important and relate to the women's image and reputation, two forms of social control and sources of *moral capital* linked to symbolic and gender violence.[6]

IMAGE, REPUTATION, AND THE MANAGEMENT OF THE SELF IN EVERYDAY LIFE

Not all the body-related gendered, gender, and other forms of violence were expressed in illnesses, nervios, or physical pain. There were dimensions that were less tangible but equally harmful; one might call these the hidden injuries of corporeal inequality, borrowing from Sennett and Cobb (1972), and they are linked to how others interpret women's behavior and attribute meaning to women's actions. Thus this aspect of violence to the body involves the construction of meaning, socially embedded but veiled injury, and the inscription of profoundly unequal power relations. Importantly, as Sally Engle Merry (1997) noted, although gossip is part of larger social processes, it is the already vulnerable who are more prone to feel its negative effects. "Gossip controls behavior when the people who gossip exercise other forms of social control over its victims," she observed (48).

Thus one of the most powerful and efficacious forms of control in the women's lives was gossip. Taking gossip out of context or placing it in a different discussion or situation may present this practice as the product of culture or tradition, unrelated to violence in the way I am arguing it is linked. However, in this milieu, where other sources of suffering act on one another, gossip becomes a form of violence because it is a weapon of social control and a source of humiliation, pain, and affliction in the women's lives.[7] The women I met worried about *el qué dirán* (what others will say), or "critiques," gossip that could hurt and perhaps ruin their reputations, and about the consequences it might have for their lives, including abandonment or diminished support and decreased opportunities to find (and keep) a partner. Regardless of their social standing, the women took extreme care to conduct themselves so as not to call negative attention to themselves and not to lead anyone to suspect them of "misbehaving," either in the streets or at home. In a manner similar to that of the Sullk'atas of Bolivia in Krista Van Vleet's (2003) study, the San Alejo women carried out their lives in a state of constant awareness of the talk and attention of others, an awareness that conditioned their actions, words, postures, and movements. Gossip, as it was explained to me more than once in San Alejo, "can destroy [women's] lives."

The anthropologist Max Gluckman (1963: 307) wrote that "gossip and scandal . . . are among the most important societal and cultural phenomena we are called upon to analyse." He observed that "every single day, and for a large part of each day, most of us are engaged in gossiping" and that talking about one another is what helps maintain a group as such and fulfills an important social function (307, 308). Gossip is purposeful communication that informs, entertains, but also influences (Fine and Rosnow 1978); it reports behavior and is based on evaluating reputations (Haviland 1977; White 2000). Thus gossip defines power relations; talking (as well as keeping silent) about others can discipline, manage, and create categories of virtue and deviance (see Foucault 1978).[8] Gossip permeates formal spheres of social control, and it is in this way that it shapes reputations (Engle Merry 1997; Haviland 1977). In this manner, as the women in San Alejo often implied, gossip can be a dangerous tool (see Haviland 1977). It can be used to control others by managing impressions (Goffman 1959) about those who gossip as well as those who are the subject of gossip (Haviland 1977).

Importantly, Luise White (2000: 60) observes that "gossip is a matter of context and convention" to which individuals attach multiple meanings (see Fine and Rosnow 1978). The context in which gossip circulates is crucial; it determines the meanings that individuals attach to the information conveyed through the act of gossiping, but at the same time it exposes underlying power structures in a particular milieu. Thus talk becomes gossip in a specific sociocultural context that is historically situated. As Ulf Hannerz (1967: 36) observes, "The same information may be gossip or non-gossip depending on who gives it to whom." My discussion of gossip is situated within these analytic observations and reflects the women's views and actions on the subject of talking about others and being talked about. Three aspects are central to the link between gossip, control, and forms of misrecognized everyday violence: women's formidable efforts to portray a positive image; their efforts to avoid a negative reputation; and the control of the women's physical movement. The first two represent two sides of the same coin; the third brings them together to highlight the injuries of gossip in women's lives.

A Good Reputation and the Construction of a Positive Image

For the women I met in San Alejo, it was key to construct a positive image about themselves as mothers, wives, and daughters. They were well aware that being *perceived* as dutiful, virtuous, and devoted would not just command respect and often admiration but also bring pecuniary as well as nontangible benefits to themselves and their families. In other words, they were quite aware that a positive image of themselves could translate into moral capital (see also Eckert 1993; Van Vleet 2003), and they accomplished this by adhering (or *seeming* to adhere) to prescribed norms of behavior. As Van Vleet (2003: 505) insightfully observes, "In contrast to men's capital, the value of which is established in the marketplace, women's symbolic capital must be evaluated in relation to community norms for their behavior. . . . These norms require regular monitoring, and because it is women [historically] who must compete in relation to these norms, it is they who have the greatest interest in monitoring." The women I came to know in both towns in Guatemala went to great lengths to be perceived in a positive light by those around them, in particular, by other women, even if doing so meant sacrifices, pain, and suffering that, as several confided, they kept to themselves. It was the way they talked about the challenges of keeping up good appearances that made me suspect that gossip, in this context, was a form of violence. And it was the kind of violence that individuals inflicted on one another in everyday interactions, words and silences, gazes, and corporeal expressions in ways that could easily be misrecognized as such.

Nena, a trained teacher, was a friendly woman in her late thirties and the mother of three children. She lived in the center of town next door to her in-laws, and her husband's family was one of the most prominent in San Alejo. They were landowners and well connected; her brother-in-law once held a cabinet-level post in the Guatemalan government. Her easygoing personality and quick smile betrayed a profound sadness and pain that surfaced easily as the conversation turned to her husband's bouts with alcoholism and depression. She referred to him as *"mi sufrimiento"* (my suffering) or *"mi tortura"* (my torture) and described a married life punctuated by pain, sacrifice, and humiliations. "I destroyed my life the moment I got married," she once commented. However, Nena made sure that her image as a proper wife and dedicated mother came through in all our conversations about her troubles. "You see," she told me, "he can't attend parties because of his problem; he is always drunk, and so I go by myself. Well, not really alone. If I go to a party, I always go with my brothers or with his parents or his family. Sometimes I really want to go out and have fun, but I can't because, well, I don't know, it's not proper to go alone [laughs], you understand, right? I swallow a lot, believe me I do. So no, I only leave the house alone when I go to church, things of God. I leave the house the way it should be. He can have his problem, but I am respectable, right [smiles]?"[9]

Hortencia, in contrast, came from humble origins. She often struggled to feed her children on the meager profits she made from selling tostadas every afternoon in the park. But like Nena, Hortencia was fully aware that she had a reputation to maintain and what that meant for concrete aspects of life. Over the years I was in contact with her, she would mention the difficulties of living alone, as a widow with five children; she would mention the financial challenges but, most important, the social cost of being a single woman. She confided that it was even more difficult for her to establish new relationships: "Look, I will be sincere with you, one makes mistakes, but the biggest mistake I have made was to start living with this señor. I didn't start living with him just because I needed a man, but because of the respect. One needs the respect of living with a man. I was also tired of working so much. I have been working alone to support my children for six years [after her husband died]. But people talk too much. It was not worth it [living with the man]." Hortencia felt the need to explain her situation, even producing witnesses to her good behavior. In her words: "Look, you have seen me living alone. My neighbors are Evangelicals, and they see that the door of my house is always closed at night, that I don't open it for anyone, that I close it at eight at night. You see, I even ask the neighbor [with whom she shares a patio] to let me out of the house through her door, so that my door is always seen closed after it gets dark. If people see my door open at night they'll think that men are coming in! I don't want problems, gossip. Bad tongues, God forbid, create problems." And bad tongues were everywhere and a source of deep concern for women. As White (2000: 59) observes, "Gossip is more aural than oral; the fact that it is heard is more important than the fact that it is spoken."

Once, when we were sitting on the only two chairs in the front room of her house, a room that functioned as living room and bedroom, Hortencia told me that she never tired of giving advice to young women about the importance of behaving well: "I tell them, look, behave well. I am not an old person, who should be giving advice, but I do know that I have been beaten by life; my life has been hard. So I know that if you behave as a respectable woman, people will treat you well. People see that I work hard, so people help me. But if people see that one is in the street, or that one talks to anyone in the street, then they will not help you, they will say, 'Ah, that *fulana* [so-and-so] is a *cualquiera* [lit. "anybody," here meaning someone with loose morals]." Hortencia stressed the link between a good image as a single woman and how people responded to her when in need.

> If one is seen alone, with children, and that you respect yourself, people take pity on you and help. Yes, this other señor comes by, but always with his wife, ah no, no, always with his wife, and they bring me beans, corn, rice. And I know they do this because they have seen my behavior. It's the same with my neighbors. They have seen my need but also my behavior. So sometimes they come and say, "Look, here's some bread," or "Here's some corn." But if they thought I was a loose one who had men in the house all the time, and even if they saw me hungry they would not lend me a hand.

Mirna also knew the value of a good reputation, of moral capital, and, like Hortencia, was always ready to share her insights with young girls. Mirna was very specific in her advice, because she did not want young women to make some of the mistakes she had made: "I tell them, don't laugh too much when you are walking in the street, because people will talk. They will say, 'Ah, so and so's daughter is probably looking for a man. She is a loose one.' One has to be *recatada* [modest, chaste]. People first think the worst."

Vera, the twenty-year-old mother of a baby girl, was also well aware of the importance of "good behavior." Like the rest of the women, she knew well that moral capital accrued from adhering to strict codes of gender-appropriate behavior. Similar to social capital, moral capital increases with use; the more women adhere to strict codes of behavior (or *appear* as if they do), the more moral capital they accumulate. Like Nena, Vera was married to a man with a drinking problem who also came from a prominent family. Both Nena and Vera came from lower social-class backgrounds than their husbands, and like Nena,

Vera felt she could go for help to her mother-in-law, who lived next door, almost any time. Vera's mother-in-law had been like a mother to her, she explained. Aware of what class differences can mean in this context, Vera remarked that her in-laws have treated her well because her mother is a hard worker and has done well financially. Vera's mother had a business renting rooms and owned a lucrative cafeteria next to it. But most of all, Vera and her sister had good reputations in town; they were serious, were never seen hanging out in the streets, and were very *de la casa* (of the home). In Vera's eyes, this made her worthy of the good treatment she had received from her in-laws; her chastity and good reputation had offset her lower social-class origins. Plus her husband was not a good provider; he got drunk, did not hold a permanent job, hung out with friends, drove fast cars, and often left her alone when their daughter was a newborn. With a hint of tears in her eyes and looking a little pensive, Vera mentioned that some people in town gossiped that her in-laws were good to her because they wanted to keep her for their son; no other woman would put up with him. These comments made Vera very sad. "My mother-in-law is always there for me because *me tiene cariño* [she loves me] because I behave well, not because I'm the only one who can put up with her son." Swallowing her pride, Vera always went to her mother-in-law for financial help even though her own mother had money, because her mother got upset when she was reminded of Vera's husband's irresponsibility as a provider. And Estrella, the proud owner of a photography studio, was aware that because she was "alone" (single) and had worked as a photographer to sustain her family, people gossiped about her. But there were some individuals in town who recognized her efforts and good behavior. Her physician often told her that he admired her for her hard work and struggles to feed her family, so instead of charging her 20 quetzales for the consultation he charged her 10. But she did not want to abuse people's kindness toward her, so she often preferred to suffer with her children in silence.

Some women went to extremes to portray a positive image of themselves or at least the image that was expected of them given their social position. Mariana was twenty-five years old when I first met her, and she told me she was married to the father of her two sons. Her family was wealthy by local standards; they owned considerable expanses of land that landless peasants cultivated (Mariana and her family lived on the wealthy side of the medianía system). Her sons' father also came from a well-off family, though everyone in town knew her family had more money than did his. The first time I visited Mariana I went to her in-laws' air-conditioned, two-story house in the center of town, where she lived. During one visit she narrated a long story about her civil marriage, describing in detail the intimate gathering she had for the *pedida* (the occasion when women are asked for in marriage) and her small reception after the wedding and that her husband picked the wedding godparents. As I got to know others in town, they told me that Mariana had never married but that she very much wanted to because given her class position, it would be expected that she be married and not just cohabitating. A nurse at the health post explained that Mariana wanted me to think of her as a respectable woman, not as someone who was just living with a man, a situation more likely to occur among less respectable women, she said. Thus Mariana opted for telling me a story she thought I wanted to hear; or perhaps she was indeed married and no one else in town knew, though this was improbable because everyone seemed to know everything about everyone else in San Alejo, in particular, about the well-off individuals who lived in the center of town (and thus were also the center of public attention).[10]

There are two contrasting stories that highlight the benefits of conveying a good impression. Leticia, the woman who was infected with HIV/AIDS, was already very ill during this conversation. Gaunt and languid, rocking on a hammock, she explained, "I have an illness that no one can find a cure for. My sister-in-law in Guate[mala] told me to go to the doctor, but I went and they gave me nothing. Besides I have to save money to go there, and since I have nothing I don't go." A nurse at the health post told me that Leticia had in fact gone to the doctor for treatment but that she preferred not to tell anyone about it for fear that people would gossip; regular doctor's visits would confirm her illness. But the nurse told me that everyone knew of Leticia's condition; in fact, everyone knew even about her visits to the doctor. Some people did not want anything to do with her because they feared they would get infected; others helped her with small things because they felt sorry for her. Apparently, Leticia had contracted the disease from her husband, who had allegedly been infected by a Salvadoran sex worker who passed through town on her way north. The nurse said that everyone knew the whole story, and because of Leticia's good behavior some people sometimes offered her help. One of the doctors in town gave her free checkups occasionally, and at the health post she got some free medication such as cough syrup. And people who themselves were renting land to cultivate would allow her to pick tomatoes there so that she could earn some money "decently." The story of Analicia stands in contrast to Leticia's. The daughter of a barber and a member of a family I came to know well, Analicia also had contracted HIV/AIDS, but she was a single woman working in Guatemala City, and people suspected she had contracted the disease in "dubious ways." When her name came up in conversation her family often changed the subject to avoid questions, and when she died her funeral was attended mostly by members of the Pentecostal church where her father was a pastor; most of her neighbors and others in town did not attend. According to a nurse at the health post, her family "suffered doubly, because of the loss of Analicia and because of what having AIDS signifies; it's like going around with a sign saying, 'I'm bad.'" Gossip about individuals' behavior and their HIV status has significant ramifications for social interactions and relationships within networks (Smith, Lucas, and Latkin 1999), often adding insult to injury.

During my time in San Alejo I had an opportunity to experience the response to a call for help from a woman who was perceived as respectable. One day I locked myself out of the room I rented, and the landlady was angry at me because she said it was going to be expensive to have the lock rekeyed. It was close to noon when this happened, and my first thought was to go to the barber's house, as his sons and sons-in-law worked at a welding workshop across the street from their house and might be able to help me. Not only did the men in the workshop help, but the entire family mobilized, even though it was lunchtime and they were getting ready to eat. Two women with several children in tow accompanied me to the welding shop, and three men came out to help, followed by a few others moments later. When I arrived to have my room opened with this small army of people the landlady was surprised and smiled. That evening at the park I ran into the secretary of the health post, and I told her about my little adventure. She laughed and intimated that it must have been my reputation as a serious woman who was not looking for men (and also was perceived as religious) that got me the help; the women in that family, the secretary explained, saw me in trouble and understood that I needed their help. I wrote in field notes that day that the response I received in a moment of need probably exemplified the importance of a woman's moral capital in San Alejo.

For women whose male partners (or close family members on whom they depended financially) were working in the United States, it was crucial to project a good image (see also Dreby 2009). They went the extra mile to make sure that they were perceived as being dedicated to their homes, devoted to their children, and faithful to their partners. The women's "good behavior" in this respect served to reassure others that the fruits of the men's labor in the United States were being put to good use. As Joanna Dreby (2009) has noted, transnational gossip affects both men and women in the home and host countries, but it is a highly gendered activity because it reinforces expectations about men as providers and women as caretakers. And Heike Drotbohm (2010) has observed that "transnational communication" is not just talk that informs; it is gossip that creates new moralities and asymmetries, and this communication becomes a powerful tool of social control across borders. Thus the women in San Alejo whose husbands were working in the United States would take special care in making sure that their children wore nice clothes and looked clean, that their homes looked the part, adorned with gifts and electronics brought from the United States; even when attending a celebration they brought a gift indicative of the success of their male partners in the United States (see Menjívar and Agadjanian 2007).

Behind these efforts there was usually sacrifice involved, as often the women were constrained in what they did and said and would act in a way that was expected of them, regardless of what they had to forgo. An entry in my field notes reads, "Especially when husbands are in the United States the women have to be even more careful about appearances." I wrote this one evening after a long afternoon of visits with different women. Isabel, whose husband worked in Connecticut, was one of them. She assured me that she left the house only when she needed to run an errand, but other than that I could stop by any time because she was *always* home. She elaborated: "These people [in San Alejo] have gotten me in problems with my husband, and I tell him, 'Look, if you want to believe their lies, it's up to you, but only God knows that I don't have any other men in my life except you. When you're not here I don't even stick my nose out the door. God knows everything.' " At the same time, Isabel was always told that her husband had girlfriends in Connecticut, and as a result she lived *"angustiada y nerviosa"* (anguished and nervous). The uncertainty of not knowing if her husband would leave her for one of the girlfriends he supposedly had kept her on edge. Thus a missed phone call from her husband when he had said he would call, a rushed call, a "disinterested tone" in his voice, or ambiguity in his plans to return could trigger a crisis for Isabel, including lack of appetite and migraines.[11]

Lucrecia's image in San Alejo and the gossip that traveled to her parents in the United States had had serious consequences. She lived with her two sisters; neither she nor her sisters were married, and all of their children had different fathers. To make matters worse, these young women were not originally from San Alejo but had moved there from the coast of Guatemala, and women from the coast, I was told, had dubious reputations. The fact that these young women lived "alone," were single mothers with seven children among them, and had a penchant for loud music served to corroborate their "bad reputation." In fact, on several occasions I was advised not to visit them because of their reputations. Lucrecia, *la costeña* (the coastal woman), as she was called, did not have a good image to maintain and along with her sisters was ostracized by others in town. However, the sisters got along well, lived in a clean house with sparkling floors, and helped one another in the house and made a living by selling food and fruit in the street and at the park; when two sisters were out selling the third would stay home with the seven children. Eleven years earlier their mother had departed for the United States, leaving them in that house in the care of an aunt, who later moved to another town. At first their mother wrote and sent money, but then the three girls started to have boyfriends. Without the presence of their parents, they had "lost respect" and brought men, sometimes married men, to the house. One by one they became pregnant, and their mother stopped writing and sending money. At the time I knew them she had recently threatened that as soon as she got her papers in order in the United States (she was still undocumented) she would travel to Guatemala and kick them out of the house. The mother had "insulted" them and called them names because of their conduct, Lucrecia said. Reflecting on the situation, she blamed herself for her bad reputation. She explained, "It's something I sought for myself; no one pushed me. When one is alone, young, you know, one makes mistakes. What has happened we have done to ourselves."

Teresa was in a similar situation. She started to live with a man who apparently did not respect her because her parents were in the United States. She was twenty-one when I first met her and had studied dressmaking but did not finish. The last time I saw her she had had two children. Her parents were upset because she dishonored them and her brothers, who also lived in the United States and did not want anything to do with her either. They refused to help her out with even minimal things; it was as if she had no family, she said. "I made a mistake. I had a child with a man, and then I went back to him after he got married.

He says he can't forget me, so now that he's married, he has come back to me. I love him too, I can't deny that. But now I am alone, my whole family is upset, and I can't count on anyone; I'm alone in this world and have to aguantar (endure)."

Both Lucrecia and Teresa were the subject of quite a bit of gossip in town; they had not been able to maintain a positive image, a situation that exacerbated their already fragile socioeconomic position, as even remittances had stopped as a result of their behavior. Their lives exemplify the destructive consequences of gossip, superimposed on structures of inequality that exacerbate the effects of gender ideology. In line with Bourdieu's theorizing on symbolic violence, the women pointed to themselves as culpable for their own misfortunes and suffering because the cognitive frameworks through which they understand the world around them are shaped by the same social order that produces the inequalities and suffering in their lives.

"Gossip Can Destroy": Avoiding a Negative Image

Gossip can be used to usher in conformity, control behaviors, and bring behaviors in line with social expectations and norms of conduct (Smith, Lucas, and Latkin 1999). It regulates behavior by conveying information about what is acceptable and what is not. One consequence of avoiding gossip is a reduced number of contacts or potential contacts, which limits the span of informal networks, a situation that can carry negative consequences for individuals' resources. One important channel of beneficial information is informal conversations with people who are not close, what Granovetter (1973, 1995) refers to as "weak ties." However, in trying to avoid a negative image of themselves (and gossip), San Alejo women often tried to keep to themselves, or at least talked about how they tried to do so. They tried to be perceived as socializing less or as sharing little about their personal lives, which in their eyes would limit the dissemination of compromising personal information. But in trying to keep to themselves, many women would avoid activating social ties, such as friends of friends or male nonrelatives (see also Menjívar 2000) and thus reduce their social circles and potential sources of information and assistance.[12]

Andrea was one of the most isolated women I came to know in San Alejo. I was told that she did not have any friends and hardly ever talked with anyone. I asked one of the workers at the health post to introduce me to her. I was told that Andrea simply did not like to talk.

When we did meet Andrea seemed a bit apprehensive, but then she agreed to talk with me and later allowed an interview. Sometimes we conversed in the street or at the park. In the course of our conversations she confided that she never talked to people, never asked for a favor, and never contacted anyone. This was intriguing to me, since San Alejo is a small town in which everyone knew each other, and it was hard to imagine this level of isolation in such a context. Andrea had resorted to this practice so that people would not ask her questions and then gossip. She explained, "I don't talk to anyone, I don't ask for a favor, nothing. Since I don't know how to read and write, I sometimes need someone to read a letter for me. But I don't even get many letters, so I don't need to ask anyone for that." Some people told me that her stepfather was to blame for her isolation; he was suspected of abusing her physically and sexually, leaving her slightly disabled mentally. Andrea had been living with him and her young son since her mother died, and people suspected that her baby daughter was her stepfather's child. The stepfather had a "terrible temper" and thus Andrea avoided any inquisitive questions by cutting ties with everyone, even if it meant almost complete isolation. In contrast to Andrea's case, at first I thought that Tita, a thirty-four-year-old mother of six with no formal education who worked picking tomatoes, would have a robust network of friends to turn to because she was in training to be a *comadrona* (midwife) and thus had to maintain regular contact with many women. However, Tita said that she was always careful to confide only in a friend she had known since childhood because this friend would not gossip about her. The two exchanged favors with each other but not with others, mostly to avoid gossip. Thus whereas Andrea had very little contact with others and Tita seemed to be very well connected, both limited their interactions and web of potential sources of support with the objective of avoiding gossip.

A similar case was that of Emilia, a twenty-six-year-old teacher by training who worked as an office clerk at a health clinic. Her husband spent nine months of the year working different jobs, mainly gardening, in Trenton, New Jersey. Because she often felt that "everything depends" on how she behaved (or was *perceived* to behave) when her husband was away, she preferred to keep to herself. In her words: "Look, the majority of time I don't talk to anyone about my worries, my problems—everything stays in me. I don't trust people. Once I had a bad experience with a friend; I confided in her, and she gossiped about me, and it got all the way to New Jersey. So now I don't talk to anyone. At night it's really bad because I'm alone. I think and think and think, and sometimes I feel I'll get sick, but I just don't confide in anyone. I just distract myself with something, a novel, a magazine, the TV. But no, I don't have anyone to share my problems with." In Hortencia's case, determination to keep a reputable image and avoid gossip had led her to separate from a good, responsible man with whom she had established a relationship after she was left a widow. She said, "Problems with this man started purely from the bad tongues of people, not because he was bad. No, he was good, never beat me, never drank too much, never mistreated me or my children. He was very good."

The situation was not so different in the Altiplano. Many women there commented on what they went through to avoid gossip, which also included cutting off ties with others, even if it meant fewer sources of support and exchange. Dalia, a twenty-five-year-old weaver and the mother of three young children, told me that she could only turn to her mother for help because everyone, especially her neighbors, loved to gossip. In Julia's case, she and her partner had almost separated five or six times because people gossiped too much about them. They were not married and had no children together, and her partner had not been completely separated from his wife when he and Julia started their relationship. She loved him very much, but her life had become a paradox: the closer she got to him, the more isolated she became from others. He gave her nice things to wear, but sometimes she refused to wear a new *corte* he had bought for her so that people would not "talk." She continued, "I don't even like to go to church so that I can avoid people. I listen to mass on the radio. I avoid all that because people talk too much, and it affects me too much."[13] Isa went so far as to assure me that much of what was wrong with her town was due to gossip: "In this town there is too much gossip. One tells someone something, and then that person adds something and tells it to another and so on. Eesh, it becomes big! My own mother-in-law doesn't talk to me these days because of gossip, because of the tongues of people who have nothing better to do. I never ask anyone for any help, to avoid bad tongues. In this town people need to be closer to God so they learn how to control their tongues. Our problems would be solved."

I do not mean to suggest that women in San Alejo (or in the Altiplano) completely isolate themselves in order to avoid gossip. My observations point to what women go through to avoid the pernicious effects of gossip, even if it costs them socially.[14] But the picture is more complex, as women do engage in multiple and varied social exchanges, though they remain mindful of how they might be perceived and guard their image from "bad tongues." Thus, for instance, although Vera in San Alejo was careful not to go to neighbors or friends for advice and personal conversations, she was far from being totally isolated with her worries and concerns. She explained, "I have my mami. I go to her for everything. Even if friends love me, it's not the same thing; they may have the best intentions, but it's not the same with friends. Besides, I don't want friends and neighbors to know how I live, what life inside my house is like! Things of the house should stay in the house, right?" She was careful not to mention to people outside her family any of the problems she had with her husband, which she confessed would just embarrass her (but, I discovered, practically the entire town knew about them anyway). "As you now know, my husband drinks, yes, he drinks [her eyes become watery and her voice cracks], and the truth is that I always speak with my mami and my sister about it. There's nothing I can do, so talking with my mami about it helps me. With her *me desahogo* [I find relief]." Or, as in the case of Lila, who considered herself very friendly and to have lots of acquaintances: "The majority of my neighbors are my friends but I don't like to visit people too much. But if there is an illness or something like that, then I'm there with them."

Social class position introduces an interesting caveat to how women socialized with others in San Alejo. Due to her higher-class background, Mariana seemed obligated to socialize more than she would have liked. She felt compelled to invite people to birthday celebrations to avoid gossip; she confessed she did this out of obligation and not because she wanted to: "If people show an interest in how one is doing, one feels obligated to invite them. So if there's a celebration and people are not invited, they talk [she smiles], so one has to invite." In contrast, María Ruth, a woman who came from one of the poorest families in town and lived in a one-room straw-and-mud house in a compound with her in-laws, said that she had never felt obligated to invite people to a celebration because most people she knew did not have the resources to be able to reciprocate. When they had a small gathering those close to her would come by, "for the pure pleasure of having people I care about here, gathered." I do not mean to romanticize María Ruth's life as more honest or sincere; I am simply pointing to an interesting class difference related to the women's social lives, a difference I was able to capture because these women's comments, reflecting their class position, were different. And Susana, one of the poorest women I came to know in San Alejo, told me that she managed to obtain a good amount of resources for herself and her family through her purposeful socializing. People understood her predicament and out of compassion would lend her a hand. Susana also noted the reciprocity involved: "My neighbor sees me, and she sometimes gives me some corn for our tortillas, so I help her grind corn. People can be good sometimes. But one can't go around [socializing] too much because that's not good in a woman." As if for effect, she paused and then added, "Bad tongues follow women with too many friends."

DOMINATION AND CONTROL

The destructive aspects of gossip go hand in hand with the control of movement. Often husbands and male partners, aided by their families (and often the women's families) and friends when necessary, controlled where their partners and wives could or should go, how long they had for errands or visits, who could accompany them, and even if the women's reasons for going to a certain place were warranted. The result was an overwhelming control over physical movement that constrained women, curtailed their social interactions, and became a palpable source of distress in their lives. It was clear that a woman's reputation had to be protected, and one way to do so was to control her movement. As with some of the other forms of violence, this intense control was normalized in the context of (male) protection of women; it was often interpreted as an expression of care and love. In practice, however, it translated into torment, as women endured unwanted and long periods of separation from friends, coworkers, and loved ones, and ultimately it served more to protect men's reputations than women's well-being.

For instance, Silvia was concerned about her situation. She was twenty years old at the time we became acquainted and had a baby boy. She and her partner met when he was stationed as a guard in her coastal hometown, but after they became a couple and she became pregnant he decided that she should move in with his parents. Patrilocality is the norm in San Alejo, but still I was curious about this arrangement. It seemed to make more sense for Silvia to stay in her town, living with her own family and remaining near him. She explained:

> Well, when we got together he said that he needed to control me more, that he didn't like to imagine where I was when I wasn't with him and that I know a lot of people in my town. Since he couldn't be with me all the time because he was working, he said that I should come to live with his parents. This way I'm not in the streets. So I always have someone watching over

> me. I can't even go to the corner store without asking for permission from his parents. Yes, very controlled. It's the custom for women.

Living in her husband's town, Silvia faced an added complication; she was originally from a coastal town and was therefore suspected of having a "bad reputation" in San Alejo. And with her husband away, she hardly left the house for fear that people would talk: "If people see me going around in the street, they'll think I'm looking for men, so my husband says that I should just stay home, so he doesn't have any problems with me or with his family. Sometimes I go out of the house with my sisters-in-law, but I don't go out alone because I prefer to avoid problems." In fact, Silvia almost never left the room in which she lived; she did not like to mingle with her large family of in-laws and preferred solitude. I came to associate Silvia with the light green walls of her room, since I rarely saw her in other parts of the house. She usually looked quiet, perhaps even sad, when she talked about her "situation." What was most distressing to her was that her partner had allowed her to visit her parents only once every eight months, when he had a day off to take her there himself. And he only came home one weekend per month. From his and his family's point of view, avoiding gossip about Silvia was much more important than Silvia's emotional well-being.

One of the most intriguing aspects of the women's explanations was not the level of control the men exerted in their lives or how much the women's physical movements were constrained by others but rather how normalized this aspect of their lives seemed to be. Silvia explained that her husband's control of her was the *costumbre,* or custom. Estrella, the photographer who supported her entire household with her work, said that it was just how things were. Estrella's need to be out of the house to take photographs at different events posed challenges for her. She explained why it was difficult for her to be "alone" when her husband, fifteen years her junior, was not in town.

> Yes, I would very much like for my husband to be here with me, you know, it's the man that lends respect to the house. For instance, he can tell me where to go, where not to go. I can't go out at night, yes, even for work, because I don't want people to talk. And it's dangerous here now, with robberies and bad things. He has already told me that I can't go out at night. He says that he worries about me. Husbands think and think, and they become preoccupied. I want to avoid giving him any headaches. As a woman, one has to be careful and not create problems for the husband, right?

Many of the women felt lonely because of the restrictions on their physical movement, and they spoke of "accepting" or enduring their situation—often rhetorically—because keeping to themselves was the custom. In some cases, however, the women spoke about the serious effects of being restricted from going to work, completing a course of study, or even visiting their parents. In such situations the women would seem to be more aware of the downside of this form of "protection," and though their words still evoked its normality, they would point to the negative consequences it had for them. Teresa's partner was "so strict" that he forbade her to continue her dressmaking classes. She explained how he came to that decision:

> I used to be a student, learning *corte y confección* [dressmaking], and one day at the end of class the teacher decided to take us on an outing. There were twenty of us, all women, and the teacher was a respectable evangelical lady. When we arrived at this place, there was swimming, and I have never liked to wear a swimming suit because I look fat. So I had already told him [her partner] that I wouldn't wear a swimming suit, but on the spur of the moment, I don't know why, I decided to wear one. We were having a great time, and this young man came to talk to us, and he quickly left. Well, it turns out he took some pictures of us and then showed them in town, including to him [her partner]. He was so furious that he forbade me from continuing with the course. So that's when I stopped going. It was my fault because I'm the one who put on the swimming suit, right? Yes, he's very strict. No more school for me after I misbehaved that time [laughs].

Emilia's husband measured the time it took her to get home from work and vice versa, and he got upset if any of those trips took longer. Sometimes she had work-related meetings in a city half an hour away, but she tried not to attend those when he was around. Luckily, she said, he worked in the United States nine months of the year, and this made things easier for her. "When he isn't in town it's fine, I can attend the meetings and work in a more relaxed way. But when he is in town I live tormented because I have to be home exactly on time. I have to leave work even if my boss gets upset, because my husband gets very angry. Yes, when he's in town I feel like someone else, almost not alive." At work her colleagues knew about her home situation and understood that when the husband was in town Emilia had to rush home as soon as she could. A coworker told me, "She looks so bad when he's around. The moment he goes back to the States her face changes and she seems to be happy, yes, she can be happy but only if he's not here [laughs hard]. No, it's true, everyone knows that." Hortencia's husband sometimes did not allow her to finish her work. Sometimes she took in laundry to make a little extra money, but he would not allow her to return it to her clients late in the day, so she had to devise strategies to return the clothes behind his back. Once she took advantage of the fact that he was not at home, but it meant she had to give the clothes to her client when they were still wet. She would do almost anything to earn money "in a decent way," but her partner opposed anything that would require her to leave the house more than he thought was necessary.

Women's emotional well-being seemed more affected when the restrictions also applied to visits to their parents. Delfina, who often described her husband simply as "*malo*" (bad, mean), complained about the rules he had imposed on her visits to her family, who lived in a town about one hour's drive from San Alejo:

> Well, he lets me go, but I can't ever stay there overnight. Since I got married I've never slept outside of our house, not even with my parents, because he's so strict about that. It's the same with our daughters. He doesn't even let them get into cars with their own [male] cousins. He says to me, "You and I know that they're cousins, but other people just see men in the car, and I don't want people to go around saying that my daughters were seen riding around with some men." Oh, you should see how he gets. I would love to stay at least one Saturday night at my parents', but that's not possible. I have to serve him his breakfast and then come to serve him lunch. One day he got upset because I wasn't home to serve him a glass of lemonade! Imagine? Another time he was looking for his black boots and couldn't find them, and I wasn't home and he got so, so angry! Men around here are like that.

Delfina said that her husband was old enough to find his own boots, but this was just a way to control the length of her visits with her parents. "I just go, quickly, and then have to come home. I think my mother suffers for me, but she won't say anything because it's my husband."

Emilia was happy that her husband had changed a little since they were first married, but he was still jealous. She explained:

> He used to control me and give me half an hour to go. So I would go in and out of my parents' house like lightning, because he would go wait for me; thank God he is not like that anymore. My mama and even my mother-in-law talked to him, because life was getting to be unbearable for me. He would have liked that I had been married to him since I was born [laughs]! He reproaches me about many things from when I was single. The truth is that we've had a lot of problems because of that. Once I thought, I'll leave [him]. This is why he probably needs to control everything I do.

And Gracia María spoke of visits to her mother's as if they were something to hide:

> You know, once in a while *me doy mis escapaditas* [I escape a little] to go and talk with my mama a little bit. But it's not good for me, because I'm always afraid. I am always busy around the house, cleaning, cooking, washing, and so I don't have time to get out. And what if nothing gets done and I'm out visiting! And he doesn't like me going out just to visit. God save me! I have to have a reason to go there, not just go there, sit, hang out. He has even gone to get me from my mama's house to bring me home.

Thus while the presence of other women can create spaces for sociality that complicates the descriptions of suffering I present, these do not tend to constitute arenas for direct resistance, only for enduring life.

Control of women's physical movements seemed more pronounced when the men lived and worked in the United States. Sometimes a husband or partner would call to express his wishes for where his wife or partner should reside or where she could go and with whom, and often his (and her) relatives in San Alejo would approve and enforce his decisions. For Lucía, a forty-two-year-old teacher and the mother of three children, life had been going well since she got married. Her husband had traveled to the United States seasonally for the previous five years, and she had been able to live with her parents in her hometown during that time. But one day, out of the blue, her husband called her from Connecticut to tell her that he had decided she should move to San Alejo. In her words: "He said, 'Either you come here with me or you go to live in San Alejo.' I was so surprised. I thought, why? But what could I say? I couldn't say no, right?" Her husband, it seemed, got the idea from his compatriots in Connecticut, who had done the same. Lucía much preferred to live with her own family while her husband was in the United States, but she said she had no choice. She understood her husband's decision, since their relationship started out because she was perceived to be a "good" girl. With a sense of satisfaction, she narrated how they were brought together. Her future husband's cousins had started "watching" her: "I had no idea I was being watched at all. His cousins were keeping a close eye on my every move! So they told him, he was in the States already, 'Look, don't marry anyone there. We have a great girl for you here.' All this without my knowing anything! They were controlling me, and I had no idea! So that's how I ended up marrying my husband." Mercedes, a fifty-one-year-old mother of eight, told me that on one occasion she was visiting her ailing father in Chicago. According to the doctors her father was in critical condition and was not expected to live through the week, but Mercedes had promised her husband that she would return to Guatemala sooner. So she called her brother in Guatemala City to intercede on her behalf, to plead with her husband to allow her to stay in Chicago until her father died. "Luckily," she said, "Beto [her husband] gave me permission to stay, but I was very nervous because he had said no before, and what would keep him from saying no this time?"

The situation was rather similar in the Altiplano, but only on the surface. For instance, Violeta did not venture out of her house very often, but in her explanation she did not mention her husband's wishes. She said she just did not have a moment to go out: "Yes, I like to visit other people, but I'm busy at home. One doesn't have the time. I have to feed my little chickens, cook, get the lunch ready, and all that. And I don't miss much by not hanging out in other people's homes anyway." Julia's situation was similar. Since the loom she used to make textiles was at home, she did not need to leave the house very often. She frequently sent her son to do the shopping because she was busy working at home; indeed, I ran into her son regularly in the street. Even when asked if the wishes of their husbands or male partners had anything to do with their staying home or not venturing far from home, in striking contrast to the women in San Alejo, those in the Altiplano emphasized other, mostly work-related, reasons. (Undoubtedly I had the San Alejo context in mind when I asked these questions in the Altiplano.)

CONCLUSION

This chapter has focused on different manifestations—physical, psychosomatic, and social—of violence on women's bodies. The framework I have used allows an examination of ailments, malnutrition, and access (or lack thereof) to health care, as well as an examination of gossip and socializing as arenas where social suffering becomes visible. Examined through other lenses, these instances could be taken as indicators of tradition, as internally driven and linked to cultural practices or perhaps inequality. However, the women's words and stories, body language, and expressions as they narrated their experiences brought out key links to multiple structures of violence. As the women related their lives, visible forms of suffering—couched in a language of fear, pain, and distress and arising from multiple forms of violence—structural, symbolic, everyday, gender, and gendered—could be discerned.

Ailments, nervios, gossip, and control of movement are the embodiment of normalized violence in the women's worlds, of the fear, suffering, humiliations, and neglect they experience each day. Even if these signs were not as evident as the effects one normally associates with direct physical violence or the observable consequences of political violence, I could not dismiss the harmful effects of this control and the deeply unequal power relations manifested in this sphere of the women's lives. Thus the women's suffering was also misrecognized as the sacrifices of "well-behaved women." Unearthing the suffering and violence in the San Alejo women's lives is crucial, because the unquestioned embeddedness and the normalization of injuries conceal structures that facilitate harming women in more direct, physical ways.

In a discussion of the somatization of socially instituted gender differences, Bourdieu (1996–97) observed that female acts of cognition are inevitably "acts of misrecognition" that make the acceptance of male domination possible. My focus on quotidian instances in the women's lives allow us to unveil (or at least to scratch the surface of) the embedded structures of violence that assault the women's lives and provoke suffering and humiliation, even when the women couch their experiences in the normalized language that obfuscates their pain. This is how inequalities and power structures shape lives and the totality of experiences in a particular social milieu and how in turn internalized dispositions (Bourdieu 1984, 2001, 2004) normalize, veil, and legitimate. In the next chapter, I move away from the immediacy of the body to discuss marriage, a facet of the women's lives not independent of the issues discussed in this chapter.

CHAPTER 4

Marital Unions and the Normalization of Suffering

Las mujeres solo servimos para darles problemas a los hombres.

[We women are only good for giving men problems.]

—Mirna, twenty-eight years old

In this chapter I discuss a sphere of women's lives that brings to the fore the normalization of gender hierachies in San Alejo. In keeping with the overall argument of this book and with the analytic lens I presented in chapter 2, I call attention to the institutional and structural dimensions of women's suffering. These include not only the role of markets and governments but also the reproduction of power differentials and inequalities at an intimate level. Thus this chapter traces the links between the women's internalized humiliations and indignities and the legitimations of gender inequalities in the home, a critical space in the lives of the women in San Alejo. Although, as Nordstrom (1997) points out, recognizing the presence of violence in certain circumstances may be uncomfortable, "failing to acknowledge particular acts as violent not only minimizes people's experiences and denies them a voice but actively undermines their pursuit of justice" (Hume 2008: 61). The focus on women's quotidian engagements in the home is an important angle from which to capture the potential and actual power of violence as well as the mechanisms of its reproduction.

The commonly accepted, normalized notion in San Alejo that men have the upper hand or the last word shapes how women see themselves and their partners in the context of their unions, as well as how they respond to male authority. The dominant notions of being a man and being a woman have very real consequences, because they reproduce power differentials and constitute hegemonic processes "by which 'normal' and ideal definitions emerge [and] how the terms of morality surface and persuade" (Barrett 1996: 130). Connell's (1987) conceptualization of how femininities and masculinities develop is instructive here, for it gives primacy to violence as the key expression of masculine behavior and as the mechanism that ensures its own reproduction. Also informing my examination is the feminist scholarship that has revealed the relationship between male dominance and violence (Campbell and Wasco 2000; see also Bourdieu 2001). Importantly, however, as Gutmann (1996, 2007) notes, instances of violence associated with "masculine domination" should be taken only as a starting point to discover the deeper roots of violence. Domestic violence, for example, "must be seen as part of the cultural politics of gender inequalities and not as deriving from some essential logic of . . . men" (Gutmann 1996: 199).

I turn to Bourdieu's (2001) notion of symbolic violence to examine the lives of the San Alejo women in their unions. Bourdieu's (1984, 2001; Bourdieu and Wacquant 1992) emphasis on the naturalization of unequal power relations, the internalization of dispositions that organize practices and sustain these power relations, the acceptance by the dominated of their condition as legitimate and as agents in its reproduction, and the centrality of nonphysical violence are central points in my discussion. As Bourdieu observed:

> Taking "symbolic" in one of its commonest senses, people sometimes assume that to emphasize symbolic violence is to minimize the role of physical violence, to forget (and make people forget) that there are battered, raped and exploited women, or worse, to seek to exculpate men from that form of violence. . . . Understanding "symbolic" as the opposite of "real, actual," people suppose that symbolic violence is purely "spiritual" violence which ultimately has no real effects. (2001: 34)

Direct physical violence is not always independent of the other forms; it contributes to normalizing inequalities and sustaining hierarchies within which other forms of violence, including gender and symbolic, become possible and acceptable. Visible and invisible forms of violence are mutually constitutive, and one does not weigh more than the other. But the men who sometimes inflict these acts do not act in a social vacuum. The active participation of women in normalizing such hierarchies and shaping interpretations of and responses to these situations must be integrated into the discussion. Thus I underscore the complexity and heterogeneity of women's relations with other women; they can have multiple effects and meanings, not always in an exclusively positive (or negative) direction.

Take the case of Emilia, the health clinic worker whom I introduced earlier. Although her husband spent most of the year working in Connecticut, he was indisputably, according to Emilia, "the man of the house." In Emilia's eyes his authority was inseparable from his responsibility as the breadwinner, so she interpreted his "authoritative behavior" in a manner that was compatible with being a good husband and father.

> I cannot deny that he is very responsible. Well, he's a Libra, so he's very loving and makes sure that we don't lack for anything. From over there [the United States], he's always attentive that we have what we need. Oh, but his temper; he has such a bad temper. What he says goes. He gets very upset about any little thing. I try not to pay attention to him, but I cannot always control myself. At first it was very hard, but one gets used to it. I got used to not contradicting him. So we avoid problems.

Emilia was not alone. Most of the women echoed her words; they had learned (from experience but also from their mothers and other women) that a good wife was one who knew how to keep quiet. Silence and acceptance therefore are powerful mechanisms by which unequal power relations are reproduced. They were, in fact, key to how San Alejo women endured life.

I present my discussion in quasi-chronological fashion, starting with the violence of robadas, when during courtship men *take* women—the question of women's will in these events is not always clear—to be their partners. I then discuss three sources of violence that take place within a marital union—alcoholism, violence in the context of marital relations, and infidelity. The "sexual double standard" (Chant and Craske 2003: 141) that applies to alcoholism and infidelity exposes the normalization of violence that results from gender inequality; indeed, alcoholism, infidelity, and violence "have become so bound up with dominant constructs of maleness that they are sometimes seen as natural" (Hume 2008: 66).[1] Thus even if alcoholism, violence, and infidelity (singly or together) can also be found among women, it is imperative to concentrate on the effects that this tripartite source of violence has on women, when the men engage in them, because of their far more common occurrence and normalization. Having said this, however, it must be kept in mind that the behavior of men is deeply ingrained in and shaped by the "social order" that generates violence in general (Godoy-Paiz 2008; Torres 2008).

Although visible and readily recognized violence in intimate spaces is deeply linked to structural, symbolic, gender, gendered, and political forms, the use of force to justify inequality is also embedded in many quotidian aspects of life.[2] Thus all these forms of violence are part of a social order that "functions as an immense symbolic machine tending to ratify the masculine domination on which it is founded" (Bourdieu 2001: 9). The chapter concludes with a discussion of the less (physically) recognizable forms of violence: those that come from accepting suffering in a union and from the participation of others—relatives, friends, neighbors—whose actions and views contribute to normalizing violence and gender inequalities.

"PEDIDAS," ROBADAS, AND THE NORMALIZATION OF VIOLENCE

> La arrastró, todavía tiene las cicatrices en la rodillas de la arrastrada que le dió cuando se la llevó. Estaba loco por ella, pues.
>
> [He dragged her; she still has the scars on her knees from being dragged when he took her away. He was crazy in love with her.]
>
> —Lucrecia

Lucrecia, speaking of a robada, points to its physical violence, which was not uncommon in the context of romantic love. Robadas contribute to the legitimation of the central element of men's authority that reinforces and nourishes gender inequality and physical violence. Significantly, robadas can involve actual physical violence, as when young women are dragged on the pavement or pushed inside an open door, or the term can be used as a metaphor to describe an elopement. But the use of the term in itself, which positions women as objects and possessions without will, is an important aspect of courtship and marriage that evinces the violent basis on which unions are built. As Wim Savenije and Katherine Andrade-Eekhoff (2003: 145) note in their examination of everyday violence in El Salvador, "Intimate relations are often confused with property relations."

Other forms of violence, including humiliation and self-blame, come to light in examining robadas. It is often the women who must go back to their parents to apologize for the deed. They go through the embarrassment of the actual robada and then the humiliation of asking for forgiveness for something that the men usually persuaded (or forced) them to do and that the social milieu sees as normal. Robadas are the way in which many unions were established in San Alejo. Of the thirty

San Alejo women I formally include here, five had been robadas (two at the age of thirteen) and two were forced to elope. Importantly, the violence inscribed in this practice was not only normalized but also formalized in Guatemalan law. Until 2006 the Guatemalan penal code exonerated a sexual violator if the aggressor married the victim, provided that the victim was older than twelve (Sanford 2008); however, in practice men were not prosecuted. Still, it was not unheard of that a young girl was forced to marry her abductor.

Lucrecia told me the story of her sister, whose boyfriend "stole" her as she was leaving school. He knew that after having stayed with him for one night she could not go back to live at her aunt's house, because it would be assumed she was no longer a virgin and was thus dishonored. However, because she acted "easy" by not putting up much resistance and agreeing to stay with him, he decided not to marry her; she ended up a single mother of two children from two different men (neither of whom had stolen her). Estrella's boyfriend stole her just before she turned seventeen; she and the boyfriend were married twelve days later. Estrella's mother did not sanction the union but had to go along with it because her daughter had already been robada. Estrella lived with her first husband for thirteen years, until he opened up a business in another city and met a woman there. The second time Estrella married, her boyfriend had not thought it was necessary to "court" her because she had been married before. In the end he also left her. Estrella resented that she had never been asked for in marriage and reasoned that this was why her husbands left her for other women. "I don't know why," she told me, "but I think that men have to feel the woman is worth the trouble to court her. They have to find resistance and conquer. In my case I was not worth the trouble, so they didn't appreciate me." Susana's and Mirna's cases were similar to those of Lucrecia's sister and Estrella's in that once they eloped/were stolen there was no going back to their parents' home, and they were forced to marry the men.

Ileana, who was thirteen when she was robada (and seventeen when we met), had vivid memories of her experience. She had a penchant for Tex-Mex music, in particular, songs by Selena, and was invited to a house where she was told they would be playing her music. The man who is now her partner was there and "took" her from that house. "Me llevó [He took me]," she said. She reflected that it had all been planned because she barely got to listen to any of the music she was promised. Mirna's grandparents were upset because, like Estrella, they assumed Mirna's boyfriend was not going to appreciate her as a wife because he had never bothered to visit her at her house and she had eloped with him. Mirna's grandparents did not blame the boyfriend; they blamed Mirna for having been "easy." Mirna explained, "Since I was a minor, they captured him and forced him to face his responsibility, but he said that he loved me, and since I loved him I had to marry him. My grandma said that at thirteen, yes, I was thirteen years old when he stole me [smiles], I could not make such a decision, but I thought I was in love and that he had stolen me because he loved me."

The cases of Isabel and Hortencia shed light on how these robadas happen, the power men have, the participation of other family members, how women see these acts, and, importantly, their normalization. When I asked Isabel if her husband had asked for her in marriage she said no and explained how it had happened.

> No, I just left with him. Because here the men say, "You're leaving with me," and the women start to lie and give excuses until you can't lie anymore. The third time he told me to go with him, I went. But by then I couldn't even look at him. It was something that came over me. I abhorred him in the end, but I had to go with him because by then we had agreed to elope. He took me to Guatemala [City]; we spent about five days there at his sister's house. We came back, but it took my parents about fifteen days to forgive me for what I did, and after that I started to visit them again.

In Hortencia's case, she had already talked about marriage with her boyfriend, though she was just sixteen and did not feel ready to start a union. Then she found out that he had been married before. She was upset that he had not told her and changed her mind about marrying him. "He was furious because I didn't want to marry him anymore, so he stole me," she said. "You know, as it is the custom we have here." "And how did it happen?" I asked. "It's the custom here; the man takes you. He has friends with him in case you resist. They hit you if you don't want to go. So that's how they did it with me. The next day I ran to my mama's, but she thought that I had left with him of my own accord, so she sent me back to him. She told me, 'Marido querías, marido tenés' [You wanted a husband, now you have one]. And I asked myself, why is she saying this to me? Nothing has happened to me yet [meaning she had not had intercourse yet]. And when I went back to him he started hitting me because I had dared to escape to go back to my mama. I had to stay with him after that."

The practice of robadas seemed to cut across social classes, but the women of higher socioeconomic positions did not refer to it as such, making robadas a class-bound concept that adds insult to injury among the socially and/or economically vulnerable women who go through it. This contrast was evident in how Vera and Mariana explained their situations. Vera, who had attended private schools in a larger city and drove a late-model car, was still considered to be from a lower-class background because her mother supported the entire household by renting rooms and running a cafeteria. As people in town commented, the money her mother had made, though decently earned, had not erased Vera's "humble origins," and her family, though "decent and hardworking," were not among the "notables" in town. Vera fell in love with the son of a powerful, "notable" family. The young man drank and was never interested in working or going to school. One day, on her way back from the city, he was waiting for her in the street and stole her, Vera explained. For about ten days she stayed with various relatives of her boyfriend until he brought her home to his parents, where she seemed to have been welcomed. Others in town said that part of the reason this family of higher status welcomed Vera to their home (and even helped the couple establish their own home) was because the young man was not the family's best "asset," so the parents were happy that he had found a woman who could tolerate him. A neighbor of this family said, "Her family has more money, but his has more *orgullo* [pride, arrogance], so they're a good match. When he stole her it worked well for all of them." Everyone, including Vera, referred to this event as a robada.

Mariana's experience was almost identical to Vera's, so when we conversed about it I asked her if she had been robada. She smiled and quickly corrected me. "Robada, no," she explained, "that's what the people here do. In my case, I just came to live with him when he told me to." It is not that she wanted to paint herself in "modern" terms or to appear "liberal," a worker at a health post told me. "It's that she wants to separate herself, differentiate herself from the *pueblo* [people]. She does not want to appear as if she is like everyone else, because her family is very wealthy. That's all. That's why she didn't tell you about her robada." I heard similar comments from members of well-to-do families, who generally did not use the term *robada,* and the town's self-appointed historian provided me with a similar explanation. Vera said that it took her mother about two weeks to forgive her for what had happened. Vera (but not Mariana) felt embarrassed and needed to be forgiven for something that was not entirely of her own choosing. Thus to be robada hurt the women triply—emotionally, physically, and in their relations at home.

Leticia's case further highlights the injuries that class inequalities can add. As was customary, Leticia's partner took her to live with his parents, and eventually they had a daughter, but they never married. In fact, she only stayed with this partner (her first) for one year, because his mother never accepted her. Leticia worked as a housekeeper for another family before she and her partner got together, and her partner's family did not accept her because of her lower-class standing. "[His mother] used to call me *la sirvienta* [the maid], never by my name. I don't think she ever pronounced my name. Yes, she would say, 'Vení, vos, sirvienta,' [Come, you, maid], or just 'Sh, sirvienta.' She made me eat in the kitchen, not at the table like the rest of the family. In that house I was always treated like an inferior. So he only stole me to be humiliated by his family. So, of course, no, we never married."[3] Leticia never questioned that given her background and social standing he would refuse to marry her after all. In her eyes, this is how things were.

Mariana and Vera were still not married even after they had been living with their partners long enough to have had children with them, something that bothered them, mostly because of what this meant in the eyes of others in San Alejo and also perhaps because it affected how they saw themselves and their futures. In contrast, María Ruth and Susana, who lived in the poorest area of town and were also robadas, had married their boyfriends. When Susana's boyfriend asked for her hand in marriage, her parents did not give permission because they did not like the young man; he drank too much and was not a hard worker. So Susana and the young man eloped and went to live with his parents. "Yes, I was robada, but not completely, because he and I had already talked about it," Susana told me. María Ruth's parents were very poor—even poorer than her husband's family, she said—and although they thought the marriage might improve their daughter's life, they hesitated to agree to it because when the young man came to ask for her in marriage at ten o'clock in the morning he smelled like liquor. Thus both men stole their girlfriends and in time married them in the church, but in hindsight both women regretted the events that led to their marriages. Susana said, "It's been suffering since the first day. Not a single day passes when I can say that I'm happy." And both thought that the robadas might have had something to do with the way things turned out; at the same time they pointed to themselves as culpable because they had disobeyed their parents and not resisted the men strongly enough.

One afternoon I was discussing the issue of robadas with Ofelia, the receptionist at the health post, and she said that the practice was common. In contrast to what I had observed, she said that many couples who start out their unions through a robaba—whether involuntary, forced, or semivoluntary—marry in due course. She remarked that many couples begin a union this way because they lack the money to have a wedding and start a family, endorsing the belief that robadas are a "custom" of the poor. She added, "So, it's the poor, the poor women, who suffer because they enter unions they don't want, a lot of times by force. Here [in San Alejo] the men are the owners. Sometimes they act out of caprice; on a whim they steal a girl." She was thinking of her neighbor's experience, who had been robada by a man she hardly knew. Her neighbor and the man had spoken a few times and he had "expressed interest in her," and then he stole her.

> Someone else had stolen his girlfriend, so out of pure anger he got drunk, and *bolo* he stole my neighbor. He used to be in the army and had a very bad temper. After he stole her he was always drunk; two weeks after he took her he started beating her. He used to tell her, "Go to your house if you don't like it here," but she had to stay because her family was angry with her. She *aguantó ese trato* [endured that treatment] for years. She had a boyfriend whom she loved when this man stole her. It was tough for her, for years. Even now, she doesn't live in tranquility.

I noticed that often when women talked about men "having interest" in the women they later stole, they referred to a period similar to stalking, in which intense control and pressure (bordering on harassment, as in the cases of Isabel and Hortencia above) is interpreted as "interest" or romantic love. This happened to Delfina. When her husband started courting her, he became "very possessive," to the point of not letting her come close to any other men, even young male cousins. He kept an eye on her every move and enlisted his friends to help him "control" her. Smiling a little, Delfina explained, "He became very jealous; I couldn't even look at other men. Once, this drunken man from the street, a dirty man, came by our house and he [at that time her boyfriend] thought that this man came to see me. Imagine! He never let me have any other boyfriends; he would chase them away. No one could get close to me." So, Delfina explained, she married her husband by default. "I knew I would never be able to see other men because he kept me watched and controlled, so I ended up accepting him," she said with a shrug of her shoulders and a slight smile.

Robadas also took place in the Altiplano.[4] I heard similar stories there, including tales of mothers-in-law not approving of their sons' brides and accounts of violence. As in San Alejo, people in the Altiplano spoke of the difference between *robada a la fuerza* (stolen by force) and *robada a voluntad* (stolen willingly). Constantina's boyfriend stole her when she was just fifteen by pushing her into the open door of a home he knew when they were walking in the street. He then put a lock on the door and kept her there for two days. His family came to get her and went to talk to her father to arrange the wedding. Although the women in the Altiplano also talked about the robadas a la fuerza in which women were pushed, hit, or dragged in the streets, they also mentioned, like some women in San Alejo did, that sometimes they left willingly with their partners but used the euphemism "robada" to describe the elopement. Dalia explained that because weddings were normally celebrated with pomp, when the families were poor the young couples often eloped in what resembled a robada.[5] This explanation was similar to the one Ofelia offered in San Alejo. In both towns the women's explanations of "voluntary robadas" pointed to a more complex situation. Adelia, in the Altiplano, explained what happened in her case: "Well, we had talked about it, but one day he saw me in the street, and he said, 'Let's go.' I couldn't say no anymore, and I went with him. He put a lock on the door of the room, and I had to stay there until he talked with my parents." These descriptions of robadas appeared exceptional to me, but the women themselves delivered the accounts as though they were not out of the ordinary, for they knew others who had experienced the same thing.

EVERYDAY VIOLENCE: ALCOHOLISM AND VIOLENCE IN THE HOME

In a study in neighboring El Salvador, Hume (2008) notes that violence, drinking, and womanizing are among the dominant constructs of maleness and thus are seen as natural; taken together, they express direct physical and nonphysical forms of violence. Latin American researchers (Alméras et al. 2002; Rico 1992) have noted that in the region, regardless of social position, women share the real possibility of being victims of violence, whether in private or in public. However, there has been a certain social invisibility of violence in the privacy of the home, justified by cultural customs and tradition (Rico 1992), embedded in stereotypes of women that seep into the judicial system. Shannon Drysdale Walsh (2008: 54) interviewed an activist in Guatemala who heard someone in court saying, "Women themselves cause the [intrafamiliar] violence. They provoke violence because they do not cook well, because they don't do the house chores, and because they do not obey their husbands." As Gutmann (1996) reminds us, however, we must be careful to separate symbolic from actual sources of violent conflict. Whereas at times the comingling of drinking, interpersonal violence, and womanizing is visibly violent, at other times it is not. Here I would like to underscore the socially prescribed roles and the broader context that permits and encourages acts that result in suffering and lead women to also actively normalize suffering. It is this embeddedness in the social context, rather than an essentialist analysis of men as violent, that contributes to the normalization and misrecognition of these acts as violent (see Gutmann 1996).

Thus violence, drinking, and infidelity are also intertwined in San Alejo. However, one does not lead to or *cause* the others, because they are all expressions of dominant constructions of masculinity. For instance, several San Alejo women talked about the violent behavior of their male partners when the men were drunk, behavior that was often linked to the men having "another woman." Tita, who became a widow just before she turned twenty-eight, explained that her husband would never hit her when he was sober, but as soon as he got drunk, which he did often, he would, and he would also hit anyone else who stood in his way. "He was so aggressive when he was drunk, it was frightening to see him. He had another woman, and she used to take all the money from him and give him liquor so he thought he was having a good time with her. This left us with no food at home, putting up with an aggressive drunk who just wasted away. To this day I've never tasted liquor, but I know the consequences it has. I've lived in my own flesh the damage it does to people." Though the tripartite frame of violence in the home is bound up and often indivisible in reality, for the purposes of this discussion I want to discuss each separately.

Vera, Mariana, Nena, Susana, Ileana, Hortencia, and María Ruth lived in dissimilar parts of San Alejo, were at different stages of the life cycle, came from diverse social class backgrounds, attended different churches, and had diverse labor market experiences. Their circumstances differed widely, but they shared, along with many other women in San Alejo, a key aspect of their personal lives that kept them awake at night and worried "each moment" of their waking hours: their husbands or male partners drank heavily. Invariably, when we got to talk about this issue, the women would break down and cry. Between sobs, Vera repeated that her partner just drank too much. She said that when he drank he had convulsions, so his mother, who lived next door, came in and took him to their physician or did something for him. Her partner's mother also taught Vera what to do in these cases. Vera was convinced that his drinking had terrible economic, physical, and emotional effects on her, and she considered it an illness that was destroying her and her family. Vera knew he drank before she began seeing him, but she loved him very much, and still did. Seventeen-year-old Ileana, who shared a similar story, put it in context. Men's drinking, she explained, was omnipresent:

> There are many bolos here [in San Alejo]. There are too many stores and clandestine businesses that sell liquor and beer; on weekends there are drunken men on the streets everywhere. Not long ago my neighbor died from drinking; he drank for two straight months, and when he wanted to stop he couldn't because the worm in his stomach wanted more *guaro* [alcohol]. It's the guaro worm, people call it. So they can't stop drinking. They die if they do. My sister's husband also drinks a lot. He goes out to work and comes back very drunk, wobbling as he walks in the street and without money. Most men, that's how they are [sighs].

Nena, a woman with a jovial disposition who was known for being nice to everyone, usually joked and smiled when we spoke, and she often interrupted our conversations to say hello to someone walking by on the street or to someone who came to make a purchase at her bookstore. However, her face changed expression when she introduced the topic of her husband's drinking. "I have a very serious problem in my home that tears me apart," she said, looking down and fidgeting with her rings, her voice about to crack. "My family didn't want me to marry him because of his drinking, and his father didn't want him to marry me because I was poor. So I never came to this house as his girlfriend. I never met his mother in the seven years we were boyfriend and girlfriend. We didn't have a normal courtship because he was a drunk and I was poor. Both were big problems for our parents." With tears running down her cheeks, Nena explained that all she wanted was a father for her children, because even though they loved him dearly and he adored them he was just not there for them. Nena was quick to note that even though there had been times when her husband was drunk every single day for months, he never hit her or mistreated her, something she appreciated. She said this with a tinge of surprise; the absence of physical violence in her case served to highlight its omnipresence in the lives of other women in similar situations. Sobbing, she continued: "He's not bad, he's good, he always asks for forgiveness afterward, when he's sober, but it's torture to live with him and his disease. Sometimes he starts to *chupar* [drink] at five or six o'clock in the morning. That's been my life for fifteen years." She got discouraged because his family, who owned large amounts of land, cattle, and properties in the region, had paid for expensive treatments, but nothing had helped. "The suffering continues; it never goes away," is how Nena described her pena.

On the other side of town—physically and socially—María Ruth's experience was similar. She was twenty-nine when we first met, and had married her husband when she was nineteen. She lived in a one-room thatched-roof house where she shared a bed with her five children (two more children died as infants). Her husband was a soldier in the Honor Guard in Guatemala City and only came home once a month for a visit. One morning I visited María Ruth just before noon. Her husband was at home, already drunk, and she looked embarrassed. Rather than point to her husband's behavior as a source of suffering for her, however, María Ruth blamed her husband's job for his drinking: "They rounded him up and took him to the army when he was just fifteen, and he drinks like the other soldiers. They have a tough job so they console themselves by drinking." However, her husband was by no means the only man who drank heavily in her family. "My papa has been drunk all his life, and my mama has suffered a lot with him. My papa was drunk like my husband. Sometimes there are months that go by when he is drunk nonstop. My husband drinks, yes, but not like my papa. My papa continues to be drunk; he has not quit, and my mama has never left him. She has endured so much. And look at me [with tears in her eyes and voice breaking], it looks like I'm headed in that direction."

Men's drinking and its effects were not a problem among male partners alone but also among other men in the family and were compounded by ideologies that position women as accepting it, all of which contributed to normalizing these situations and to exacerbating other forms of violence. Estrella's neighbor attended school for just one year; she barely learned the alphabet and could read a little but never learned how to write. Like other women, when this neighbor reflected on her limited opportunities in life she pointed to her father's drinking: "I only went to school one year because my papa was always bolo. There were too many of us kids, and my mama didn't have enough money to send us all to school because my papa would drink all the money he earned. I wish I had learned at least a little so I could defend myself and not live the life I've lived." And although knowledge of other men's drinking contributed to its normalization, it elicited responses on the part of friends and neighbors that the women appreciated, responses that were mostly based on "pity." Symbolic, structural, and gender violence coalesce vividly in these situations. Susana said that everyone knew about her husband's drinking: "All the neighbors know how we suffer, and they know when he *anda chupando* [is drinking], so they come by with a pound of beans, corn, just for us to survive. My mama also brings us food. They take pity on us. That's how bolos are, and people understand what it is to live with one."

The situation was similar in the Altiplano. Flor, a woman who seemed to know everyone and worked at the local health post, explained that drinking was a major problem in her town, that it "leaves destruction in any home it touches." As in San Alejo, men in the Altiplano could drink for days or months straight, with similar consequences for the women and other family members.[6] Lilian, a young woman with five children, said that she had often regretted marrying her husband but that it was too late. "El es malo [He is bad/evil]," she said, "and my papa warned me many times about him. And now my husband's younger brother is drinking a lot too. And when he gets drunk he comes to our house and breaks things here too. I just hide at my neighbor's when they're drunk." Azucena also ran to her neighbor's house when her husband was drunk, because she was afraid that he would beat her. Alberta said that the moment she saw that her husband had come home drunk, she and the children ran out the door; and often he chased them down the street until they found refuge at a neighbor's house. "He becomes crazy, and he can hit anyone who stays home," she said, "so we all have to run out, no matter the time of day." When he was sober, her husband would explain that he drank because he was desperate from all the problems he had, especially his inability to provide enough for his children. In Alberta's view, "Well, that's the way men are; they drink when they have a problem, but actually their biggest problem is the guaro." And Constantina, who married her husband when she was fifteen and was happy to obtain a divorce after twelve years of marriage, still found it difficult to get any financial support from him. "Since two days after our wedding he started to *chupar* [get drunk]. He lived drunk all his life, giving me a life worse than a dog's. Once I begged him not to drink anymore, and look what he did [showing me a scar on her forehead]; he broke a bottle on my head. How would I expect him to give me even a cent for the children now?" In a twist that highlights the symbolic violence in these situations, Constantina had resorted to selling *cusha* (or *kuxa*), clandestine liquor, to make extra cash, because she did not make enough working as a housekeeper, and her former husband did not help her. As these accounts demonstrate, one cannot lose sight of the fact that men's lives are also shaped by the multilayered context of violence, a context that normalizes drinking but also severely constrains men's economic activities and threatens their social roles and status.

Violence in Married Life

The U.N. Declaration on the Elimination of Violence against Women, which serves as the epigraph to this book, lists the different forms of gender violence that can result in women's suffering. Applying that definition, nearly every woman I met in San Alejo was experiencing or had experienced one form and often multiple forms of violence in her life. Some spoke about it openly; others did not. However, what is important here is not only *what* the women said but also *how* they talked about their experiences and perceptions. Attending to these subtleties permits us to capture the women's recognition of their suffering but also the acceptance and naturalization of the various sources of pain in their lives. I focus on violence in the context of married life, an area that is central for many women, which shapes the cognitive frames women use to interpret their lives and those of others.[7]

Hortencia described her first husband as a hardworking man who was a good provider. She remembered how caring he was when she was ill; he worried if she did not feel well and made every effort to take her to see the doctor as soon as possible. He even took care of the children if she was bedridden. "He was good, caring; he would take pity on me," Horencia said with a hint of contentment. But she often qualified her positive assessment with comments like "Oh, but he had a bad temper," or "The ten years I lived with him were *años de amargura* [bitter years]," or "The scars I have on my body and in my heart remind me of my life with him." After eight years of widowhood she still had flashbacks and nightmares from the days when he used to beat her and chase her around the house and out into the street with a knife, shouting insults at her, all because the beans were not salted the way he liked or because he thought she stared at a man who passed by their house. If he was too drunk she would manage to wrestle the knife from his hands and run to a neighbor's house. With a slight smile, she revealed that deep inside she wished that he would come home very drunk, so she could outmaneuver him. One incident stood out as especially painful to her. It happened right after their first child was born.

> Twelve days after the girl was born he beat me badly because the tortillas got cold when I served them to him. So I escaped. The neighbors told my mama what he had done, just twelve days after the girl was born, so my mama took me to her house, right here, around the corner. But he went to get me from there by force. I was very afraid of him and came home. My mama thought that I *wanted* to come back with him. She was very upset and told me never to come to her if I had a problem again. I said to myself, if I'm going to stay with him, then I'm going to suffer in silence. I never went back to my mama or my sister. I had to endure all this alone. I realized that I was an adult. Uno de mujer sufre [One suffers as a woman].

Although most assaults happened when Hortencia's husband was drunk and she recounted the more egregious incidents with sadness and a lingering look of fear on her face, she described the physical violence matter-of-factly, as "the way things are around here." Although her husband acted alone when these incidents happened, the tacit (but sometimes open) participation of other family members lingered as a backdrop. It is this social context that makes possible violence on the part of individuals (men in this case) and the consequent suffering in the lives of women not only possible but also acceptable.

Delfina said that even though her husband insulted her every day, telling her that she was good for nothing and that she should just leave the house, he had never hit her. He insulted her family, who also owned a significant amount of land, about their supposed arrogance and wealth and threatened Delfina with sending her back to them as soon as his mother died. However, he was nice to her relatives when they visited, so no one ever guessed what he said about them; thus Delfina reasoned that the only reason he unleashed the litany of insults at her was to get her, not hurt her family. She observed, "People don't believe me. He is so nice to everyone. He is capable of taking the shirt off his back to give it to someone who needs it, even if it's an American shirt. But it's different with me." However, friends and family who were close to them had seen how Delfina's husband behaved toward her. Delfina explained, "When he gets upset, he insults me in front of anyone, no matter who it is, and calls me everything from bitch on up, it's never below that. If one of his friends comes over and he asks me to serve them something to eat and I don't do it quickly or if he tells me to look for something and I take longer, oh God, he starts shouting at me. 'Stupid,' 'bitch,' ay, he shouts anything that comes to his mind. In front of the workers who built this house; you should have seen how he insulted me every day. I would just ignore him, *ni modo* [what else]. Ay, a los hombres hay que aguantarlos [one has to put up with men]," she said shaking her head.

This was the reason Delfina never went on trips with her family or engaged in much socializing; she was afraid that her husband would lose his temper at any moment and start insulting her. "I don't want to *martirizarme* [mortify myself]. For any insignificant thing he starts to bother me." At the same time, it intrigued her that he had never asked her for forgiveness, as other men seemed to do after mistreating their wives or partners. Delfina explained, "You know how men are here, they mistreat, insult, hit, and then they go, 'Oh, my love, forgive me.' Every man does that, but no, not my husband; he is very proud, so when he is angry he mistreats and is awful, but then he wants me to talk to him like nothing happened." A painful aspect of being married, Delfina mentioned, was that her husband's insults and his attitude, all together, made her feel unloved:

> I used to be very expressive. When we got married I thought I had married a romantic man because that's how he behaved. And then my surprise came. I spent a good five years crying. Right after we got married, we started sleeping in separate beds. Only lately he bought a huge bed for us, but no, I used to beg him, you know, come closer to me, and nothing. He wouldn't even cover himself with the same sheets. It has been very painful to feel so *rechazada* [rejected] all these years. It's all part of him being so awful with me.

And although Delfina seemed well aware of the source of her suffering, she sometimes blamed herself for her husband's behavior; she thought she provoked him because she had never learned how to obey him fully: "I do everything in the home, whatever he asks, but I know I could do more, so maybe it's me. If I were different, more docile, maybe it would be different at home."

Almost all the women who spoke of some form of violence in their marriages echoed Delfina's reflections: they tended to find culpability in themselves or attributed the men's expressions of violence to "custom." Emilia spoke at length about her husband's short temper, his requirement that she be the only one to serve him, and his constant control; however, she did not find it out of the ordinary because she was not the only one in that situation, either in her family or in San Alejo in general. Gloria, a busy mother of toddler twins, understood why her husband was so upset on his return to Guatemala from Connecticut. Neighbors' rumors that questioned her decency had reached him, and he was furious with her. "We had this problem because a neighbor started saying that I was getting home late at night, when I was just coming home from the *culto* [evangelical church]. He got angry, and he hit me. It hurt me a lot, but you see, I understand him because what husband would stand that a wife makes a mockery of him when he is away working, don't you think? So I don't say it's right to hit, but if a woman goes out with who knows who, then she deserves it." And Andrea, whose marital situation was uncertain because apparently she had become her stepfather's partner after her mother's death, mentioned routine beatings from this man. Speaking in a low voice in the garden of the house where she lived with her son and her stepfather/partner, she said that this señor did not like it when other men showed interest in her: "He becomes very angry and hits me if some man talks to me. The other day, there was a young man who talked to me at the park. He doesn't tolerate that. The next day he came to the kitchen to hit me with a sauce pan in the head. I live in fear because if he finds out that I talk with anyone, he can hit me." Her stepfather/partner would tell her that he was looking out for her, making sure that she did not get entangled with some irresponsible man, as had happened after her mother died. Andrea explained, "I was fifteen when she died, and I was lost; I ended up having my baby alone. So to prevent another accident like that, he does not let me have a boyfriend; I'm twenty-two, but he says no." In a framework of protection, itself bound up in symbolic and gender violence, this man ended up controlling Andrea's romantic life by means of psychological and physical violence.

In the Altiplano the situation was no different; many of the women there experienced similar violence and also spoke about it in normalized ways. And racism shaped images about men's behavior in marriage as well. Ivette's husband, who was Maya, was perceived in San Alejo as being strict, aggressive, and rude, even though he had never behaved openly so toward Ivette or to anyone else in the family. People talked about his *"malcriadeces"* (misbehavior) as part of his being Maya, even though San Alejo men's acts seemed to me more violent in many ways than Ivette's husband ever was. The physical violence in Gina's marriage in the Altiplano was compounded because, as was the case in San Alejo also, patrilocality was the norm after marriage, and other members of her husband's family would also mistreat her. Like Gina, Isa endured physical assaults during her pregnancies, but Isa could not leave her partner because she was unable to provide for her children on her own, though she worked nonstop on the textiles she sold on market days. It must be kept in mind that this kind of violence took place in the social order in which masculinity was enacted in specific ways and in a broader context of political and structural violence that has created deep inequalities that have contributed to cheapening and diminishing life for most people.

This chain of causality was not lost on the women I came to know. One hot afternoon I was sitting at a small convenience store in the center of San Alejo chatting with the owner, and two religious women, who had come to have a soda, joined in the conversation. One of the religious explained her views as follows: "Look, in this country we have lost our fear of God and we have learned to fear each other. We fear everything and everyone. Yes, violence is all around us. Here it's like in Israel, the land of Our Savior. And the violence enters the home and our families, and it destroys us. But why? Because we don't fear God." The owner of the store, not fully convinced, nevertheless nodded in agreement and said that in her country values about basic humanity had been lost, which is why so many people were being killed. During one of my last visits to San Alejo, a nurse at the health post provided the following assessment: "What do you expect in a country that has not respected its citizens? From a government that only has fomented violence to deal with violence? Of course, if we live with violence every day, that penetrates the minds of people, no? So it's *la ley del machete* [the law of the machete] for everything!"

Many of the women mentioned their moments of consolation and the people in whom they found comfort, the spaces in which they might even resist the gender subordination in their lives but that also sustain the reproduction of violence. Delfina, for instance, lighted up when she talked about her sister, who lived in the United States, but who lent a sympathetic ear when she visited Guatemala, and in whom Delfina confided because she would not gossip. Delfina's mother, whom she visited on short *escapaditas* (brief escapes), or even a colleague at work, with whom she talked and *se desahoga* (finds relief). "As they say, *el mal de uno es el consuelo de otros* [the problem of one person serves as consolation for others]. Hearing what my colleague at the school says about her husband, who is triple as evil as mine, is somewhat comforting to me [smiles pensively]." Even shy Emilia did not always heed her partner's demands and managed to keep working, although he had clearly stated his disapproval, mostly because, she noted, "It is helpful for me to go to work. It serves me to console myself." These conversations and friendships among women highlight how the violence the women suffer is inscribed in the specific context, how responses to violence are also embedded in the social world, how such ties also provide a framework to make sense of the world around in a normalized way, and how they can also engender a collective sense and not a self-contained, individual experience.

Infidelity and the "Other Woman"

Closely related to their concern with the men's drinking, the women were fearful of their partners' philandering. Men's extramarital affairs represented a real threat to the women's livelihoods and to their families' and their children's well-being, but also to their sense of being. At the same time, infidelity was seen as men's behavior but not women's.[8] Thus when Nena described her torment over her husband's drinking, in addition to never beating her, she also noted that her husband was not a womanizer. Proudly, she said, in eighteen years of marriage he had had only two affairs. She explained, "What happens is that women, especially *patojas* [young women] who are poor, when they see him, that he drives late-model cars and pays for rounds of booze, the young women start to flirt with him. And he, being a man, even if he's very drunk, he reacts, right? It's men's nature."

One of those affairs had an added complication for Nena and the family. Her husband had started to attend Alcoholics Anonymous meetings and had stopped drinking; as a result he was working hard and making quite a bit of money from his land and cattle. But his prosperity made him popular, with men and women, and he started to visit "women of the streets" and fell in love with an eighteen-year-old sex worker. Nena had not realized what was going on, even though she found it strange that he came home from his AA meetings at 2:00 or 3:00 A.M., when they were supposed to end by 10:00 P.M. A neighbor informed Nena about the affair, and Nena needed to confirm it. "Since I've been a mother and a father here in the house because of his [drinking] problem, I have a strong temper. I started to watch him and his schedule and realized that, yes, he was having relations with this young woman. So I went over to where they met and hit him first and then her. Then I sent her to jail for interfering with my marriage. After that he started drinking again."[9] Nena was emphatic in noting that his affairs had not been consequential for her marriage. But even if in her eyes her marriage was not affected, Nena and the young women ended up hurting each other, a situation that highlights the gender and symbolic violence in their relations and how these affairs are constructed. And her mother-in-law usually became involved in these situations. Nena explained, "My mother-in-law quickly interferes and puts an end to these relations; she is the only person my husband listens to. It was with her help that I sent that young woman to jail. So it's her intervention that has prevented my marriage from having even more problems, maybe from totally disintegrating."

Mirna's situation in many ways paralleled Nena's, but it also differed in crucial ways, in particular, regarding social class, power, and influence. In contrast to Nena, Mirna came from a poor family in San Alejo and lived with her husband on the outskirts of town in a one-room rented house with sporadic running water and electricity and a latrine that had been promised but had not materialized. Right after they got married, when Mirna was thirteen, Mirna's husband started to have affairs; he was known as a *mujeriego* (womanizer), a reputation that deeply hurt Mirna. Her husband's women friends would sometimes come to Mirna's house to tell her about their affairs. Mirna told me about one such instance: "One time, when I was like fifteen or sixteen, this woman came to the house and insulted me and threatened to kill me if I didn't divorce my husband. Can you believe that?" She confronted her husband, but instead of accepting his culpability and putting an end to the affairs, he blamed Mirna for not trusting him, and he hit her. "He would tell me, 'Do you believe other people instead of me? What kind of a wife are you? Don't you trust my word?' But it was the women themselves who would tell me about their relations. And then he would say, 'Oh, who have you been hanging out with? With women of the street? Are they your friends now and you talk and confide in each other what you do with men?' He would blame me and get angry at me for finding out about his businesses." But Mirna actually knew a "woman of the street," her aunt, who used to work at a bar, and Mirna decided to turn to her for help. One night Mirna went by a bar and caught her husband with another woman.

> Now I was sure [about the affair], and so my aunt got two of her [male] friends from the bar where she worked and went to talk to the woman. They threatened her that if she ever bothered my husband again they would have to fix the situation and would even use a gun if necessary. You see, my aunt's

> husband was killed like that, entangled with a woman of the street. So my aunt told me, "Look, my *negrita* [little black one], we'll take care of this so you don't suffer anymore." And thanks to God, that's all gone. The woman, a Salvadoran she was. To this day I don't know if she's dead or alive. She disappeared from here forever, thanks to my aunt and her two big guys.

Extramarital affairs were deeply hurtful and worrisome to the women both directly and indirectly. In my rare conversations with men, they implied that extramarital affairs should not surprise anyone and, in fact, were very much part of being a man. The women's reflections on this issue supported the men's views. Isabel, who argued that she had gotten ill with headaches and stomachaches as a result of her husband's philandering, explained how she had dealt with this issue since the early years of her marriage:

> You know, men will always look for other women. That's just how they are. No man in this world is different. I have never heard of any man who is different in my entire life. As men, that's what they do, whether they are in San Alejo, in Guate, in the United States, or in China. It doesn't matter where they are. So I can't argue with him, I can't demand an explanation, because that's normal in men, right? At first in my marriage I used to get sad and cry, but my mama would tell me, "No, don't argue with him, don't fight with him, all men do that; he'll leave you if you bug him too much." So I would be very upset—trying to change him would have been like trying to keep a monkey from going up a tree.

In addition to talking to her mother, Isabel often talked with a friend, who told her that she should not believe everything she heard about her husband's affairs. "Believe it when you see it," the friend would advise Isabel. And one day Isabel saw it: Her husband decided to ride in his car with the woman he was seeing then and go right past Isabel's house. Isabel recounted her reaction, the upset stomach and the dizzy spell, and then said, "Ay God, you can't imagine how bad that feels; I felt awful because he had no shame. I saw him with my own eyes, all my neighbors saw him, and the whole town saw him. I felt like my soul was leaving my body [lifts both arms]. It's the worst feeling. But one who is married knows that that's how men are. What can one do?"

Although in San Alejo extramarital affairs and womanizing were normalized for men, women often talked about the hurtful effects this behavior had on them. Evidence points to traumatic, life-altering effects on women on discovering their partners' infidelity, and to important gender differences in this respect. Indeed, one study found that women suffer more prolonged effects as a result of their partners' infidelity than men do (Meldrim 2005). Two instances underscore the deeply painful consequences extramarital affairs have for women, even for those who are not at the center of the affairs. Two men were so open that their relationships were indistinguishable from open polygamy. Teresa, a young woman who fell in love with one of these married men, had accepted the idea of going to live in her boyfriend's sister's house. When a relationship got serious and the couple intended to form a union, custom dictated that the woman would go to live with the man and his family or close to them. However, because Teresa's boyfriend lived with his wife, he decided to take her to his sister's house, a situation that created problems for his sister, Gracia María, as well. Gracia María explained, "I do it because I love my brother, but I live very tense knowing that people are talking, thinking that I have no shame, and that I approve of extramarital relations. And I worry every day that, as the Bible says, someday someone will do the same to me. I live with that thing in my heart, worried and embarrassed, and I don't know what to do." Teresa beamed when she spoke of her boyfriend and their plans and said she would do anything for him. She realized this was not an ideal situation, but what mattered to her was that she was with him, sort of.

> I know you probably think this is embarrassing, shameful, and the whole town is talking. But I love him very much, what can I do? I even did something that most people don't know. I couldn't get pregnant, but I love him so much that I took medications so I could have a baby with him. I'm very happy now because I'm pregnant with the second one. I don't know what will happen in the future, but I know I will never be able to live without him, even if it is in this condition, hiding and exposing my family to embarrassment, having to walk with my head down. He tells me that I have always been and will always be his.

Anthropologists who have examined extramarital affairs cross-culturally have noted that regardless of a culture's notion of descent, level of social complexity, or the degree to which a culture is normatively permissive or restrictive in sexual matters, sexual propriety is the presumed right of both sexes (see, e.g., Jankowiak, Nell, and Buckmaster 2002). Though in principle this was also the case in San Alejo, such expectations were suspended for men but strictly enforced in women. Although Teresa's boyfriend was very open about his relationships, she said that he could not tolerate it if she (or his wife) did something similar: "Oh, no [laughs], no, I can't even go to the street alone or take a bus on which there are many men. He won't let me. I went to my aunt's house because she can take care of me while I'm pregnant. But he refused. Right away he went to get me from there and brought me back and told me to stay here. He said that he couldn't spend a night without me. Can you imagine, someone telling you all these things? Yes, I'm very romantic." So I asked, "Does he spend every night here in this house with you?" Teresa responded, "No, half there [with his wife] and half here." However, no matter the positive slant she tried hard to put on the situation, Teresa confided, this situation embarrassed and ostracized her in San Alejo because she had become so obviously and openly "the other woman."

Estrella's situation differed from Teresa's in that Estrella had a job that allowed her to provide for her family. Like Teresa, Estrella had a current partner who was already in a relationship with another woman when he and Estrella started their relationship. Her partner did not help her much financially because he did not feel obligated; as he saw it, Estrella was well aware of what she was getting into when they got together. But she did not ask him for much either. It was a conscious effort on her part, which she had hoped would help her to save the union, but it was not working: "He's gone back to the woman he had before me. But he sleeps here, eats here; I iron and wash his clothes, so he lives here. Yes, I do feel bad about this situation, but one does it so that one can have a family, you know, one tries to save the marriage, well, the union. People didn't ever say anything about me before him, because I used to be very well behaved, with an intact reputation, you know, from home to work and from work to home. No one could talk about me. Then I thought about getting together with him, you know, to have some company, as a woman one needs the company of a man—and also because I thought things would be better. Sometimes one says, 'Ah, I'll be better that way, but it doesn't always turn out that way' [laughs]."

As a result of these living arrangments, Estrella made all the decisions in the home. Rather than empowered, however, she felt lonely and overwhelmed at times, because all the burden of the house seemed to rest on her shoulders, from decision making to actual expenses. He contributed some beans and corn from his harvest, but Estrella was in charge of everything in the home. She was willing to put up with this situation, blaming herself for her two previous failed marriages and thinking that it was now her responsibility to work hard on this union. After her first husband had left her for another woman when the children were little, she started living with a man who moved in with her and her children. Her children loved him, and eventually Estrella had a baby boy with him, but since there was hardly any work for him in San Alejo he decided to migrate to Canada. For about eight years he had to stay put in Canada until he "established himself," but during this time he started living with another woman there and Estrella got involved with another man in San Alejo. Thus, when I met Estrella she was with her third partner and considered herself unlucky in love: "I am not lucky in love or in marriage. I have five children and three marriages." But she blamed herself for her situation and prayed to God that he would help her by sending a good partner her way, so that she would have "the respect that a man brings to the house" and would not spend her old age alone.

A common thread in most of the stories about infidelity that I heard was not only the embarrassment and hurt the women felt but also the looming fear of abandonment if their partners chose to go with the other women and the potential decrease in men's economic contributions. During the time they were having affairs, the men would sometimes make less of a financial contribution to the home (and would not necessarily feel responsible for the other home either), a situation that compounded the vulnerability of women.[10] A nurse at the health post explained, "Of course, when the men go around with other women, you tell me, how will men have enough money to pay for the women and also for food for their kids?" This situation had a parallel in the Altiplano. For instance, Azucena complained that her husband, who worked in Xela, contributed little to the household, even when the children were ill, because he was spending money on other women and alcohol. Azucena's mother thought the entire problem started the day of the wedding; apparently the groom was drunk at the ceremony and did not seem serious about his commitment. At first Azucena went to live with him in Xela, but she decided to return to her hometown because her husband had become abusive physically and emotionally. "He treated me badly," she said. "He sometimes hit me, but he would also go around with women almost in front of me." In a twist I observed a few times in both towns, Azucena ended up being accused of the consequences of her predicament. Her husband not only refused to contribute to the household but also had threatened to take the children away; he told her that she was not caring for them well. "He said it was my fault that the children were not eating well, and I worry because he wants to take them away, so I got a job preparing the thread for a woman who weaves. I got Q.15 for that." But Azucena's worst moments were when her husband would yell that he regretted marrying her. She would refuse to have sex because his words were so hurtful; he then would tell her that she should not have married him, or anyone else for that matter, and that no one would ever love her.

Whereas men's extramarital relations were bound up with constructs of maleness, women's sexuality was restricted to marriage; thus women's premarital or extramarital relations tended to fall in the category of "social evils" (see Rydstrøm 2006). In San Alejo even women's *perceived* infidelity was enough to have serious consequences for them, even when their husbands were no longer around. When Estrella started to live with her third partner, her older son moved out because he thought it was disrespectful of her to bring another man into the house, even though she had been alone for some time and had been careful to guard her behavior so as not to invite gossip. Her second husband refused to allow his son to live with Estrella after she began living with her third partner; as a result the boy lived with his paternal grandparents and visited Estrella daily. "He can't sleep here," Estrella commented, "but at least he [her second husband] didn't take him to Canada, like he had threatened; that would have devastated me. This way I see my boy every day." Hortencia's son left the house too when he suspected that his mother was seeing another man, even though his father had been dead for a few years. And Tita, also a widow, spent a few years alone after her husband had died from spraying pesticide while drunk. She had finally decided to start her life anew and became involved with a man with whom she had a baby. But her former in-laws were furious and accused her of having become a "woman of the street." They refused to help her anymore with the beans and corn they would sometimes give her. Tita was embarrassed: "I felt bad, like I was sinning, but I don't think I was doing anything wrong. I was tired of living alone, and it was the first man I ever had something with after my husband died." In other cases the mere suspicion of a woman's infidelity justified violence in the home, a comment I heard more than once, from both women and men, and also reported among criminal justice professionals (see chapter 2).[11]

THE PRESENCE AND INTERFERENCE OF FAMILY AND THE ACCEPTANCE OF SUFFERING

The women's experiences did not occur in a social vacuum; they lived in regular contact with their own parents and siblings, in-laws, neighbors, and compadres, and it was from within these webs of social interaction that women interpreted their experiences. Thus although women found solace and comfort in the people who were close to them, at the same time the actions of these individuals often reinforced the structures of inequality and violence in which the women lived. While a mother's words might have helped to soothe her daughter's pain, they also encouraged the daughter to continue to endure a husband's abuse, because this was better for the woman and her children or because this was the way things were. In Bourdieu's (2001: 9) conceptualization, "The strength of the masculine order is seen in the fact that it dispenses with justification. . . . [It] has no need to spell itself out in discourses aimed at legitimating it." Thus this discussion is not meant to present only the palliative effects of the presence of others in the women's lives as "networks of support" but to problematize such relations in the context of symbolic, structural, and gender violence.

For instance, Mirna remembered that whenever she confided in her mother about how she was suffering in her marriage, her mother would console her. Mirna found that talking with her mother was a good way to *"desahogarse"* (let it all out). "She advises me to be patient," Mirna explained, "to remember that this is what it means to be married, that young women think it's all going to be good, but this is not how it is. So my mama advises me *que aguante me dice* [to endure, she tells me], not to despair." And often those close to the women made comments that would make them think they were the cause of their problems. Mirna continued, "My mama is right. I think that we, women, are only good for creating problems for men. It's the women who are coquettish, who invite the men to sin, and it's the women who reproach the men at home. Old women are wise, and they know." But Mirna's mother-in-law also helped her quite a bit; she would tell Mirna's husband that Mirna was a "woman of the house, not of the street, so she deserves respect." She would also advise Mirna not to be so afraid of her husband. Years later her husband suspected that someone had cast a spell or had performed *brujería* (witchcraft) on him, because he noticed that Mirna was not as afraid of him as she was when they first married, and she even answered him back on occasion. Indeed, several women, both in San Alejo and in the Altiplano, spoke of having been afraid of marriage. Rosita, in the Altiplano, spoke of being sad when her husband asked for her in marriage; she had heard so many horrible things about marriage that she was terrified. However, it turned out that this was never her experience; up until her husband's disappearance in the violence that swept the Altiplano, they had a good, respectful marriage.

When Susana in San Alejo wanted to separate from her husband because she could not stand his behavior and irresponsibility anymore, her in-laws insisted that this would not be good for the children or for her and reminded her that she could go to them in emergencies. It was the same in Vera's case. Since she and her husband lived next door to her in-laws, whenever Vera's mother-in-law overheard an altercation in their home she would quickly come over to "calm things and keep the peace." They argued only when Vera's husband was drunk, so her mother-in-law kept an eye out when she saw that he came home drunk. Vera explained, "To be sincere with you, I'd prefer that she not get involved in my things, but she has saved me. Without her I don't know where we would be." And to this day Hortencia remained grateful to her mother-in-law because the woman "saved" her from her husband's beatings more than once. Hortencia did not complain and never talked to anyone about her situation, but when her husband became aggressive her neighbors or her eldest daughter would run to call her mother-in-law to "come to defend me." Her mother-in-law would run to her house and stop him and even hit him if necessary, Hortencia said, because she understood how it felt to be abused.

In-laws, however, would sometimes "help out" in ways that sustained symbolic, gendered, and gender forms of violence. For instance, Delfina recounted the times when her husband came home drunk at 3:00 A.M. and demanded that she prepare dinner for him. She would need to get up and prepare the outside oven to broil his steak over charcoal because that is how he liked it prepared. Her mother-in-law would "rescue" her, Delfina explained. "She helps me get the fire going with small corn husks so that I can prepare his steak. He doesn't want me to prepare it on the stove, which is much easier. No, he likes it in the most difficult way. Yes, at 3:00 or 4:00 A.M. And his mother sees the injustice and helps me out." Delfina's mother-in-law would also prepare a completely different lunch if she thought that her son would not like what Delfina had prepared before she left for work. "Sometimes I'm in a rush," Delfina said, "and I prepare a pasta dish or chow mein [a popular Guatemalan dish]. My husband loves beef, steaks, so his mother rapidly changes the meal so that I don't get in trouble when I come back from work. She is very good. She interferes in my marriage but in a positive, not in a negative, way. Without her around I think that he would have already done who knows what to me." Delfina was especially appreciative that if her mother-in-law wanted to criticize something Delfina had done or make an observation to her, she would pull her aside and speak to her alone, not in the presence of her husband, because he could explode in a rage if he ever heard that his mother did not like something that Delfina had done.

Nena's in-laws also interfered in different ways in her marriage, for which Nena said she was immensely grateful.

> When my father-in-law finds out that my husband is misbehaving here at home, he takes money away from him. The other day he took away most of his cattle. When my husband was in the States we found out he was drinking again there, so my mother-in-law sent her daughter to go get him and bring him back. He was in such bad shape in the States that his parents would send him money from here. You know how the immigrants send money from there to their families here? In this case it was the other way around. His parents even sent him clothes to the States one time! When he came back he apologized to his parents and promised never to do it again. But now he is back to drinking. He has been in the hospital. Well, his parents are the ones who do everything. His parents love me and support me because I *aguanto* [put up with] their son. I don't know what I would do without their help.

But Nena's in-laws were not the only ones she could count on. In my field notes I wrote, "Nena seems to have a battery of people to help her deal with her situation." Her neighbors knew that when her husband was drinking Nena might need help calling the doctor or taking him to the clinic. So they were there to help. The doctor and nurses at the health post, and even the families of these workers, also were ready to help and come to the house if Nena had an emergency with her husband in the middle of the night. In her words, "I need help, and all these people are beautiful with me. They know my situation and probably feel sorry for me. I know that *yo doy lástima* [people feel sorry for me]. So they help me, and I am grateful to them with all my heart. Without their help I probably would have left my husband. Or I would have lost my mind." Nena's social position, according to others in town, had something to do with her extensive network. "They're well known and have lots of people to do favors for them," a woman at church said. And Hortencia, though with a much narrower network of people who put fewer resources within her reach compared to Nena, knew that she could count on her neighbors and compadres if she ever needed to deal with a serious situation at home: "My compadres have been my friends for eleven years, and they know my situation. They knew that my husband would sometimes leave us without anything to eat, so they would tell me, 'Look, come iron and wash for us,' and they would pay me for that. They are good. And my neighbors sometimes would call for help if they heard me scream. So even though I never talk with anyone or complain, I know people look on me with eyes of mercy and help me out." In such cases the women gained the support of their in-laws, friends, and neighbors, because they conveyed an image of dedicated, suffering, and principled women who put up with their husbands. Those who endured were helped to continue to put up with their situations. Thus these practices were possible and reinforced by the structures of gender and symbolic violence in which the women, their friends, and family lived, and where images of morality, propriety, and devotion were constructed.

In this respect, women's experiences in the Altiplano were similar. Like other women there, Lita was very appreciative of her in-laws' help, especially with the children, during her husband's drinking bouts. She spoke of her mother-in-law as a caring woman and of her father-in-law as a fine man. Once a neighbor ran into Lita's in-laws in the street and informed them that Lita's husband was drinking and kissing the woman who sold *atole* in the plaza, so the in-laws, anticipating a problem, immediately came to the house, even before the husband arrived, and told Lita that she could count on them for anything she needed. And Adela, a young woman from a well-respected family in town, mentioned with gratitude her mother-in-law's intervention in her marriage. Though she said that this was a delicate issue because her mother-in-law's good intentions could easily become unwanted intrusions, she nonetheless appreciated them, as well as the good advice given to her husband. She described one of those instances as follows:

> Once, for the Feria, my husband gave me Q.200 to buy things for the house. I fell in love with a beautiful set of china dishes and bought it. It was expensive; I was left with only Q.30 for food and other things. My husband was enraged when he saw that I had bought pretty dishes but nothing more practical, like beans and corn. He said, "Now, see what you can do about buying what we need." He scolded me and yelled at me every day for this, and once he hit me and I left and went to my parents' house. Both my parents and his parents scolded him for hitting me, so I came back. Then his mother said to him, "Look, dishes are needed to eat; even if you have food, how will you eat it if you don't have dishes? It's good that she bought that for the house." Yes, it was helpful that she talked to him because he listened to her.

But Gina, who was married at fourteen, said that whereas her in-laws were helpful at times, sometimes they exacerbated the problem. They did not trust her when she married their son, because they considered her too young to assume the responsibility of a household. But they changed their minds ten years later, when, with the help of her compadres,[12] she decided to take her husband, father-in-law, and brother-in-law to AA meetings, because the three men used to get together to drink every week. In order to convince them to go Gina attended the sessions and became involved in the group. She said that to "cure" her husband, she also had to take care of the "other two problems"—her husband's father and brother. But in the Altiplano, as in San Alejo, relations with in-laws were not always smooth. Some women had direct and open complaints about their in-laws. Constantina went through rough moments with her in-laws because they accused her of being the source of their son's problems. By the time the marriage ended the in-laws were not on speaking terms with her. She explained, "I see them in the street, and I change to walk on the other side and look the other way. They thought that I was too smart and coquettish and lied that I was having a lover. My mother-in-law wanted her son to hit me and not let me go out. But he wasn't like that. They saw no other alternative to separate us, so they evicted us, yes, together with my husband. They even took us to the municipality to get us evicted and accused me of hitting them. The authorities came to throw our belongings out of our house, because the house belonged to them [the in-laws]. We went to my parents', but things were difficult, and then my husband and I just ended up getting a divorce anyway."

CONCLUSION

The intimate sphere of courtship and marriage in women's lives in San Alejo presented an opportunity to examine the everyday, routinized forms of visible and invisible forms of violence. The women (and their relatives and friends) recognized behavior such as direct physical maltreatment as violent, and often they would interpret abuse and mistreatment—whether in its direct or indirect form—as the way things were. My task in dissecting these interactions and calling attention to the suffering they embody is not to point a finger in the women's direction (or, for that matter, at the men in their lives as individuals committing violent acts). Nor am I drawing simplistic, deterministic relationships between larger structures and individual behavior. I am, however, linking these to the larger systems of oppression that produce and reproduce hierarchies based on class, ethnicity, and gender. I focus on the larger context that molds these situations, but it is the individuals in this context who shape and transform what is considered ordinary.

Thus I have paid attention to notions of normalized violence that lend a sense of the ordinary to suffering in women's lives. In Bourdieu's (2001: 9) words, "The social order functions as an immense symbolic machine tending to ratify the masculine domination on which it is founded: it is the sexual division of labor, a very strict distribution of the activities assigned to each sex, of their place, time and instruments; it is the structure of space[,] . . . the stable, the water and vegetable stores." It is important, therefore, when focusing on symbolic violence to note the internalization of dispositions and unequal structures, such that women *and* men "remain largely unaware that it is the logic of the relationship of domination that imposes on and inculcates in women . . . all the properties that the dominant view inputes to their *nature*" (Bourdieu 2001: 31; original emphasis). Thus the violence that takes place in intimate relations (some of which is interpreted as romantic love or as demonstrations of *cariño* [caring]) as well as the insults and verbal denigration and humiliations embedded in everyday life leave similar, often deeper scars than direct, physical forms of violence. Although I have emphasized instances of violence and suffering (for the purposes of uncovering them), these cases occur within social structures that also contribute to buttressing gendered agency and mitigate suffering. The women's complex relations with their parents and in-laws, for instance, while they reinforce constructs of masculinity that normalize violence and often are present in the lives of the women as sustaining suffering, also create spaces for a collective dimension of the women's experience. This collective dimension "socializes" the women's experiences to foster gendered agency and survival.

CHAPTER 5

Children, Motherhood, and the Routinization of Pain and Sacrifice

Le dije a ella, cuando llegue al cielo, puede por favor pedirle a Dios que me ayude a aguantar mi vida con mis hijos, que me ayude a aguantar a ser madre?

[I said to her, "When you get to heaven, can you please ask God to help me endure my life with my children, help me endure being a mother?"]

—Mirna, talking to her aunt on her aunt's deathbed

Mire, yo he sido dedicada a mis hijos en todo. Si se enferman, hago lo que sea sin pensarlo dos veces. Fíjese que ninguno de mis hijos se me ha muerto. Y si algún día uno se me llegara a morir, eso es porque ya Dios así lo quiere no por descuido mío. He luchado por ellos, Yo creo que eso es lo que me voy a llevar conmigo cuando me muera, que he sido amorosa con ellos.

[Look, I have been dedicated to my children in every way. If they are ill, I do anything without thinking twice. None of my children have died. If one day one of them dies, it's because God wants it that way, not because I have not taken care of them. I have fought for them. I think that's what I'll take with me when I die, that I have been loving with them.]

—Estrella, forty-six years old

Maxine Molyneux (2006: 427) observes that although Latin American women have entered the workforce and gained access to health care and education, "by broad consensus their primary duties lay within the family." Thus images of Latin American women as devoted mothers, as Estrella sees herself, are prototypical and often based on *marianismo,* "the cult of feminine spiritual superiority that teaches that women are semi-divine, morally superior to and spiritually stronger than men" (Stevens 1973: 91), a concept that is thought to be in "reciprocal agreement" (99) with *machismo.* The substantial body of scholarship on this topic finds these representations rooted in a secularized veneration of the Virgin Mary (Bunster-Burotto 1986; Fabj 1993; Stevens 1973), in which sacrifice, suffering, and self-denial are integral. But the term *marianismo* and these representations are not unidimensional or unilinear (see Gutmann 1996).[1] For instance, whereas some scholars point to Latin American women's "inability to resist the desire to take care of people and to indulge the wishes of others" (Fitch 1991: 264), the term *marianismo* itself has been used to resist and challenge oppression and to fight for human rights (Sternbach et al. 1992), with the Madres de la Plaza de Mayo in Buenos Aires being emblematic in this respect (Borland 2006; Bosco 2001; Navarro 2001). Indeed, this concept has shaped and reshaped ideas of motherhood, feminism, activism, resistance, and social action in Argentina and beyond (Abreu Hernandez 2002; Lucchetta 2003). Thus although Latin American women's nurturance of their children and families has been highlighted and stereotyped, images of Latin American women who have protested laws and conditions that threaten their ability to fulfill their role as mothers (Miller 1991) often coexist in the same spaces.

In this chapter I focus on the San Alejo ladinas as mothers, noting (as other scholars have done) the suffering, self-denial, and sacrifice that this identity carries but without relying on the uncritical binary of women as *abnegadas* (self-sacrificing) and men as detatched (see Gutmann 1996). Instead, these are my starting points for a deeper examination of motherhood experiences that bring to the fore aspects of the broad context of violence I am calling attention to, such as the conditions in which women mother, the lack of resources in their mileu, the deeply unequal health care system and women's dramatically constrained options within it, and the consequences all this has for women and their perceptions of themselves as mothers. Focusing on the centrality of motherhood, I examine the complexities of the women's experiences of reproduction—fecundity, birth, children, and child rearing—

that expose the confluence of multiple forms of violence in their lives. Thus rather than link their suffering and pain to the myth of marianismo and other cultural constructs that ostensibly position women as nurturing, altruistic, and selfless caretakers, I trace links between their sacrifices and the broader structures of inequality that buttress their suffering. In line with the overall objective of this book, I expose the mothers' suffering that comes from structural violence, which leaves them and their children without access to good-quality health care and nutrition; from the hidden injuries of gender, gendered, and symbolic violence behind gender ideologies and internalized inequalities, including a preference for male children; and, indirectly, from the political violence that has ravaged the entire country and contributed to the cheapening of life and the promotion of other structures of violence. As I have done in previous chapters, here I note the visible forms of violence as well as those that enter the picture indirectly or under the subterfuge of language and quotidian practices, which contribute to their normalization. And although in the women's lives suffering and pain coexist in complex ways with the moments of boundless joy that motherhood can bring, in unearthing the violence in this sphere of the women's lives I give primacy to their suffering. In short, I seek to defamiliarize what seem to be natural aspects of motherhood and link them to structures of violence and internalized dispositions—at the root of subordination, domination, inequalities—that sustain suffering (see Bourdieu 1984, 2001, 2004). I also highlight the presence of others as an antidote to an image of utter hopelessness and misery. However, one must keep in mind that this presence is not simply a source of comfort and solace, for it contributes to normalizing unequal structures.

VIEWS AND MEANINGS OF MOTHERHOOD

Like other forms of social identity, a central aspect of motherhood for the ladinas in San Alejo entailed perceptions of themselves as good, dedicated mothers, perceptions that were framed in the language of suffering, as the literature noted above would predict. Thus, for instance, the women were prone to point out that *los hijos cuestan* (children cost) or *uno de madre sufre* (as a mother, one suffers). One afternoon I ran into Mirna at the health post and kept her company while she waited to see the doctor. At that time my son had not been born yet, so Mirna took the opportunity to explain the experience of being a mother, so I would be prepared when my turn came: "Only when going through it [motherhood] can one understand what it really is. I tell my sister. Like you, she doesn't have children yet. Look, I say to her, 'You are a *señorita* [single, no children, a virgin], you don't know what a mother suffers when she bears a child and then raises him.' It's suffering that's difficult to explain but that all mothers understand." To help me understand what she meant, she recalled the time when her aunt was on her deathbed, Mirna asked her a favor. "When you get to heaven, can you please ask God to help me endure my life with my children, help me endure being a mother?"

Most women spoke of motherhood the way Mirna did. It was not only important for them to show what good and dedicated mothers they were through the suffering they endured, but also to be *perceived* as such, as mothering and suffering went hand in hand in the eyes of most people in San Alejo. Along these lines, the women also recognized the importance of their mothers in their lives. Vera said of her mother, "She is everything for me; I go to her for big problems and for little things; she's my consolation." Andrea explained that she had a rather difficult relationship with her mother: "Well, I left my mama because she hit me after I broke the jar that she gave me to get water from the creek, so I said, 'No more.' But then, what could I do alone, without my mama? I had to go back to look for my mama because even though she was angry and had her temper, she was my mother. And *madre, sólo hay una* [there is only one mother]." Andrea also brought up a link between different forms of violence and how they can lead to the internalization of feelings of devaluation: "Then when I went to live with my boyfriend, he hit me too. My mama hit me, and then my boyfriend did too. It's like I have written on my forehead, 'Hit me.' I'm treated like nothing."

As the women spoke of their sacrifices for their children, they often said that this was expected of them. For example, one of the women commented, "Uno de madre tiene que sacrificarse" (As a mother one has to sacrifice). But they also alluded to material conditions that exacerbated their suffering as mothers because they were unable to provide what they wanted, or were expected to, for the children. Mirna, like other mothers who were very poor, said that when she ran out of beans to feed her children she felt a sharp pain in her heart. "Ay, no, it feels terrible when the kids ask, 'You don't have any beans to give me?' and I tell them, 'Ay, papaíto, no tengo nada, mi vida, nada mi cielo' [Ay, little papa, I have nothing, my life, nothing my heaven]. And I just feel like crying. And I ask God, why do you send me these tests? I don't care if I don't eat. But for a mother to not be able to feed her children when they are hungry, it's torture." Silvia said that because her son ate sand when he was younger, he had to be hospitalized for eleven days, during which time she never left his side, sleeping on the floor and buying the boy food from outside because the public hospital's food was not adequate. Silvia also faced the delicate situation of seeming to compete with the wives of her husband's brothers and sisters-in-law over who was the better mother; they all lived in the same house with their in-laws, and Silvia lived away from her own family. Although in the individual interviews none of the women in this household implied any competition, in informal conversations with them in the presence of their in-laws each commented on how far she went to make sacrifices for her children, perhaps to position herself as the better mother.

Ivette made sure that everyone around her knew what a good mother she was. She was Silvia's sister-in-law but lived in the Altiplano with her husband's Kaqchikel-speaking extended family, a respected family of means in the region. Ivette explained that her husband had told her that when their daughter starts to cry, she needed to immediately stop whatever she was doing and give the child a bottle or change her diaper, because "he doesn't want the baby to be wet or hungry even for a minute." "So I immediately jump to take care of the baby when she cries," Ivette continued, "no matter what I'm doing." When I asked her if her husband also "jumps" when the baby cries, Ivette laughed and said, "No, he only tells me to do it." Then she added, "He is very demanding, and I have to be constantly alert." Ivette said that even her husband's sister had asked him not to be so demanding with his wife, because Ivette was all by herself caring for the baby and the house. The sister explained to him that it is not a big deal not to change babies right away. But Ivette's husband demanded that she "behave like a good, dedicated mother." During one of our conversations in the living room of her house, Ivette's young daughter started to cry. Ivette turned to me and said, "For instance, right now, my husband would have immediately told me to go take care of the girl, no matter what I'm doing." I asked Ivette how she responded to his demands; with a nervous laugh, she said, "What I do is do what he tells me fast so he doesn't get upset; he is happy when I obey quickly." Then she added, "It's that he loves the girl so much. It's all because of his great love for the girl."

Not all women shared Ivette's views. Some did not seem especially concerned about their image as devoted mothers. Such contrasting cases highlight the normalized assumptions about motherhood among other women. These mothers were generally perceived as *desamoradas* (not loving), mostly because their behavior put in question conventional images of motherhood and the suffering it entailed or they were not inclined to demonstrate what mothers go through. And these women were well aware that they were seen as "not normal." Delfina, for example, said, with a smile that betrayed her awkward situation, that her daughters were closer to their paternal grandmother than to her. She also was aware of her reputation for not being a good mother. She linked this to how her husband treated her; in her eyes, his treatment also shaped how her daughters perceived her. She explained:

> My mother-in-law has been spoiling my daughters since they were born, so they love her more than they love me. You see, the girls have been exposed to all the things that he [her husband] tells me, all the insults, how he rejects me and mistreats me, so they imitate him, right? The girls get ideas from him that I am a bad wife, so then they don't think I'm a good mother. In their opinion I'm not a good person. And to top it all off, my mother-in-law buys them good things; she gives them bracelets, necklaces, and clothing that I don't even buy for myself, expensive jewelry and suits that cost Q.350.

Sometimes suffering during pregnancy, birth, and child rearing left women with less than enthusiastic views of motherhood and of children in general, views that then shaped these women's images as desamoradas. Such was the case with one of Gracia María's neighbors, who was known for not being a loving mother. Gracia María explained, "Her character—what she says is that she just doesn't have much love for children because she suffered too much with her own children. So when her daughter brings the grandchildren to see her, she says hello and is friendly, but you'll never see her picking up and carrying the children, and she mostly stays far from them." When constructed as *madres desamoradas* these women also experienced loss of control over their children, for which their husbands and family blamed them, a situation that amplified what the women perceived to be their own shortfalls. Delfina continued, "So the girls spend most of their time at their grandparents'; the grandparents even take the girls to the doctor if they get sick. Sometimes I don't even know about it until they come home with medicine. But this creates huge problems because then my husband blames me; he says that I'm not attentive to the girls, that if his mother has to take them to the doctor it's because I am not caring, that I'm not a good mother. I'm desamorada. Well, yes, it hurts [looks down and rubs her hands]."

PRENATAL CARE, PREGNANCY, AND BIRTH

Practically everyone in San Alejo knew that prenatal care was vital for a successful pregnancy and raising healthy children; however, not all pregnant women obtained prenatal care.[2] The gap between what the women knew was good for themselves and their children and what they actually did serves to reveal how structural violence keeps them from fulfilling their expectations about motherhood. Structural violence, expressed in material scarcity and poverty, is perhaps the most commonly associated factor with the women's restricted access to prenatal care.[3] For instance, whereas Mariana, the daughter of a wealthy family in San Alejo, never missed a prenatal visit with her obstetrician in the city and delivered her two boys at a private clinic in Guatemala City, Leticia, a tomato picker who often did not have enough money even for a bus ride to see a doctor in a nearby town, had missed almost all of her prenatal visits at the health post. Leticia's explanation for skipping prenatal visits might give the impression that this was her decision alone. "I didn't have time, especially with the second one, no time at all," she said. But links to her material conditions began to emerge: "Well, I didn't have time because I had to work; my husband was already sick [with AIDS], and I had to do laundry for people, iron, clean a house, pick tomatoes in the fields. I had to feed him and the older girl, and the clinic was not open when I had time, late at night. So, no, I only went to prenatal care when I had time." Other women, who could not afford the time or money required even for a free prenatal care visit, would go only when they did not feel well. Gracia María received prenatal care for only one of her five previous pregnancies, and only because she had morning sickness, a recurring bloody nose, and weakness, likely symptoms of undernourishment.[4] Andrea tried never to miss these visits and was quick to recognize the added bonus they provided. In addition to vitamins and other care during her pregnancy, she received food. "No one told me to go," she told me. "I went on my own; I know it's a good thing. And the food they gave was super important."

However, as powerful as the effects of structural violence were, this factor alone could not account for the range of situations I found in San Alejo. It began to interest me that in spite of the vital place of motherhood and the care of children, there were women, even those with some means, who would forgo prenatal care. My seemingly naive observation prompted me to explore this situation in the context of my other observations in San Alejo. Closer examination revealed factors besides material resources that played a part in these decisions. In Tita's case, for instance, it was not so much material conditions that kept her from seeking care (although these also weighed heavily) but other circumstances that seemed more closely tied to gender and symbolic violence. She had her youngest baby with a man who was not her husband; they had been together for some time after her husband died, but they were not married. She explained, "I was embarrassed about my situation so, no, I didn't go to the Centro de Salud [Health Center] for prenatal care. I felt like everyone was looking at me, that everyone saw my face, but I couldn't explain my pregnancy. So then I stopped going to work too because I was embarrassed that my patrones would see me too. I lied to everyone. One day I had to go to work because I had a great need of the money, and I started to get sick at their home, so the patrones took me to the doctor." She said that this attention made her feel even worse, because then the patrones found out that she was pregnant and irresponsible as well. "The doctor scolded me because I had not gone to prenatal care and said that the baby was not doing well. Then my patrones reprimanded me for endangering the baby and for lying to them. So I ended up *regañada* [reprimanded] by everyone." Tita was happy when her youngest baby, her only boy after seven pregnancies and six live children, weighed in at nine pounds four ounces and was born healthy.

Lucrecia also avoided going to prenatal care visits because she felt uncomfortable about her situation. People suspected her of having sexual relations with married and single men in San Alejo, so she avoided most contact with institutions, including the health post. "I don't like to go [laughs]. No, I didn't go with either of my children. The people at the [health care] center ask too many questions and I don't like that, they ask too much [laughs]," she explained when I asked why she had not gone to prenatal care visits. Delfina, who came from one of the well-to-do families in town, also said that she mostly avoided going to prenatal care. I was surprised to hear this because I did not think Delfina, a teacher with the means to pay for private medical care, would skip prenatal care. Her explanation underscored the connection between these decisions and the broader social context in which they are made. She explained, "Look, I don't like it when people tell me that I need to lose weight, that I don't look good. I know that, and I don't need doctors to tell me that I'm not attractive because I have extra pounds. My husband says that every day; even my mama says that. So I didn't want one more person to tell me that I'm fat and ugly.

I have enough daily reminders with my husband at home." Estrella was always proud to note that she never sought assistance from the health post or from other people, but this meant that she suffered a great deal while raising her children. And Susana's sister, from one of the poorest families in town, also avoided any contact with physicians or medical practitioners during her pregnancies because she was embarrassed. In her case it was because her husband abused her physically, and she did not want the medical professionals to see that; they had already scolded her for not protecting her babies, acting "irresponsibly," and placing them at risk by putting up with the abuse. In the end, regardless of the source of embarrassment that kept the women from seeking prenatal care, they (and others) often pointed to themselves as culpable for their "mistakes" or "faults," even if they found the situation mortifying, as they knew well the importance of care during pregnancy. In this way statements from people in San Alejo—"Women don't want to go to prenatal care"; "They only care about themselves and not their babies"; "They are irresponsible and should not be mothers"—served to reinforce symbolic, structural, and gender forms of violence in the women's lives.

Equally important, when the women could not become pregnant or when they had a miscarriage they were mostly held responsible for the situation, even when external factors played a key role. Silvia's experiences reveal how such unfulfilled expectations of motherhood, in situations largely out of the women's control, led to feelings of inadequacy, self-doubt, and self-criticism. Silvia was quite concerned about her capacity to bear children, which led her to doubt herself and to question whether she was fit to be a mother, something that tormented her greatly. She experienced problems that almost caused her to miscarry when she was six months' pregnant. She was put on bed rest, and her husband and family decided that it would be best for her to stay with her parents during the last months of pregnancy so that they could take care of her. About two years after we first met she was deeply saddened and obviously distressed over a recent miscarriage she had had, especially because all the other women in her household continued to have children and Silvia and her husband had only one baby boy. I wrote the following observations after a visit with Silvia: "She is extremely sad and insists on seeing her difficult pregnancies as something that is less than womanly or motherly about her; she is convinced this is her own shortcoming. This is made worse when she sees her sisters-in-law having additional children seemingly without any problems. People have insinuated that if she continues to have problems with her pregnancies, her husband might leave her. This creates more stress for her, which she told me affects her health overall. She is then more vulnerable. She is worried about the future and sad."

About half of the San Alejo women in this study mentioned having had miscarriages, stillbirths, neonatal or post-neonatal deaths, often more than once. Mercedes had had twelve pregnancies, but four had resulted in a stillbirth, a neonatal death, or a miscarriage. Like Silvia, regardless of the reasons for the outcomes, these events made the women feel inadequate and sometimes incapable of fulfilling the important role of motherhood, which exacerbated the doubts and other perceived shortcomings the women had about themselves. For instance, Mirna, who had five living children by the time she was twenty-eight, lamented her first and only miscarriage and attributed it fully to her own immaturity. Her miscarriage happened in the first trimester of her first pregnancy, when she was fourteen. She fell in the patio of the house where she lived with her in-laws. She and her husband, both children themselves at the time, were playing around with water. She explained:

> We were patojos, children. We were thirteen when we got together, so we used to play around, like kids do [laughs]. Like tag; we used to play tag, and he would chase me to throw water on me. And I would throw water on him [laughs hard]. And my mother-in-law would have big fits and scold me because I wasn't making tortillas or doing my chores. I was so immature! I wanted to fool around! One day, I was already pregnant, my husband and I were playing tag, and I slipped and fell on my back. I felt my period coming. I told them to call the comadrona,[5] yes, Chavela, that one. But she didn't do anything to help me. Instead she boiled some herbs and gave me that to drink. I think that provoked an abortion. If I had gone to the hospital my baby would have survived. I was so immature and irresponsible. Yes, it was my fault because I behaved like a child and not like a mother.

Years later she still felt guilty about losing the pregnancy, though it was completely involuntary. "An aborted child makes you suffer even more," she said in a sober tone.

As with other aspects of life in San Alejo, different forms of violence compounded to create situations that increased women's self-recrimination over things that were beyond their control, especially in matters that dealt with motherhood. For instance, Hortencia's in-laws blamed her because she did not become pregnant soon after she got married. Her sisters-in-law would come by the house to tell her that if she could not bear children her husband would certainly leave her and that if she was barren she should just be honest about it. Hortencia said that her husband's family never imagined that it could have been his problem: "Men also can have problems having children, right? So I had to go to the doctor for treatment, and I was finally able to have children; we ended up with three [laughs], one after the other." Hortencia was malnourished and severely anemic, which might have affected her ability to conceive, her doctor said. "They gave me vitamins, *suero* [serum], because I was in bad shape," Hortencia explained. "When you spend years not eating enough and your family is so poor, there are consequences later on. One suffers from poverty, like one suffers from a disease."[6]

Women seldom if ever made reproductive choices alone; but when things went wrong they were blamed (and blamed themselves). And when confronted with difficult decisions such as terminating a pregnancy, the women would choose to put themselves, rather than the fetus, at risk. For instance, Lucrecia was unsure about her ability to raise more children alone, especially after her mother stopped remitting money and gifts from the United States. Lucrecia did not mention the word *abortion* in our conversations, but she implied that for a moment she had contemplated ending her pregnancy: "I told my friend, 'Look, I think I'm pregnant, and I don't know what to do this time.' 'Look,' she said, 'you better shut up, don't have those thoughts. Let's go see the doctor to see if you are pregnant, and if you are, and if you want, go to the United States, but don't you ever do something terrible. It's better that people talk about you having a thousand children than think that you're an assassin.' I think it's better for a mother to show that you can be responsible even if you're dying from fear inside because you don't know how you'll raise them."[7] And Gracia María knew that another pregnancy would be too much for her body; she lived tormented (if she died she would leave small children behind, she said, and this is what worried her the most) but went along with another pregnancy. "And what?" she said. "Take the baby out? No, I think that if that's the option, then I'd prefer to die. A mother can die for her baby, but a mother cannot kill her baby."[8]

There were some striking differences between the women in San Alejo and the Altiplano that have implications for gender ideologies and inequality. For instance, I came across a couple of cases of male sterilization in the Altiplano but none in San Alejo. Gina's mother in the Altiplano wanted to be sterilized, but her husband did not allow it because he thought it would not be good for a woman to have this procedure; instead he volunteered. In contrast, at the health post in San

Alejo the nurses laughed in unison when I asked about this. "No, here we don't do that; it's because here we have real machos [all laugh]! No, seriously, here the women are the responsible ones, which in my estimation is good and bad because that means they take responsibility but then are culpable when things don't turn out the way the husbands want," a nurse explained. These observations do not mean the situation is black-and-white in these towns, or that clear-cut differences always apply, or even that gender ideologies are always more relaxed in the Altiplano than in San Alejo, though relatively speaking there is a measure of gender equality in the Altiplano that I did not perceive in San Alejo. Thus although I am sure I did not capture the entirety of experiences in either location, these observations point to a nuanced picture that underscores the complexities that the combined effects of gender, structural, and symbolic violence bring to the two settings.

In other respects the experiences of the women in the Altiplano resembled those of the women in San Alejo. Women in the Altiplano also talked about the pressures of conforming to expectations of motherhood in a context of unequal access to goods and services. Alberta, for instance, a woman with five living children who had suffered one miscarriage and one stillbirth, said, "Other women go to prenatal care and see doctors; I haven't been able to do that. I don't have money for vitamins or tonics, so I eat what I can, and the neighbors take pity on me and sometimes give me corn." And Gina, who had had four pregnancies and one miscarriage, received prenatal care sporadically. Her husband's drinking kept her from going to see a doctor regularly, so she would consult with the comadrona in her neighborhood when she did not feel well. When she worked at a maquila in Guatemala City, she applied to the Instituto Guatemalteco de Seguridad Social (Guatemalan Institute of Social Security; IGSS) to receive prenatal care regularly, but she was not allowed to take time off from work to see a doctor once a month. She tried to go before or after work, but it was just too taxing, and sometimes they would not see her if she arrived at the clinic just before closing time. She explained, "The supervisors [at work] would not let me go because we had a lot to do; we used to work like thirty-six hours in a row. If you got in at 8:00 A.M. on Monday, then you would leave at 6:00 P.M. on Tuesday. No rest, not even on holidays. One could see a doctor at the factory, but only if you fainted or something like that. Just to go for a checkup, like prenatal care, no." And Gina had learned not to trust the factory doctor. One morning she went to him because she was not feeling well; he told her that she had anemia (which was correct) and a venereal disease (which was incorrect) and gave her penicillin. Gina instinctively decided not to take the penicillin and instead went to the comadrona back in her hometown who immediately diagnosed her pregnancy accurately and suggested *remedios caseros* (home remedies) for her morning sickness.

The San Alejo women who came from families with more resources generally delivered their babies at hospitals or private clinics, and poor women (the overwhelming majority) tended to have their babies at home.[9] If the women had complications with their home births, they were taken to the health post, or a relative would consult at the pharmacy to see what to do. Sometimes a private doctor would help out and charge them less. "He's good to the poor; he knows we have nothing," Susana, who had been in that situation, said about one such physician.

Two salient aspects about births emerged in my observations, interviews, and informal conversations in San Alejo and in the Altiplano. First, in both towns many of the women who gave birth at home (always the poorer women) routinely told stories about birthing alone without anyone's help;[10] second, most of these women mentioned the presence of other women helping after the birth, though in the Altiplano (but not in San Alejo) men also assisted. These observations help to capture the complexities of social position and gender expectations and highlight the importance of the presence of others in the women's lives.

Mirna said she was embarrassed to have anyone with her during the birth of her first child, when she was fifteen. She did not think it was a childish or immature whim due to her age, because she said many women felt that way. "I was embarrassed and did not want anyone, not even the comadrona to see me. I went to my aunt, who is a comadrona, and she helped. I felt fine because I know her and can trust her. But I tell my husband, 'Let's stop having more children because she's already very old, and when she dies I won't have anyone to assist me.' Yes, we can find someone else, but I will have to have a stone face to get used to someone else." Tita had her first child at a hospital, when she was sixteen, but decided to have the other six at home, alone, because she did not like people watching her give birth. She explained, "I don't like it; it's a private thing for a woman. When I feel it's time, I tell the kids to leave, to go play in the street. I deliver quickly. So later on they can come in and see their new baby brother or sister." She was being trained to be a comadrona and said that this was teaching her it was okay to have someone there during a delivery but that it was still difficult for her to have someone "watching." "It's quick; I give birth,

I don't stay there because I just don't have time, so I try to get up as soon as possible and start doing my chores. I have to wash the sheets and cook; no, no time to just stay in bed [smiles]." Tita brought up the cost of delivering her children at the hospital or with the help of a comadrona: "Tell me, I've had seven deliveries, and for each I would have had to pay. I better spend that money on the chidren who need food." Mirna was thinking along the same lines; she tried her best to have her children alone, but her husband became worried during one of her deliveries and went to get a comadrona to help. Mirna explained, "He worried because he thought I was going to die, imagine if I leave him a widower with all these children? He worried. So he went to get the comadrona, but she arrived late. The baby had already been born, and she only arrived to cut the umbilical cord. But she still charged the Q.35, because she said that it was still a delivery for her. I tried to bargain with her, but she didn't reduce the fee even though she didn't do anything."

Hortencia also made it a point to deliver alone after the birth of her first child. Her husband wanted a son, and the first two children had been girls. "The third one *had* to be a boy," she explained, and she feared a different outcome.

> So I wanted to be alone, to deliver by myself, because I was going to have problems with my husband if I delivered another girl. I didn't tell anyone that I was going into labor because of the fear I had. He was going to leave me if I had another girl. Thank God, it was a boy! Otherwise I would have had to leave the house with three girls. My husband's young brother was walking by our house and stopped by and saw me, so he went to get my mother-in-law and everyone, and then they got the comadrona to come and cut the umbilical cord.

But Hortencia had delivered at home before for the same reason and had to cut the umbilical cord herself in her previous delivery. She explained: "I would put pieces of cloth in my mouth so that my neighbors would not hear my screams, and I would just pray and cry until the baby was born." Mirna also said that her husband and his family wanted her to have at least one boy, so when her fourth delivery was a boy she jokingly told her husband that it was a girl. "I had him [the baby] all by myself, and then my husband came in and I said, 'It's another girl!' and he said, 'Another *molendera* [miller, grinder], but what can I do? God sent us this, and we have to accept it.' He looked disconsolate [laughs]. But then my aunt went to tell the others that it was a boy, and when my mother-in-law and my husband heard, she was so happy that she even lifted him from the floor, embracing him! Ah, no, with the girls, she only says, 'Ah, that's fine. At least the baby is alive.' With the boy it was great joy." One afternoon when I was waiting for Mirna at her house her sister was there, so she and I got to talk about all this. The sister was single, had no children, and said she had no intention of having any. Her statement intrigued me, because I had not heard anything similar in San Alejo. She wryly replied, "Because I wouldn't want to have a girl. Girls just come to suffer and have problems in this world. The danger of having a girl is what keeps me from wanting to ever have children."

In the Altiplano I also came across women who, for reasons similar to those in San Alejo, had also delivered their babies on their own. Lita, who had miscarried in three of her six pregnancies due to "weakness," had had to deliver several of her babies alone, because she did not have the money to pay a comadrona in the middle of the night when the charge was higher. On one occasion she started delivering alone, but the labor lasted a while, and a neighbor went to get the comadrona. Lita's house had no electricity or running water. Knowing this, the comadrona arrived with a candle, but the wind blew it out so she ended up delivering the baby in the dark. "Sí pues, dí a luz en lo oscuro [Yes, I gave birth—lit., "brought to light"—in the dark]," she said, laughing at the play of words in Spanish. Azucena delivered her babies by herself for the same reason: she had no money to pay the comadrona. "I kneeled and cried and thought of what my mama told me: 'Don't have any more children.' My mama later told me not to cry because God would help me. And yes, my neighbors came to help me with beans and corn and sugar." Isa, who had had six children, also had some of them at home without help. She had come to live in the Altiplano with her husband and did not fully trust her neighbors, she said. "I had to give birth on my own because my husband was not home, and no, I didn't want to call the neighbors because they could have said no; I don't trust them with favors. Since I had watched what other people do when delivering children I did the same. I even saved the umbilical cord in the way it should be." And although Constantina had assistance at her deliveries, like some women in San Alejo she usually only rested for a day or two "at most" after a birth, because she had to resume working in order to provide food for her other children.

Thus even though motherhood and the pain and struggles associated with raising children are defining moments for the women's identities, the birth itself embodies the pain and suffering that come from the conditions in which the mothers live and give birth. Often the women did not have the means to pay for a comadrona or to be taken to a hospital or a clinic and had to have their children alone. In the often harsh environment for women in San Alejo (and the Altiplano), the natural act of birth was couched in notions of decency and propriety. A preference for baby boys, itself an expression of gender asymmetries, also shaped where and how the women gave birth. Women would give birth alone rather than have others assist them for reasons beyond a scarcity of material resources and access to care; these reasons were bound up in discourses of morality and propriety that shed light on the gender ideologies that dictate the pace of life in this context. But delivering alone did not mean that the women ended up alone *after* a birth; they seldom did.

Whereas some of the San Alejo women gave birth alone and others had their babies with assistance, I noticed the consistent presence of others after the baby was born. Susana spoke at length of the help her sister usually provided to her when she gave birth. Her sister would bring her tortillas, food, and "some cents," so Susana did not have to worry about such things right after giving birth. Susana considered this a great help and spoke affectionately about her sister: "She helps me prepare lunch. Because she's my sister she's always helping me. If it's not one thing it's another, and she helps me." Susana also mentioned that her mother usually helped out by washing clothes, making tortillas, and looking after the other children.

For the most part, the same was true in the Altiplano. Women had others to assist them after a birth, even if they delivered on their own. In the Altiplano women used the *temescal* (traditional steambath) after a birth, and other women were there to prepare it and help the new mothers. In the Altiplano, however, I noticed a significant difference in the women's comments. According to my field notes, "Maria's father was very helpful when Maria's daughter was born. He held her and kept her going during childbirth and followed the comadrona's indications. Filita's husband was with her at the birth of all their four children, and he took care of her after she gave birth. Brothers, fathers, husbands are much more likely to be involved in the Altiplano than in San Alejo. And Antonia's husband was present for the birth of two of their children, and he did all the household chores for a few days after the birth, while her brother helped with the care of the older children when the youngest was born." These observations do not mean that this happens all the time in the Altiplano (or that it never happens in San Alejo), but the fact that I noticed the presence of men during or after childbirth several times in the Altiplano but only came across similar cases twice in San Alejo might point to important differences in this regard.

Reactions to the two cases in which men helped out with household chores after a birth in San Alejo underscore its rarity and the universal expectations that women were in charge. Mirna explained that after her baby boy was born her husband would get up at 5:00 A.M. to wash their clothes. When his mother arrived around six o'clock to help out, he would show her all the clothes he had already washed and was readying to dry. And when her daughter was born, she said, "he even made tortillas! He made beans. He never went to the mill—he would send the older girl—but he would make the tortillas." Mirna explained that because her husband's help was so unusual some neighbors considered him weird, and a Nicaraguan woman who lived in town could not stop laughing when she saw him making tortillas. Mirna said that he told the woman, "Look, don't laugh, don't make fun of me; instead you should help me out." But the woman explained that she was not making fun of him; she was simply amazed at what she saw and could not believe it, and she told him that she admired him. Victoria had a similar experience. Her husband helped out by mopping the floor when she needed to rest during a complicated pregnancy, which the neighbors noticed. Victoria said they thought he had learned such behavior during a stint working for a family in Connecticut. They needed to find an explanation for such unusual behavior, even though Victoria had already told them that he was like that even before he worked in the United States.

CARE OF CHILDREN

One of the ways in which women define their position and demonstrate their devotion as mothers is of course in the care of their children after they are born. The women in San Alejo beamed as they narrated the details of how attentive they were when their children needed them, their long nights when the children got sick, and the lengths they went to to ensure that their children had food, clothing, and medical care, as well as the unparalleled joy and rewards that their children brought to their lives. At the same time, the care of children exposed aspects of the women's lives that are intimately tied to multiple spheres of suffering, aspects in which the effects of structural, symbolic, and gender violence were compounded in ways that highlight the social and structural bases of mothers' sacrifices. The care of children made more vivid the constraints that poverty and exclusion imposed on the women; what it meant to have to decide between feeding the older children or the younger ones, or between purchasing medicine for one child or buying beans for the others. Expectations of mothers' dedication and sacrifice based on gender ideologies cut across social class, but the structural violence in the lives of poor women turned the fulfillment of such expectations into a series of impossibly difficult tasks that aggravated their vulnerability and led to suffering. In many ways the same acts of sacrifice that enhanced the women's position as mothers were also sources of incalculable pain. Contrasts across class position shed additional light on these observations.

Mariana, in San Alejo, always seemed to have an army of people caring for her and her two boys and did not seem to lack for anything. She lived on the second floor of the building in which her in-laws operated a large store, in the center of town; the living quarters were air-conditioned, and there were several people working in the household. Each of her two boys had his own nanny, and there were drivers to take them around on errands. In addition, there were domestic workers in charge of cleaning, washing, and ironing, and there was a cook who dedicated long hours to painstakingly preparing the boys' meals, even as she did not seem to have very much food for her own children. When I commented to Mariana that she probably had a lot of help caring for her children, she immediately corrected me and gave me a long explanation about how she was the one who was in charge of telling the workers what to do and that this, in essence, put her in charge of the children's care. I noticed that Mariana was more emphatic in her assertions when we heard footsteps in the hallway of the house; her mother-in-law would occasionally drop by when we conversed. At one point Mariana looked over my shoulder to see if someone was coming and said, "I dedicate a lot of time to the children. I overprotect them. I take care of their illnesses before I take care of my own. Because of my children I don't have time to visit my own family, to care for anyone else."

Mariana was not exaggerating or simply putting up a front; I had the opportunity to observe and corroborate what she said. In the middle of our converstation, she would excuse herself to tell the cook to mash the potatoes well, to cook the chicken just so, to prepare for the boys orange juice only from the sweetest and freshest oranges, and she would get up to go to the kitchen to supervise all this. Or she would call one of the workers to immediately change a child's clothing if he spilled anything on himself or just to check if a diaper was dirty. She would sometimes order Pampers from the United States because they were softer for the boys. And it was obviously important for Mariana to show her in-laws that she herself was doing all this, especially when her husband was away in the United States. She never tired of explaining all the things she did for her children, and how she spared no expense to make sure they were well taken care of. One afternoon we talked in a bedroom where one of the boys was taking a nap, and I had a chance to observe all the U.S.-bought clothes the boys had, including a brand-new Bears jacket that an uncle had sent from Chicago. She was thinking of asking this uncle to be the boy's godfather, she explained, but could not decide, because the boys had another uncle living in Los Angeles who also sent expensive presents regularly. But she was particularly touched by yet another uncle who had fully paid for the older boy's birthday party at a McDonald's in Guatemala City. When I asked Mariana about birthday celebrations in general, she smiled and said that she preferred not to have them in San Alejo, because she wanted "the best of the best, and that's usually in the capital, not here." She also did not want to invite "everyone" in town to those celebrations. Elvira, a nurse at the health post who was not originally from San Alejo, mentioned that Mariana's boys received so many gifts and so much attention because of the family's influence and position: "Everyone wants to be on good terms with them. Do you think they would be getting all that if they were poor?"

The situation was different for Mercedes, who was fifty-one years old when I first met her and who had the first of her eight living children when she was sixteen. Even though she now lived in a large Spanish-style house with a beautiful garden, she did not come from "a family of means," as she put it, so she had to work outside the home most of her life, during pregnancies and after her children were born. She quit going to school in the fifth grade and started working to help her parents, because they could not support her and her twelve siblings on her father's agricultural work alone. She worked at a factory that made popsicles in a large city in eastern Guatemala and was lucky to have a government-supported day care center nearby; so five of her eight children were cared for there while she worked twelve-hour shifts, until one by one they turned seven and transferred to school. She was quick to point out that even though the children spent most of their waking hours at day care, it was she who did not sleep at night if they were sick, she who ate less so her children would have enough food, and she who would wear the same clothes year after year so the children would have good shoes to go to school. "A mí me cuestan [They cost me]," she would say repeatedly, as if to dissipate any doubts about her devotion to her children that might arise because the children went to day care while she worked long hours at the factory to support them. The situation was even more complicated for the poorer mothers, like Susana, Mirna, and Hortencia, to whom I return later.

Mercedes mentioned that she only sent her first five children to the day care center because by the time the younger ones were born, the older girls could help care for them. The practice of having older girls care for their younger siblings is common in San Alejo, as elsewhere in the world. As in other societies around the world, girls are socialized into being the caretakers of their families and households from a very early age. With a mix of laughter and pride, Isabel in San Alejo recounted that when her younger daughter was in the first grade, the child would sometimes get up during class, around 10:00 A.M., to tell the teacher she needed to go home because it was time for her to go to the market and get things ready for lunch. Isabel and I laughed, and she said, "See, she was little, all her front teeth were gone at that time, and she was already thinking like the responsible woman that she is going to be. I guess we women are born with that; first the house and then everything else, like school, and even us." I came across girls as young as eight or ten fully in charge of the care of their younger siblings in both San Alejo and the Altiplano. But even though I heard about it and had the opportunity to observe it in both towns, I noticed that there were two or three day care centers, in addition to other programs to care for children in the Altiplano, but none in San Alejo, even though both towns were approximately the same size in population.[11]

From the time I first noticed this difference, I asked in both towns why this might be the case; most people provided vague answers or said they did not know. A physician at the health post in San Alejo, who was originally from Guatemala City, laughed, and tongue-in-cheek said, "Ah, because this is a *machista* town that expects only the women to care for the children." I talked to others in San Alejo, and some mentioned that a corn-packing factory had to close because fewer female workers than expected showed up for the positions. The factory managers had mentioned that the absence of a day care center was the reason women could not work. The issue of the day care center became a topic of conversation for me with several people in San Alejo, as it provided me a window into local expectations of motherhood. At one point I had a meeting with the mayor to discuss the possibility of having a day care center in town (it did not materialize for lack of resources). He was very open to the idea, saying, "I'd do anything for the well-being of our children." When I mentioned that this would also open up opportunities for the mothers to work and earn incomes, he tilted his head a little to one side, squinted his eyes, and said, half-jokingly, "Hmmm, but keep in mind that we don't want the mothers to abandon their children in the day care center; we want mothers to continue to be dedicated to their children and not use the center to deposit the children while they go to do who knows what."

Indeed, many people in San Alejo agreed with the mayor. Such expectations put enormous pressure on the women. Gracia María, for instance, said that she was completely in charge of all her five children, who ranged in age from five months to twelve years, because her husband left the house early every morning and came back late in the evening. However, even if her husband were home more often, she would still be in charge of the children.

> He almost never sees the children. If I want to tell him something about the children . . . well, I've been in that situation, the kids get sick and he just comes and goes in the house and never finds out that the kids have been sick. So I have to make all the decisions because he knows that if it's something that's related to the children, no one will stop me from doing whatever I can for them. My husband, well, really me, I am the one who has to see how I can treat the children when they're sick, how I want them to be, how I want them to behave. I have to oversee everything. Only when they don't listen to me, then I have to tell him. Otherwise it's just me, by myself. So, yes, even when he's home, I'm the one in charge of the kids [smiles].

Some of the women in the Altiplano shared similar experiences. On occasion they would call on their husbands or elders in the family to discipline the children. When Marta had problems with a teenage daughter who would not go to school, she called her in-laws, and they gave her advice. But "they always say, spank her, she needs that, and I don't like that, I am not a person who spanks, so I don't obey them." Alberta was fully in charge of caring for her deaf daughter, who at one point needed to go twice a week to Guatemala City for therapy, a two-and-a-half-hour trip. In order to pay for the bus fare to Guatemala City, Alberta would skip breakfast and lunch and only eat at home on returning from the city. She finally convinced the doctors to change the girl's treatment to only once a month, because it was becoming too costly and too taxing on her to go more frequently.

Thus expectations associated with motherhood meant that women would be devoted, self-sacrificing, and always thinking of others before thinking of themselves, all images that fit well with the "traditional," culture-based concept of marianismo. However, from the perspective I adopt here, these expectations—on the part of the men, other women, and the women themselves—revealed gendered ideologies of parenthood that placed women in extremely difficult situations, as social and economic inequalities constrained their actions and the resources they could muster. When the expecations were not fulfilled, the women felt, but also were held, responsible. Ideals of motherhood that place women at the center of children's care therefore expose the suffering these women endure as mothers and the pain involved in one of the most important aspects of the women's lives.

Illnesses

One aspect of the lives of these women that brought into sharp relief their centrality as primary caretakers and the paradox of the suffering and joy of motherhood was a child's illness. An illness underlined the consequences of living in a context shaped by the daily assaults of structural violence, the indignities and self-recriminations linked to symbolic and gender violence, and the devaluation of life exacerbated by political violence. It also revealed the routinization of suffering as part of life among mothers and the normalization of the children's illnesses among the most vulnerable.

"Everyone knows," Mireya, the mother of five, told me, "that kids always get sick. It's part of their nature to have *asientos* [diarrhea], to have fever and colds. They are like that because they're still little, not strong yet. So you don't even take them to the doctor if they're sick like that, only if they get grave." In the case of María Ruth, her children were "always sick, more sick than not." So she did not treat diarrhea and persistent cough as out of the ordinary; she usually waited until a child became seriously ill before taking it to the health post. "The kids always have something," she said. "They live with worms in their little stomachs because they always eat soil, but that's how they are. If they get sicker then I give them *yerbitas* [little herbs] that people say are good; it's good to talk with people about these things. And if they get worse, then we go to the health center. And then if they don't get better with the medicine, we go to the doctor here in town. But most of the time we don't have money for medicines, so a visit to a doctor is when we think the situation is grave, the last thing."[12] María Ruth's second daughter suffered from bronchial illnesses since birth and had been hospitalized twice in a nearby city. But María Ruth said, "When we have money we buy the medicine, but sometimes we can't. The man at the pharmacy gives us medicine on credit, and thanks to his charity we can sometimes give her medicine." Then she added, somehow resigned to her lack of access to medicine and good health care, "But if you are not meant to suffer, you will get better even with some yerbitas." The only problem with this approach, the nurses at the health post explained, was that by the time the children were brought in, they often were in critical condition, and it was difficult to save them. A physician chimed in, "And you will probably notice that this happens all of the time to *la gente más pobrecita* [the poorest people]. The skinniest dog gets all the fleas, isn't that how it is?"

Indeed, it was "la gente más pobrecita" who suffered the most in this highly unequal and brutal system. There are some images of life for mothers in San Alejo that are etched in my mind as vivid examples of how the confluence of multiple forms of violence shapes life in this town. One of these is the home of Concepción, a twenty-nine-year-old mother of six children who had lost two babies soon after they were born. Concepción and the father of her children never had a chance to attend school; neither one knew how to read or write, and they resorted to odd jobs to make a living. Concepción made cusha, which she sold from her home, a construction that looked more like a hut. The entire family slept, ate, and cooked in this same small one-room place, which had a permanent film of smoke from the wood stove, was always too dark to make out faces clearly, and invariably felt cold and damp. I remember my difficulty trying to discern one of her kids, who was sitting on a foldable bed looking listless. The dirt floor would turn to mud in some areas next to the stove, and outside, by the entrance, there were puddles of water where mosquitoes bred abundantly. The *promotores de salud* (health promoters) were constantly getting after Concepción; they said that she was responsible for breeding enough mosquitoes for the entire neighborhood. But Concepción was not entirely responsible for the puddles of water; her cusha clients sometimes hung around to drink, and they littered the place. The promotores also complained that she kept her children inside the house, breathing the smoke all day, but Concepción saw no other choice. "They say that this is unsanitary, but what else can I offer my children? This is my life." Concepción even asked me to stop in the middle of the first interview, because she felt too embarrassed when she described her conditions but especially when I asked her what her husband did for a living. (I never quite understood what he did.) One of the promotores, however, saw her as a careless mother who was not *willing* to do more for her children. "See," he told me, "another of her babies just died, and what does she do? She continues having more, living in those unsanitary conditions, and exposing them to illnesses, only for them to suffer."

These situations not only exposed the daily struggles and vulnerabilities of poor women but also highlighted how they internalized the deep inequalities of their lives and their perceived inadequacies as caretakers of their children. It was not uncommon to hear the women (and others in town, including some medical professionals) blame themselves for a child's grave condition, even as they were also acutely aware of their limited resources. Tita's only boy was usually sick with bronchitis, and it was always a struggle to buy him the medicine he needed. However, Tita refused to ask the boy's father for any financial assistance because he had accused her of not caring properly for the boy. Once when he found out the boy was ill, he threatened Tita with taking the boy from her. Gracia María, who was supposed to take one of her boys to therapy monthly, sometimes could not afford the trips to Guatemala City. She noted the dire need for more and better medical care in rural and semirural areas of Guatemala because the hospital in the nearby city did not have the apparatus her child needed for his therapy. Gracia María said it was out of need that she took her child to the IGSS; to take him to a private clinic was enormously costly. Then she added, "I do what I can, believe me. I take good care of my children. I am a good mother, I am [her voice breaks and her eyes become watery]. I do everything for them. I sacrifice my life for them [tears run down her cheeks]. It's so difficult because I also have the five-month-old baby girl. And I am alone in this; I attend to all of my children's needs on my own. My husband doesn't help. But please, don't take it the wrong way. Don't think that I'm complaining. I'm only talking to you about my situation."

Even though the women were often the sole parent in charge when a child was ill, they seldom ended up alone dealing with these adversities.[13] Hortencia said that she had spent many a night awake, looking after her son, when he fell gravely ill. The boy had had chronic bronchitis and also pneumonia a few times, as well as the "normal" intestinal infection. During an especially acute episode, the boy was vomiting, had a high fever and diarrhea, and seemed to be dying, but Hortencia did not have a cent, not even a "sad quetzal" on her, so her uncle's wife gave her three quetzales so that she could "face the doctor" with the boy. She also had to make some tough choices. Her words highlight the painful decisions and the experiences of poor mothers in a context of highly unequal access to medical care.

> With that money I left the house in a hurry, with the anguish of thinking that my boy was not going to make it, but with my heart in pieces knowing that I was leaving my other children hungry. I hardened my heart and asked God for help. I asked the doctor to please see my child, even if I only had 3 quetzales, and Seño Angelina's husband—he's a very good doctor—saw him. He gave me a medicine and a prescription for another one, but that one was expensive, well, expensive for me. But when I got to the pharmacy, they gave it to me for free. I think the doctor, seeing my situation, and he also knows me well, paid for it in advance. I am eternally grateful to him because going to see a doctor with only 3 quetzales, forget it, they won't even look at you. If you don't have the 20 quetzales for the consultation they don't see you. So thank God this doctor is there; they gave me medicine for free. When I have money I pay only 10 quetzales at the health post. They know that I have nothing in this world.

Sometimes assistance from others did not come as expected, and sometimes it did not come at all. The women's relatives and friends were not always in a position to help, or had recently helped, or simply were not seen as trustworthy. However, as in Tita's case above, sometimes the women did not ask for help lest their relatives would suspect them of not taking care of their children properly. Gracia María said that she was sometimes embarrassed to ask her mother-in-law for money to take the chidren to the doctor: "Me da pena [I get embarrassed], because you know that kids always get sick, but it's not the same with her. She'll think that I'm not taking good care of them." Gracia was especially careful about not asking for help to care for the other children when she needed to take the boy to therapy, because "a mother always has to find a way to care for her children and not ask others to do what she's supposed to do." And María Ruth said that she sometimes was apprehensive about asking her in-laws for help: "No me gusta molestarlos [I don't like to bother them], because then they think that I'm good for nothing, that I don't care for the children and all that. This way they won't think that I'm irresponsible, right?"

The situation on the other side of town was quite different for the mothers who came from the (fewer) families with resources.[14] A salient aspect of illnesses that marks class differences is that whereas among the poor there were a series of ailments that were normalized and not treated as illnesses, among those with more resources "even a sneeze" became a cause for concern that required a doctor's visit, as Hortencia noted. Vera said that as soon as her daughter got sick she would take her to the private physician in town or the larger city to see their private physician there.[15] Mariana preferred to take her boys directly to specialists; in addition to the pediatrician they saw in Guatemala City, she took the boys to a series of specialists she knew were among the best in the country. And she always drove to the capital city with the boys' nannies, just in case, she said. Nena did the same. She and her family only went to the best doctors in the capital city and some of her husband's relatives had even traveled to the United States to obtain the best medical care. However, these women were still expected to be primarily responsible for making sure that their children got the medical care they needed, as soon as they needed it. One time, Delfina left with her daughter to see the doctor in Guatemala City at four o'clock in the morning. "See," she said, "I am capable of sacrificing for my daughters too [laughs]. My husband thinks that I am incapable, that I'm not a good mother, but I am. I can behave well."

The experiences of mothers in the Altiplano were slightly different. In addition to having husbands or partners who sometimes helped with child care, the women (and sometimes men) went through different stages in seeking a cure for their children's ailments. As in San Alejo, in the Altiplano they would do something at home, a combination of herbs, infusions, and remedios caseros. If the child did not improve, they would take it to the health post, and those who could afford it would go to a private physician in town or to the hospital, which was financed with donations, mostly from the United States, for a small fee. If this did not work, they would turn to a hospital or clinic in Antigua, about a two-hour drive from the town. Lita said that it was sad to take a gravely ill child to the health post only to be told they did not have medicine, and there was nothing they could do. Like the poor women in San Alejo, those in the Altiplano also saw the children's illnesses, the deficient health care system for the poor, and their own lack of resources to purchase treatment as the way life was. Isa, a thirty-two-year-old mother of six, explained what she saw as being a regular occurrence: "As soon as they are born they get sick; they get diarrhea, fever, and cough, and some come close to dying." Just before we met for the first time, one of her children had been quite ill; he was going to be hospitalized because he was already dehydrated, but instead a doctor in town gave him serum, and the child recovered. Isa liked and trusted this doctor because she could openly tell him that she had no money for medicine, and this openness had helped her deal with her children's constant, "normal" illnesses. The doctor also gave her medicine on credit and told her to pay him back whenever she could, "little by little." Sometimes the women saw *naturistas,* who charged one or two quetzales, a much more affordable fee than that charged by private physicians or even the health post. Lita said that the lower fee was the reason she went first to the comadrona and then to a naturista, even if in the end she ended up taking a child to the hospital.

Like the women in San Alejo, those in the Altiplano turned to others for help. Mirian learned to provide advice on home remedies for a variety of illnesses and also gave *sobadas* (rubs) for stomach illnesses. People sought her out quite frequently, even in the middle of the night. Eliza would ask her mother or a trusted friend or neighbor for a small loan to pay for treatment, and when she felt she had borrowed too many times she resorted, she said, to "selling my clothes, like a *huipil* or a *faja* or a corte, that I make. In an emergency, if I need money for a child's illness, I would rather sell my clothes." Lita raised chickens so that in an emergency, which usually meant a child's illness, she could sell one to get some money. But that was when an illness became acute or grave; otherwise, like the poor in San Alejo, those in the Altiplano were used to "normal" illnesses. Lita, for instance, mentioned that anemia was "normal," so endemic in her town that one could usually tell right away if a person had it, and most people did. However, she said that sometimes the person just had "*susto*" (fear; or a "folk" illness with multiple symptoms), which had some of the same symptoms. In her words, "Here everyone gets it [anemia]. But I have a niece who married a man from the capital, and he's never had it. I don't know why that's not the case among you [probably outsiders or perhaps non-Maya], but among us, it's common. People get pale and thin, and sometimes they're so weak that they can't even get up. We do different things for it here, different secrets. Sometimes a tonic, or we call the spirits, and sometimes we go to the river with all the family and neighbors and have lunch at the river." But, as in San Alejo, at times the women in the Altiplano did not seek help from others, either because they feared they would be branded as irresponsible mothers or because they were simply too embarrassed about their conditions, which highlights the symbolic violence that shaped their lives.

Death

The death of a child highlights several of the points I make in this book. It is often the culmination of a general lack of good health care for most of the population together with other forms of exclusion, and it highlights how gender ideologies position women not only as the chief caretakers of their children but also as those to blame if things go wrong. In life as in death, class and gender matter a great deal. According to UNICEF statistics, Guatemala's child mortality rate (those under the age of five) in 1999–2001 was 58 for males and 51 for females per 1,000 live births (UNICEF n.d.a). Similar to what Scheper-Hughes (1992) notes in her research in Brazil, children's deaths were normalized in San Alejo and in the Altiplano. They occurred regularly, and though mourned, they were not seen as extraordinary.

Of the thirty women I came to know in San Alejo, six had experienced the death of a baby or a small child (in some cases more than once), and another four had lost their babies through late-term miscarriages or stillbirths (also more than once). Those who, like Estrella, had several children all of whom had lived were quick to point out how proud they were because children's deaths were so common. Others who, like María Ruth, experienced these deaths more than once also pointed to the ever-present deaths of babies (in particular, among the poor). Both instances reveal the ubiquity of death that could be avoided with an equitable health care system.

María Ruth's first two children died several months apart, one at eighteen months and one at eight months, both apparently from bronchitis, one of the main causes of death among children in Guatemala.[16] María Ruth was not sure what kind of treatment they had received at the hospital, but she was told by the doctors that little could be done, and both babies died at home soon after they were discharged. "They said that they could not be saved; they said they had bronchitis, but I don't know for sure. That's what I was told. The older one only coughed a lot. So they gave them to me after almost a month in the hospital so they could die at home," María Ruth explained. And though she pointed out that her remaining five children were "healthy," she enumerated their multiple episodes of diarrhea and respiratory illnesses. As we sat outside the thatched-roof construction that was her house and her youngest two children played on the dirt floor wearing only tattered shirts, she said with a hint of sadness and a forced smile, "God willing, they will be here next time you visit us." I responded that I was sure I would see them all next time, but she replied, "You never know with kids. Only God knows." María Ruth's neighbor, her sister-in-law Susana, was well aware of the fragility of children's lives, though all of her four children were still alive. A devout Catholic, she had all four children baptized soon after they were born, "just in case, because they can get sick and die. A kid gets gravely ill from one moment to the next." Besides, she had observed that the babies who were baptized got sick less often. However, it was even more important to her that the babies were prepared to die as Catholics.

The practitioners at the health post highlighted the close links between malnutrition and infant death and between poverty and lack of resources and morbidity. They noted the lack of resources and the constraints that they believed kept them from providing better care. It made the practitioners sad that they could not do more for the children. But not everyone in town agreed with this assessment. A woman who lived in the center of town said that the deaths of the babies and young children were the women's fault, because they were ignorant about sanitation and nutrition and in the end were irresponsible for bringing so many children into this world only to suffer. Indeed, Tita said that people had often told her to just give away some of her children so they would not suffer. One of Tita's daughters died at a few months. According to Tita the baby girl had blisters from the waist up, and Tita would lay her down on plantain leaves to soothe her pain and cure the eruption, but then the "fire" went inside the baby. Her mouth developed blisters, preventing her from eating, and eventually she died. Tita did everything she could, even took the baby to the doctor a few times, but the girl could not be saved. Some people had advised Tita to give "at least some of the children away" to ease her burden of providing and caring for all of them. Tita commented, "People think that six children are too many for a single woman to support. But I can't just give away my children, as if they were mangoes. No matter how many I have, how can I give them away? They are not dolls; they are kids [laughs]." Neighbors and acquaintances also advised Andrea, who only had two children, to give them away because, they believed, her income from selling tostadas at the park was not sufficient to care for them properly. The same person who faulted poor women for their babies' deaths added that she thought the government should not let the poor have children and should take their children away from them. In sharp contrast to Tita's (and Andrea's) views, this woman said, "Look, those mothers give their children away easily. They have a lot of them; one more or one less doesn't matter. If their children mattered to them they would have fewer and would care for them better." This woman's words expose the devaluation of the lives of those who suffer the most from inequality and exclusion, as well as the added injuries of blaming the women who cannot provide adequately for their children.

Blame for the deaths of their babies and children, however, was not directed only at poor women. For instance, though Delfina knew well that the death of her only son when he was nine months old was something that no one could have prevented, her husband and others in his family often made her feel that it had been her fault. The baby boy was born with congenital heart disease and required surgery before he turned one; he died half an hour after the surgery was performed by a well-known specialist in Guatemala City. Delfina noticed a change in her husband after the baby died and attributed a lot of the abuse she suffered from him to this sad event. Somehow, she said, he thought she had something to do with the baby's death. She explained, "He has not always been *malo;* there were some times when he was better. But after the baby died he just turned angry; it's as if it was my fault. How can that be? [She sheds some tears.] But since I was the mother, he blames me. He blames me for the condition that the baby was born with. In his mind this is how it is, but it's not true. He knows I would have given my life for the boy. He is so cruel to me."

Research has consistently pointed to worse health and social indicators among the Maya. Eight of the twenty-eight women I interviewed in the Altiplano had lost a baby or a young child to an illness, and one had lost nine out of twelve, often complicated by malnutrition. There, too, women rushed their babies to be baptized because they were seen as being likely to die from one moment to the next. For instance, Marisela had to baptize her children even when her husband was not around, because "*se me estaban muriendo* [they were dying on me], and I had to make sure they were baptized; my parents went with me to the church." Luckily, some of her children survived, but she blamed her mother-in-law for being an "alarmist," because she was the one who pushed for the emergency baptisms and then those babies survived. Lilian, whose youngest daughter died at the age of two, explained that the girl would not grow, and she was embarrassed to take her out in public because people often thought the girl was much younger than she really was. Like other women in the Altiplano, Lilian connected her children's illnesses to the abuse she suffered from her husband: "When

I was pregnant she [the baby girl] swallowed everything that happened to me, everything that he [her husband] did to me went directly to the baby, and so naturally she was born with malnutrition." And for Julia, the survival of her only live child was bittersweet: after three baby deaths due to diarrhea and colic, the fourth baby, a boy, made it, but by then the father had been disappeared during the political violence, so he never got to see his son. Her husband had blamed Julia for her apparent inability to first conceive and then "keep" the babies, and when she finally had a baby who survived her husband was gone.

In the Altiplano, too, the women could not do everything they wished to save their babies, often because they did not have enough money to buy medicine or pay a doctor. Lita regretted not having taken small gifts to the hospital's staff so that her baby daughter would have been seen more quickly; people knew that such gifts to the staff helped. As in San Alejo, the women in the Altiplano often turned to others when their children died. Lita said that neighbors felt sorry for her and helped her out with money for the bus fare when she needed to take her baby to the hospital. And it was the vecinas who showed up promptly at the door with sugar, coffee, and bread when one of Lita's babies died from "lack of vitamins." Although Lita had to sell a huipil in order to cover the funeral expenses, the neighbors helped too. In the Altiplano, more than in San Alejo, godparents played a rather central role in the lives (and deaths) of the children. Flor, the woman who worked at the health post, explained that when children died at home, if they were Catholic, the godmother was in charge of buying the little coffin, and if they were evangelical, the church had to help out because those children had no godparents. Not long before our conversation, Flor had had this experience. From the moment her godchild was born, she knew it would not be long before he died. The baby looked sick, and the mother was malnourished and abused by her husband—sure signs of an imminent baby death, Flor told me. Ever the practical woman, since the day the baby was born Flor had been thinking of the preparations for the funeral and had been putting money aside for the little coffin; she did not want to be caught unprepared.

CONCLUSION

Taking apart the different moments of motherhood in San Alejo provides a close-up look into how multiple forms of normalized violence and internalized domination impinge on the women's lives and how social inequalities are encoded in the dominant beliefs about and cognitive repertoires of motherhood. The complex and vulnerable relationship between mother and child in San Alejo highlights the consequences of scarcity and unmet need and of gender ideologies that position women in charge of their children's well-being, an especially difficult position given the scarcity of resources to care for them. I have focused on depicting motherhood and its expectations not as "natural" in the women's lives but as a site to scrutinize this "naturalness" and link its "normality" to multiple sources of violence. Ideologies of motherhood that position women as nurturing and devoted and create expectations of sacrifice must be understood in the specific context in which they occur. As Scheper-Hughes (1992: 22) notes, the practices she described among the women in the Alto do Cruzeiro in Brazil were "not autonomously, culturally reproduced. They have a social history and must be understood within the economic and political context of a larger state and world (moral) order that have suspended the ethical in their relations toward these same women."

One of my first reflections on violence in San Alejo came after a conversation about malnutrition in children with a nurse at the health post who stated how sad it was for her to see children suffer and that she saw a chain of violence that went all the way to the babies. She explained as follows: "So what do you expect when people grow used to killings everywhere, where a crime of passion is the order of the day in the newspapers? Then that gets transmitted, and people behave violently to each other. All respect and decency are lost. And men become more inclined to use guns and *puños* [fits] to get what they want; they spend money on alcohol and other women, and then everyone suffers, the mothers more. I would say that principally it's the mothers who suffer because they're in charge of their children. One doesn't feel like continuing to work."

Motherhood in San Alejo is not only about suffering and pain; I would not want to portray the lives of the women I came to know only in those terms. As the mothers told me (and as they tried to convince me to have my own children), the joys that a child can bring are second to none. Also, the women turned to others for comfort, material support, and a sympathetic ear, though these forms of solace in the women's lives were themselves bound by gender ideologies and expectations that prevent me from presenting a decidedly postive image of women's informal sources of support. Paralleling other research (see Sear and Mace 2008), I found that not all potential sources of support provided the same kinds of help, even if they were family members and lived close by. In keeping with the overall objective of this book, I have highlighted aspects of motherhood that involve the suffering and pain that come from a mother's inability to purchase medicine for an ill baby, from watching her children die from treatable diseases, or from her inability to fulfill expectations imposed by rigid gender hierarchies and ideologies. Although class differences dictate access to resources, the consequences of symbolic and gender violence in San Alejo were present in the women's lives regardless of social class standing.[17] These contrasts reveal the multisided violence that makes suffering a natural "part of life" for most women in San Alejo.

CHAPTER 6

Women's Work

Normalizing and Sustaining Gender Inequality

Cuando uno trabaja, uno trabaja para ayudar al hombre, entonces el trabajo de la mujer no es así, tan importante, diría yo. Bueno es importante, pero no tanto como el del hombre. Así lo veo yo.

[When one works, one works to help the man, so women's work [outside the home] is not that important, I would say. Well, it is important, but not as important as men's work. This is how I see it.]

—Mercedes, fifty-one years old

When issues of women's status are discussed, particular attention is given to the link between women's work—reproductive and productive, remunerated and unpaid—and equality. Indeed, interest in this link developed from feminist critiques of theories that emphasized the separation between home and work, "ignoring the household as the locus of social reproduction" (López Estrada 2003: 174). Thus this nexus has been examined from a variety of analytic angles, disciplinary approaches that range from the social sciences to the humanities, and through a vast range of empirical observations from around the world. As a result, there is a voluminous body of work on the topic. Some scholars have looked at the links between paid work and equality in the home (Becker, Fonseca-Becker, and Schenck-Yglesias 2006; Benería and Roldán 1987; Dutta 2000; Safa, 1995); others have examined the implications that economic activities have for women's living conditions (Chant 1996; González de la Rocha 1994; Moser 1996; Roberts 1995), warning of increased vulnerabilities when women's participation in paid productive work is not balanced by fewer reproductive demands in the home (Chant 2003; Floro 1999; Olmsted 2005); while others have looked at the effects of structural adjustment policies on women's and men's labor force opportunities and gender relations (Hite and Viterna 2005; Menjívar 2003), concluding that such policies have increased women's participation in the labor force and their incomes but mainly as a result of the deterioration of men's once-privileged position (Hite and Viterna 2005; Safa 1995).

Although the questions raised in the research described above are crucial ones and have produced a fundamental body of work, in this chapter I do not seek to assess whether women's work leads to greater equality in the home, to empowerment, or to parity with men more generally. I examine the sphere of work in the lives of women in San Alejo primarily because it permits another view, away from the immediacy of the spheres of family and household, into the lives of the women. It allows an examination of the misrecognized violence resulting from the lack of social services, from neoliberal policies that disproportionately affect the poor and women in particular, and from the insecurity of life in a "postconflict" society. Attention to this sphere of life also helps to redirect attention to how violence is structured and normalized in social relations outside the home, not only in the intimate spheres I examined in previous chapters, how experiences in one domain are deeply linked and reinforce those in the other, and how violence resides in realms beyond the willful intentions of individuals.

To be sure, I do not wish to argue that work itself is a source of violence in the women's lives. Rather, I focus on the *meaning* that the presence and absence of paid work has for the women, as it brings to the fore the confluence of multiple sources of violence in their lives and renders visible the gender and gendered forms of violence that mark them. The lack of or limited access to paid work, the abundance of poorly remunerated jobs, and the common practice of child labor and children's abandonment of school are aspects of work with roots in structural violence, for they reveal deep inequalities and multiple forms of exploitation. Issues related to gossip and suspicion of women who work for pay, as well as the male partners' opposition (and that of other family members) to the women's paid employment, expose the symbolic and gender violence that buttress ideologies disallowing women from fulfilling their wishes and castigating them for exercising their will. This examination exposes the vulnerability of life in a context of fear, which is often rendered invisible and normalized in everyday life. Often this backdrop exacerbates other circumstances, as when women are kept from participating in paid work for fear they may be exposed to crime and the new wave of feminicide in Guatemala today. At the same time, the sphere of work offers those women who are employed outside the home opportunities, limited as they may be, to earn an income to support their children, to interact with other women, and to create spaces for sociability and potential solidarity.[1] I examine aspects of work the women brought up in our conversations, including the availability of paid work, low pay, working conditions, work at an early age and school abandonment, gossip, and men's disapproval of women's paid employment, while at the same time noting the positive meanings work can have when it provides an avenue for the women to engage in friendships and collegiality with other women, as well as to earn an income.

LIMITED OPPORTUNITIES FOR EARNING AN INCOME AND LOW-PAID WORK

Most of the women I met in San Alejo spoke of the limited opportunities for paid work in town, whether they had directly experienced this shortage or someone they knew had. The shrinking agricultural sector that has further marginalized the rural poor and the proliferation of insecure industries beyond urban areas, such as those in the maquila sector, lend an urgency to the women's narratives and expose the toll that structural adjustment and neoliberal policies take on their lives. Of course, jobs for men also have disappeared or become more precarious, so it is not only women who have suffered the consequences of neoliberal policies. Indeed, the women in San Alejo told me that the decline in jobs in agriculture was the main reason for men's migration to the United States. A nurse put it this way: "Agriculture these days doesn't give; it doesn't feed families. In this part of the country, to have land meant a lot before, but now, even those with lands, no, it's sad. So what do people do? The men leave for the United States. But they become separated from their families here, and many problems happen. This situation, one can say, *violentiza* [does violence to] families, right?" In this overall context of structural violence, which includes work insecurity, low wages, exploitation, and precarious conditions that, in the words of the nurse, "violentiza" people's relations, women and men experience it differently.

Paid work is not only gender-bound (there are jobs in agriculture and in other sectors that women do not do) but also profoundly class-bound (there are jobs that well-off women simply do not do). Thus gender and class ideologies permeate this area of women's lives in ways that can mark women who engage in paid work as deviant. "Imagine," Nena said with a smile, "I can't go work on the land with all those men my husband works with; I can't even give them orders. That's men's work, not women's work. So when he's drinking I have to find a trustworthy man to organize the workers for me." Similarly, at the other end of town, on the marginalized outskirts, María Ruth explained, "Working the land is man's work, so if there are no men in the house, the work does not get done. My brothers go work on other people's lands, but I can't. I could work in their homes but not on their lands. Yes, even if we have need, one, as a woman, can't because it exposes you to too much danger." However, Leticia, who also lived in one of the poorest areas of San Alejo, had to work the land herself to harvest a small amount of corn on a rented tiny plot. Her case, though, underscores the heightened vulnerability and insecurity at the juncture of multiple forms of violence, as she was not only a woman eking out an existence in marginal agricultural activities but also a widow, a single mother, extremely poor, and living with HIV/AIDS.

In general, when the topic of paid work came up the San Alejo women spoke mainly of limited opportunities and of the poor working conditions and very low pay in the few jobs that were available. The women's words evoked key links to structural forces that shaped their lives. Although she described herself as a housewife, as did many other women, Susana stitched together different ways to earn "even a few cents," as she put it, by cleaning, washing, and ironing in the homes of the better-off people in town, and her sister-in-law, María Ruth, earned some money by selling tomatoes or any produce that her husband harvested when he was home on leave from his work as a security guard in Guatemala City. Leticia explained that for her going out to work meant working the land to harvest some corn or pick some tomatoes for someone else, she was allowed to keep a small amount of produce to sell, because "the owner feels pity for me and allows me to keep some so I can earn some cents." Working took on special meaning for Leticia, not only because as a single mother dying of HIV/AIDS it was vital to earn even a small amount of money, but also because while she was with the father of her eldest daughter she was humiliated by his mother, who called her simply "la sirvienta." After her husband died from HIV/AIDS, several people refused to hire her to work in their homes because they were afraid she was contagious. "No one wants to give me work, so I go harvest corn and pick tomatoes and live from the charity of others," Leticia explained, looking with watery eyes at the surroundings in her humble abode. Leticia's sister, Tita, also picked tomatoes, and as a widow and single mother herself, she had to be creative "to earn money in decent ways, in ways that won't make me feel ashamed." Picking and selling tomatoes paid very little, mostly because both Tita and Leticia worked for people who themselves were already poor and were renting the land from others. "Let's say that they are at the margins of the margins," is how a physician at the health post described Tita's and Leticia's positions. Tita and Leticia knew this well, as others in town occasionally reminded the sisters—in derogatory ways—of their marginal status. To increase her earnings, Tita had just started training as a comadrona, washed clothes for several people in town, and worked a few times a week at the health post helping to distribute medicine.

The women's work varied but was generally confined to activities that generated very low incomes and was performed under difficult, often exploitative, conditions. Like others, Hortencia felt the pain of her working situation sharpest when her children were sick or hungry. Hortencia had worked as a housekeeper, but when she got married and started to have children she decided to try out having her own business. She began by making *hojuelas* (flaky flatbread with syrup), tacos, and tostadas for sale. This was a risky move, since sales were generally unpredictable. Sometimes she borrowed a few quetzales with which she purchased some corn to make tortillas or tacos for sale; then she would repay the debt but also generate some money for her children's needs. Her children, Hortencia explained, did not know if she had been able to sell or not; they wanted food when they were hungry and medicine when sick. Even when sales were good, she barely made ends meet, but she set aside a few quetzales for times when sales went down. For this she worked ten to twelve hours a day and ended the day exhausted, which was the least of her problems.

> For instance, right now, I'll start preparing the tamales for this Saturday, and I let my clients know that I'll be selling. I walk around eight to ten blocks with the tamales, which is not bad. But then I have to still do *la limpieza* [housecleaning] at the home of this family; they give me Q.50 a month [about U.S.$12 at that time]. Then I can have enough for the rent. I worry everyday about not having enough money. When the patojos tell me

they're hungry and I don't have money, it rips my heart. So, no, being tired doesn't worry me; for me being tired means I have had work, and that's a blessing!

Mirna also sold hojuelas on weekends and made 70 or 80 quetzales on good days, but it was extremely tiring. "Sometimes my husband tells me to rest because he sees that I've been standing all day making the hojuelas, sometimes a hundred. I have to stretch the flour and fry them, and it's very tiring. Then I walk to sell them. Imagine how tired I must look for my husband to say to me, 'Rest a little'?" In the case of Concepción, who did not live far from Mirna, it was cusha, the clandestine liquor that she sold from her house, that was the main source of support for the family. Concepción was well aware that "people talked" because of the drunken men who congregated by her house, but she did not know how else to sustain her family.

Andrea sold tostadas every afternoon at the park, and in fact sometimes we would converse there while she was working. She said that what she earned was enough to cover the bills for water and electricity and to buy some firewood, beans, and corn, sometimes sugar, too. Andrea had to support the entire household, even her stepfather/partner who was middle-aged, because he did not feel healthy enough to work. Others in town commented that he was taking advantage of Andrea, for he seemed fit and healthy. Andrea had another small source of income, occasional remittances from the United States sent by her boy's father. "That's help, right?" Andrea asked. "Even if it's a few cents once a year, he sends money once a year. I used to write to ask for more, but he never responded. But now he sends money. The problem is that he doesn't send the money to me; he sends the money to him [the stepfather]. And he [the stepfather] then gives me a few cents here and there. But at least it's something. Now that we both [the stepfather and Andrea] have had surgery, I hope he'll send a little more because I can't work as much now, even if I try. It's painful sometimes; my side hurts when I bend. But what can I do? I have to work again."

Lucía, a teacher who came from a family of landowners and was well known socially in San Alejo, explained what she thought were the work options that poor women had in town: "Look at me. *La muchacha* [the housekeeper] quit, and I went to ask another one if she wanted to work and she said, 'Look, señora, excuse me, but I won't work for Q.200, because I earn more picking peas.' These pea harvesters came here from Antigua, and they are hiring the young women who used to work [as housekeepers]. The patojas earn more there, and they like it better than working in a house; they go there singing, with young men, so they have more fun doing that than working [as a housekeeper] in a home." In the end, Lucía recognized that the options for poor women and men in San Alejo were highly constrained and that even if they worked more they did not earn enough, "The poor people here live with *la soga al cuello* [a rope around their neck]," she said. Lucía, as well as others who had more resources, would quickly point out the benefits of an education in alleviating poverty but then would blame the poor for not educating themselves. And although Nena, a teacher by training, echoed Lucía in this regard, she corrected herself and said that education had not helped her out of poverty as much as her husband's wealth did: "When I got married, my father-in-law opened up a butcher shop for me; I've always liked to work. And sometimes when there is a need for interim teachers around here, I go work for a month or three months." She confessed that she had never lacked for anything, and her children would not know what it means to be hungry or not to wear good clothes *de marca* (with good labels).

As I mentioned in the previous chapter, during the time I visited San Alejo a corn-packing factory came to town, and though the managers were looking for women to fill the jobs they had not found women willing to work. A year later I asked about the factory and was told it closed down a few months after it opened. I was surprised because I had heard so many women complain about the lack of work opportunities and knew about the young women who worked picking peas. The responses were varied: some said the factory was located too far from the center of town, and it was dangerous for women to make the trek there. Some said that because women were receiving remittances they had become *used to* receiving "money for nothing," so they would not look for work at the factory. Others (mostly men) said that women did not *like* to work outside the home, because they were good mothers and preferred to stay home to look after the children. Related to this, others said that it was the absence of a day care center in town that kept the women from finding employment outside the home (this prompted the conversation I had with the mayor; see chapter 4).[2] And others (mostly women) said that the factory simply paid too little. "To leave your children at home, travel that far, and expose yourself to who knows what, no, it's not worth what the factory was paying," Isabel said. It is also worth noting that an association between factory work for women, especially when it involves traveling by bus, and the threat of danger has been cemented by the general insecurity of life and the wave of killings in postwar Guatemala.

Even though paid work was scarce and when opportunities presented themselves the conditions under which women worked were harsh, sometimes even brutal, one common aspect of the women's lives as workers was the possibility that through working they would be able to come into contact with other women, clients, neighbors, and professionals. As Rocío Guadarrama (2006) remarks in her study of Central American female workers, networks of female workers have provided a basic social framework on which women have built their identities, sometimes in ambiguous or even conflictive ways, but these networks have become indispensable for women's own life projects. Thus, in San Alejo, informal contacts would put resources—material or emotional—within the women's reach, something I had the opportunity to observe. Through selling tomatoes, for instance, Leticia and Tita came into contact with people who helped them out by giving them old clothes for their children; Ana sold tostadas to the people from her church, an activity that helped her reinforce key ties that boosted her emotional well-being; and Hortencia, through selling tamales, was able to talk with others and find out what to do in case of illness. Hortencia also made sure that she reserved some tamales for the doctor who saw her children for half the price of a regular consultation and dispensed medicine to her at no charge. When I saw her delivering two tamales to the physician, she turned to me, saying, "This is my way of thanking him because I have no other means to express my gratitude." Leticia, too, picked extra corn for the women who gave her food or lent her money for a bus fare to visit her husband when he was sick, or for her sporadic medical checkups in Guatemala City.

The importance of these work-related ties was also evident among the women from more affluent backgrounds, because they too established similar ties and recognized their importance. One of the most poignant examples of the centrality of these ties in women's lives was Delfina. With a big smile and a twinkle in her eyes, she explained what her job as a teacher meant to her:

> I love going to work. There, I talk to my colleagues who live in similar situations as I do. One of them, her husband opposes her working, like mine does. My work, my colleagues, all that is so important in my life that my husband complained to his mother that I only talk about the school. "Only the school," he told her, "so then she doesn't take care of the house." But even if I have this huge *stress* [she uses the English word][3] when I go to

> the school, because I don't know if he's going to like what I left prepared for lunch, if he's going to like what I left him for his breakfast, I like to go there and talk to my colleagues, because they talk with me; all that makes me forget my torment at home. They tell me, "Don't retire, don't ever stop working, come here, distract yourself a little." Even the bus ride there distracts me a little. One forgets, even for a moment.

For those reasons, Delfina hung on to her job for as long as she could, even when her husband ridiculed her for going to work: "He tells me that I should quit, that I really don't need the money, that he makes in one minute what I make in a whole month, so I should quit. He says that I'm crazy getting up at 5:00 A.M. to go to work. That I don't take care of the girls because I'm so involved with my job. Ay, a thousand things he says! All insults. And my work is something he throws at me. I think that it's for this reason that I don't quit! [Smiles] Don't think I'm crazy, that I want to contradict him, but I won't quit working." And during my last visit to San Alejo, when I visited Nena, she looked like a different person. She was smiling, had makeup on, and was elated. After years of wanting to go back to a permanent position in teaching, she had finally realized her dream. She could not find enough words to explain how satisfying this was for her, her self-esteem, and her overall outlook on life. Like Delfina, Nena said that working for pay was an *option;* she did not *need* to, she emphasized. "Work helps one's mood, one's health, and I think that's why I am so happy to be working now," she said with a big smile.

Hortencia had grown tired of her situation, tired of *luchar* (fighting). One afternoon she confided that she was contemplating migrating to the United States in search of work, even though she was aware women often did not fare well in the journey north.

> I feel like leaving. I would like to go there. Here I'm suffocating little by little. But you know what's my real interest in going? To save enough so that I can buy the house where I live, so I don't have to pay rent. I don't want luxuries; I don't want clothes or anything like that. I just want a house for my children and not to pay rent; all this is killing me. All the time I think, what am I going to do? Where to get money for this or that? What else can I do here? I live anguished, and no matter how much I work, it's never enough. So, yes, I would like to go to the United States.

When we spoke of the dangers of migrating by land to the United States, Hortencia replied, "I know that very well, everyone here knows that, but what's the difference between dying on the road and dying little by little here? Aquí me estoy acabando [Here I'm dying away]."

Women in the Altiplano shared some of the experiences of the ladinas in San Alejo; their work was also low paid, and they often worked under exploitative conditions. However, there were significant differences in the place and meaning of work for women in the two towns that merit discussion here. Women in the Altiplano also saw paid work as a necessity, because through it they, too, supported their families. However, in contrast to the ladinas in San Alejo, they did not seem to associate work so strongly with necessity, because even for the women who had more resources paid employment was a central aspect of their lives (as in the cases of Nena and Delfina in San Alejo).[4] And significantly, their husbands and other relatives did not put them down or humiliate them for working for pay, as happened in San Alejo. Carmen, a deeply religious, successful businesswoman in the Altiplano and the owner of a well-stocked pharmacy, explained, "Thank God, we have work, and we do it well; God has a plan for us, and I saw God's power in my work. I have worked for seven years nonstop, not one day. I work in weaving, and there was a period of time when I was producing four hundred coin purses per week. And I've always been able to deliver all the orders we get on time and in the exact quantities they request." Thus, for Carmen, it was "natural" to work essentially two full-time jobs, in the pharmacy, which she co-owned with her husband, and in weaving, and she had recently invested a small amount of money in raising chickens for sale, all while caring for six children. She smiled when she noted the look of admiration on my face and said that her situation was not at all unusual; practically every woman she knew worked the same way, and in her own family she had never seen any adult woman or man (or older children) not working long hours to earn an income. "Look at her," she said gesturing to one of her young daughters, who was tending the cash register at the pharmacy, "she is learning already, and she's good in mathematics and responsible, so God willing she'll do well in any business."[5]

Although the women's views of paid work might have been different in the Altiplano, when women were employed their wages were low and their working conditions tough. Carmen mentioned that sometimes she did not get paid for the weaving she did, even though she was well aware that the product was sold at several times the amount she charged for making it. Azucena cleaned houses but got paid half in money and half in food, mostly tortillas, an arrangement that lent itself to exploitation. And Constantina, who also earned a small amount of money by mopping and cleaning houses, said that she had no other choice but to sell clandestine liquor out of her house. At first she did not want to mention this business to me, even though others in town had told me that visiting Constantina's house was not seen as respectable because of her business activities, which attracted a male clientele. But one afternoon while I was visiting Constantina some of her clients knocked at the door, and she confessed that they were looking for cusha. "What else can I do to feed my kids?" she noted. "I don't sit idle at home. I clean, mop, wash clothes, and even tend the small plot that my father had. I look like a *trompo* [spinning top] and still don't earn enough to live on, because every single thing I do leaves me only a little bit of money. Even the cusha. None of this will make me rich; I only make small amounts. So I don't know why people criticize me." Constantina's cusha business (and Concepción's in San Alejo) exemplifies how symbolic violence permeates the women's lives; the vulnerable end up inflicting pain on themselves. Both women had suffered the violence that came from drinking in both towns, but poverty, lack of access to goods and benefits, and structural violence in general had pushed them to earn an income from selling liquor.

In contrast to women in San Alejo, women from the Altiplano worked in other parts of the country, either selling their textiles on market days in towns throughout western Guatemala or laboring as housekeepers and in factories in other urban centers, mainly in Guatemala City.[6] Whereas working at jobs away from their town opened up opportunities to earn more money, sometimes the conditions under which they worked there were even harsher. For instance, some of the women who went to sell their textiles in other towns had to leave home at two or three o'clock in the morning, often not returning for days at a time, sleeping wherever and whenever they could. It was not unusual for those working in Guatemala City to be underpaid or mistreated. Gina worked at different jobs there, but through it all she kept in mind that the patrones were looking for a profit, not for the well-being or the health of their employees. She worked at a *cevichería* (restaurant where ceviche is served); it was, she said, "*trabajo matado*" (work that can kill, exhausting work), because she had to do everything there. She then worked at a maquila, but she could only stand it for fourteen days because it was too tough. After trying a few other jobs, she landed one at another maquila that had its own day care center. She liked it there for that reason, but then one of her children got to be too old for the factory's day care and she had to quit. This was the best job Gina had ever had in Guatemala City, a factory where all the workers were Maya women of different groups and the owners were an American man and a Guatemalan ladina. But even at this job, the conditions were far from optimal.

> Well, we started work at 7:00 A.M. and didn't have a break until 1:00 P.M., half an hour for lunch. Then we were supposed to stop officially at 4:00, but we never did because we had a lot of work. No, no breaks. But they were good, the owners were good. They would send us to see the doctor; there, at the factory they had a doctor. Or if one of the children got sick, the doctor would see them there. And if one of us got sick, for something that had to do with work, like if we fainted, the doctor could see us there. The owners used to say that instead of sending us to the IGSS, where one wastes a lot of time to have a consultation, they would rather have a doctor right there at the factory. Going to the IGSS was like, for them that was a loss, right? If a container with the product left the factory late because one of us got sick, that's a loss for the owners because that product could get canceled. So that's why we had medical attention right there. *Sí pues* [Yes, right], they cared for us, the owners, they were good. I think.[7]

Thus work for the women in the Altiplano was seen as "natural," and there seemed to be more opportunities, however constrained, for their work. There was a steady demand for the textiles they made, which are distributed and sold in stores worldwide.[8] There were weaving cooperatives in town, and some of the women I met were members of these "clubs," as they called them. These clubs provided important spaces for the women in the Altiplano, who, like the women in San Alejo, came together in places of work with other women to exchange views, talk, and provide various forms of assistance to one another. One of these women commented on the importance to her of the "club of weavers" to which she used to belong: "We would help each other. Like one of us would make an adornment, and if the other one didn't know how to make it, this one would make it for her. If one was late with her own work, others would help out so that the order we had would not be late. So it was good. We all collaborated, and it was very good for everyone." She lamented, however, that this cooperative dissolved when the organizers left town. "It was two gringas who came and did this with us; it was a great thing for us. We would weave, make our textiles, and the gringas knew how to sell it well, so we all cooperated. But they left. We couldn't continue because they knew where to sell the textiles better than us." Thus even though there were some short-term development projects available to the women in the Altiplano, some tended to come to an end when those who implemented them left town.[9]

Due to the precariousness of work, the presence of other women in the Altiplano, often evidenced in borrowing and lending, was crucial to survival. Martina said that it was *favores* (favors) from others, particularly women, that helped her in her day-to-day struggles. She explained, "Yes, they do me favors. Sometimes one needs a *quetzalito* [a little quetzal]; sometimes I don't even have money to buy a tomato. And so I borrow from others, and when my husband comes to town he pays them back. Sometimes he can't pay because he hasn't earned, so I pay back our debts, too. Sometimes it's five quetzales or ten quetzales, like that. I try to pay it back on time, so next time they will do me the favor again. My husband says, 'But I give you money,' and I tell him, 'But it's not enough.' Things are too expensive. So I borrow, pay, borrow, pay, and like that." Antonia had asked for a big favor from her neighbor and friend, who also did some weaving with her. During the time of the violence her husband had to be out of town, and Antonia could not stay alone because she always felt as if she was going to be killed in the middle of the night. So she spent each night for a year at her neighbor's house, which was a tremendous *"alivio"* (relief) for Antonia. In addition, it must be noted that, as was the case for many men in San Alejo, most men in the Altiplano did not escape the injuries of insecure and low wages and shrinking employment opportunities. In the Altiplano, too, men had to stitch together whatever work they could perform, migrate to other cities, and, increasingly, go north to the United States in search of work.

WORK AT AN EARLY AGE AND SCHOOL ABANDONMENT

One aspect of life that brings into sharp relief the multisided violence in the lives of women in San Alejo is the common practice of child labor, in particular, among girls, which usually results in nonattendance at school or abandoning school.[10] Often, poor parents did not send their daughters to school because they could not afford it; the girls were needed at home to help with domestic chores but also were sent out to earn some money. Dary Fuentes (1994) notes in her fieldwork in eastern Guatemala that girls start assisting with household chores from the age of ten or twelve and boys of that age run errands, but as the boys grow older they refuse to help out while the girls continue to lend a hand. This practice underscores the normalization of gender differences and hierarchies (and the misrecognition of these practices as harmful): having young daughters working at home and later working for pay, while abandoning or never attending school, was not an extraordinary occurrence in San Alejo. According to UNICEF (n.d.a), the primary school enrollment rate for girls in 1999–2001 was 82.9 and for boys 89.9. And fewer Guatemalans continue to higher educational levels, but the gender inequalities persist: the rate of secondary school enrollment for females was 35 percent and for males 39 percent during the same period (UNICEF n.d.a). Of the thirty San Alejo women whom I knew, five were teachers, one was a nurse, one finished a sewing course, and one attended two years of college. However, there were nine women who had never attended school, two who had been in school for six months, nine who had between two and six years of schooling, and two who had seven or eight years of schooling. When I talked with Ileana about school, she first mentioned that her in-laws had not attended school, but she then continued to add names to the list of people she knew, including herself, who had never attended school. It turned out that the three neighbors she knew had a similar experience. "No one in this area, like from that store to here, knows how to read," Ileana noted.

Although many of the women mentioned the benefits of education, not attending school or abandoning school, for girls especially, was an act so embedded in the "order of things" that most did not blink an eye when the subject was brought up for discussion. A nurse at the health post, who was not originally from San Alejo, reflected on this situation as follows: "The families here, even those who have resources, don't send their daughters to get more education (outside San Alejo) because in their minds, they think that these girls won't be virgins anymore. People think that if someone leaves the town, that means they'll have sexual relations. They have these strong ideas about women, and this becomes part of what the children learn and how they will be when they grow up. So it becomes, let's say, tradition, but it really keeps women from going forward."

The ordinariness of abandoning school obscured the harmful consequences of the lack of access to education or abandoning school because a girl is needed to contribute to the household income and help with chores at home. And among those who recognized the long-term detrimental consequences of a lack of education in the life of a girl, it was also easy, as it is in other instances, to blame the parents for taking their female children out of school. "As you know," a teacher said matter-of-factly, "it is the custom here not to send their kids to school or to take them out, so the kids can go to work. It's the ignorance of our people. We'll never advance." This teacher's words added insult to injury. Placing culpability on the individual parents and not on the larger structures of inequality that have kept the majority of Guatemalans from gaining access to increasingly limited resources and services contributes to their marginalization. Indeed, the teacher's words veiled the harmful effects of structures of inequality in a language of "custom" or even "culture" that blames those who are suffering.

Several of the women I came to know in San Alejo had been earning an income since they were young girls, having abandoned their schooling early. Now they were also sending their own daughters to work, taking the girls out of school as their parents had done with them. Such a practice, seemingly part of "tradition," exposed the response of generation after generation to economic and social vulnerability and exclusion. For instance, on a follow-up fieldwork visit, I stopped by to visit Hortencia and found her very happy with good news: Her thirteen-year-old daughter was now working as a housekeeper in Guatemala City. This surprised me, as I thought Hortencia had other plans for the girl, who seemed to show potential at school. Hortencia explained that the girl had received an offer that was too good to pass up; she was going to earn the equivalent of U.S.$20 a month and was going to send most of it back to San Alejo, to Hortencia and her siblings. Hortencia was obviously moved by her young daughter's generosity and recounted one of their conversations: "Look, mama, don't worry, my siblings and I love you, and even the little ones will one day realize how much you've done for us, that even without a husband you've sustained us. You've worked so much, and now it's my turn to help." Wiping her tears of emotion and satisfaction with the corner of her apron, Hortencia mentioned an added benefit of her daughter's new job: she had been given permission to phone her mother every Sunday afternoon. "She calls me every Sunday, and so every Sunday is a reminder for me that I'm not alone in my *angustias* [anguish], that I have her."

Susana had a similar experience. She also started work at an early age in order to help her parents. We were talking about the time she married her husband, and I asked her if it had been difficult to get used to living away from her parents. "Well, I had lived separated from my parents before," she explained. "I left my parents' house when I was ten. I was in second grade. That's when I stopped going to school. Never went back, how? A cousin got me a job in the capital, and I worked there for six years. I was the only one that family had working for them, so I did everything. I washed, ironed, cooked. I burned myself I don't know how many times. I did everything." She was in charge of washing and ironing the school uniforms of the children of the house, and sometimes they would give her the old uniforms that the children had outgrown for her to wear as a regular dress. But that proximity to what school-age children wore did not make her feel as if she could be one of them, she said, because that was simply unattainable. This is how deeply ingrained and internalized structures of inequality remain for many in San Alejo.

Young boys also were taken out of school at an early age, to help their parents, no doubt. However, it occurred more often for girls because it was assumed they could work for pay in a wider range of activities, such as domestic chores, selling, and even harvesting. Similar to almost a third of the San Alejo women in this study, Andrea was never actually taken out of school. "My parents just never sent me," she said, "because we were too poor, and they needed hands, hands to work so we could eat. They didn't care if I learned the letters or not; food was important." Thus, as soon as she was able to, she started earning some money by doing domestic chores and selling fruit in the street. When I asked her how old she was when she started earning an income, she could not remember exactly; she said with a smile that her front teeth were still missing (meaning she was around seven) when she had to start cleaning other people's houses, for which she got paid a couple of quetzales or sometimes a pile of tortillas to take home. Selling fruit taught her a little about how to run a business, she said; as an adult she sold tostadas and tacos at the park and had regularly added more products, like cold sodas and enchiladas. She knew it was important to evaluate her competition before deciding on what merchandise to add; she thought she learned that from her early experiences in selling on the street. "My mama couldn't go out [selling] with me, so I had to think quickly when I was selling fruit. Maybe that taught me something. I still don't know how to read and write, but I do know how I can make some cents from my sales," she said with a smile of satisfaction.

Never attending or abandoning school at an early age usually meant blocked opportunities for most of the women I came to know in San Alejo, and many were well aware of this. Hortencia attributed her life of hardship directly to the fact that she was never sent to school, and Tita put it in a way that underscores its normalization: "As *uno de pobre* [a poor person], one doesn't think of these things, like school. One knows as a poor person that these things are for others, but not for us." Although Dalila also realized that these goals were not for the poor, she was not altogether content with how things had turned out. She went to school for six months and barely learned how to sign her name; after that her mother kept her at home to look out for her young siblings. When she was a teenager she married a man twice her age. Strikingly beautiful, she was thought by her family to have married well, to a good provider who owned a *pinchazo* (tire repair business). By the time she was twenty-four, she had had three children and two miscarriages. Something that always caught my attention when I visited her was that she never smiled. She normally looked away when we talked and appeared withdrawn, and she always seemed a little sad, no matter what we talked about. One afternoon, while the entire town was quiet and the only noise one could hear was the sound of the machinery in the tire repair shop next door, Dalila spoke up. "This life, what you see around me, everything is fine, he's good, but I wish my life could be different. For example, I could have learned more at school. Maybe my life wouldn't be what it is. Who knows? It's fine now, I don't have any complaints. I don't have anything to complain about. But I feel like, I don't know, tired, bored, I don't know why. Some moments I wish I could read better," she explained, lost in her thoughts as she looked out the window.

School abandonment did not affect only the very poor women; it had a marked effect on other women as well. For instance, Lucrecia finished sixth grade and started seventh, as she was supposed to have continued her education, but for this she needed to travel to the larger city because San Alejo only had elementary schools. For a girl, she explained, it was not only complicated and dangerous; it had also started to get expensive to travel by bus every day, because her sister also traveled to school. Both Lucrecia and her sister had to drop out three months short of finishing seventh grade. The sisters explained that "when you are a young girl, the men in the buses start to say things to you, *molestan* [they bother you]. What if something happens to you? Even if you liked going to school, tell me, is it worth it? The dangers—you know, the money, the travel, and the exposure to who knows what?" The sisters' words expose the vulnerability of the young women, the limited access to education beyond the sixth grade in rural areas, and the constraints that a general lack of resources impose.

Women in the Altiplano had also been pressured into not attending or abandoning school at an early age, and, as in San Alejo, conversations about this topic were couched in normalized language. This way of talking about such practices could sound as if people were describing a "custom," something that could be interpreted as part of tradition when divorced from the context in which these decisions are made. Of the twenty-eight women I interviewed in the Altiplano, twelve had never attended school, fifteen had between one and six years of schooling, and one had a ninth-grade education. There were no teachers or college students in the group, though in that town I came across teachers and women with higher education degrees, such as a dentist. Some women either avoided the question or said something vague about their schooling, which signaled to me not to press for an answer. Constantina and Azucena were among those who were vague about their educational level initially; later on they confessed that they had never set foot in a school in their lives and were embarrassed about it. They both mentioned that whether or not girls (or boys) go to school, most learn to weave when they are between the ages of seven and nine. Constantina's fifteen-year-old daughter had been working for pay for several years already, and her twelve-year-old son had been working in the fields fetching water since he was very young. Both children had learned to weave, and they worked occasionally with professional weavers in town. Rosita only finished the first grade; she was taken out of the second grade, at the age of twelve, so that she could work as a housekeeper for a family in the capital and later as a sales clerk at this family's store. Rosita worked with this family for five years, during which she learned to speak Spanish with the children of the house, who would show her their homework, and thus she learned a bit more beyond the first grade. "The children taught me some things from school," she recounted, "as I basically grew up with them. I used to also care for the youngest girl in the family, yes, I was her baby-sitter. This family was very nice to me; they treated me like one of the family. They taught me how to add and subtract; that's where I learned more than first grade. At the end, they taught me how to write receipts at the store. They were kind to me."

PERCEPTIONS OF WOMEN'S WORK OUTSIDE THE HOME

The women's own perceptions of their work also reflect gender ideologies that shape views of men as breadwinners and of women as earners whose incomes *supplement* the men's, of women working for pay in order to *help* the men, even when it is the women who are supporting their families. However, these views do not yield clear-cut differences; perceptions were more nuanced and complex, particularly when men could not fulfill their role as breadwinners in the context of a general lack of opportunities for well-paid work. The cases of absent men or of homes headed by women are instructive: when men were present in the homes of San Alejo, or even when they were thousands of miles away but sending remittances, they were seen as the indisputable breadwinners, in spite of the fact that the women were also working in remunerated activities and sometimes generating more income than the men.

For Leticia, work for pay was a necessity because she was a widow, and her young daughters had no one else to support them. So on the days she felt "more or less" well, when she did not have chills or other ailments associated with HIV/AIDS, she would go to work. In the last months of her life Leticia's workdays amounted to about one or two a week, but she had no choice. "Her body is weak but not her desire to be a responsible mother for her daughters," a worker at the health post commented. Victoria shared a similar view of work as a necessity, except that she had never "needed" to work outside the home. "No, I've never worked in my life" she smiled. "Thanks to God, I've had all the comforts here at home, and I've never lacked for anything. So, no, I don't need to work, so I don't." Mercedes compared her two marriages as follows: "My first husband gave me a hellish life; he used to drink and had other women, so I had to work to support my children. So when my mother died I took the opportunity to move back to my father's house to help him raise my younger siblings. With my second husband it's very different. I don't work. Thanks to God I don't *need* to work." Vera and Mariana stayed at home and would not change anything, because in their eyes this is how they were fulfilling their roles. The contrast between their lifestyles and their not working for pay was something that others in town would comment on. "All they have is from inheritance, not from their own work. No one in that family [referring to Mariana's family] works, but they live well thanks to the inheritances they have received," a worker at the health post commented after we saw Mariana drive by in a late-model car.

Among the poor, however, women were not only expected to work for pay, but it was also a part of their lives. Mirna pointed this out to me when she remembered her aunt who had worked "all her life" until her very last days. Mirna talked about a photo of her aunt: "We are sad now because she is gone; our Lord took her with him. She left a remembrance for us; she left us this photo of her grinding corn to make tortillas. She didn't leave anything else, only this photo of her working. We put it up so we remember her, and we remember her working, grinding corn, working. She wanted us to remember her as always working."

For women whose husbands were in the United States, staying home to care for the children was more meaningful than paid work because it was evidence that their husbands' migration had been successful (meaning their spouses were remitting regularly) and that they had not forgotten their obligations as breadwinners (or the women themselves). And caring for their homes—and working in the home—meant that they were putting to good use the remittances they received. Mirna described her cousins' experiences: "Their husbands are there [in the United States], and the wives, my cousins, are here. One, the one who is my *comadre* [lit., "co-mother] she has a small *tienda* [store] at home, but she mostly dedicates herself to her household chores. And the other one, she too stays home and does her chores. If the husbands send them [money], tell me, why are they going to kill themselves working? It's much better to be home, in charge of the home, the kids."

An important aspect of women's work as complementary or inferior to men's is its formalization and codification into law. Until 1998 an article in the Guatemalan civil code required that women obtain permission from their husbands to work outside the home (Steinsleger 2005). This article was removed from the civil code, but article 113, which states that a married woman can practice a profession or be employed only when these activities do not impair her functions as a housewife and mother, was left intact (Steinsleger 2005). Indeed, a series of articles in the Guatemalan civil code, the Interamerican Human Rights Commission declared, institutionalized a disequilibrium in the rights and obligations of a married couple and subordinated the rights of women to men's decisions. The Commission made these observations after a Guatemalan woman filed a complaint with the international body because Guatemalan law could not protect her rights (Morales de Sierra 2001).

Not surprisingly, the image of women working outside the home only when there is a need for it is the other side of the coin, as far as the view of men as breadwinners is concerned. But the disconnect between the ideal of men as the breadwinner and the reality that they could no longer uphold that role sometimes carried harmful consequences for women, limiting their access to informal networks and thus exacerbating their precarious situation. Gracia María's brothers sent remittances to their own spouses and to their parents but only occasionally sent money to her, even though they were aware that she needed financial help. "Well, because if one has a husband, then why would others send you money? The husband is the one who needs to know what he can do to procure money," Gracia María explained, when I asked why her brothers did not send money to her if they knew she was in need. Providing for some other man's family, even if the woman is closely related, she later added, was interfering in another man's affairs, and "once you marry, you pass to being his and not your family's anymore." Mirna's other aunt and her husband had a hard time providing for their three children because they could never find any work that paid enough. The aunt's husband had been killed in a cantina altercation three years earlier, but only after the tragedy took place did others start helping the aunt. Mirna explained, "When he was alive he was the one responsible for the house, even if he spent the money on guaro and women. But now she is left alone, so naturally people see this and give her some help, like some tortillas sometimes or some coffee, or like that, something for her and the children."

Reflecting reduced work opportunities and incomes among men, the men had reduced their contributions to the household—but in a way that would not directly reveal their reduced earning capacity. For instance, some of the women mentioned (and this was corroborated by a nurse) that their husbands or partners would give them less money for daily expenses (mostly for food) but expected them to continue to keep up the household as before. A nurse explained, "The men give their wives Q.10 a day to buy food, and we know that's very little. Tell me, what are they going to buy with that? But if the women buy less food, the men say, 'Ah, what did you spend the money on? Something for yourself? Some nail polish or lipstick?' But no, the women are simply unable to buy as much with so little money." Although this nurse pointed out that the men never ventured to the market and therefore likely had no idea how much anything cost, still they might have known that their contributions did not meet their households' needs and in fact did not expect the women to make do with less. Telling the women that they expected the same amount and quality of food, for example, might have helped them to uphold the image of being the breadwinners in a way that transferred the pressure to the women to cope in the midst of reduced economic opportunities.

The absence of a husband who would be responsible for his family's well-being led Nena to a life that was different from that of other women, highlighting the normalized image of the man as a breadwinner. Nena's husband was not dead, as in the case of Mirna's uncle, but he was largely absent from the family's life because of his drinking, Nena pointed out. Thus when it came time to discuss how they were going to support themselves, Nena's father-in-law decided to open up a butcher shop, supplying meat from his own cattle, for Nena to sell. His own son was not responsible enough to be the breadwinner, and Nena's father-in-law wanted to make a statement about it, so he put Nena in charge of the business. Nena explained:

> I ended up being the one in charge of my family, can you imagine that? I made money in the butcher shop, but my husband would take the money to go get drunk. So we had to close the shop. Then my father-in-law bought me the bookstore. I have been in charge of it for eight years now; I've been responsible for being the sole provider for my children. Can you imagine to what degree drinking has affected us? We can't even be a normal family with the father at the head. Then my father-in-law got tired and took away my husband's truck, and so my husband went to the States. Of course, he never sent us even one dollar. He continued to be an absent father. This is why his father had to step in.

Estrella spoke at length about what work had meant in her life, especially after her first husband abandoned her and the children. When she found herself alone and with small children to support, she decided to start taking photos for a living. Little by little she established a clientele and then opened a small studio, which, she proudly told me, has been the source of everything good in her life, and she had done it on her own. "It's my work that has sustained me. Through my work I've supported my children, have sent them to school. So I care about my work a lot. I don't even have time to go visiting because I have to see to my business. And it's all been me, me and my work. When I work, I save so that if later I don't have something I don't have to bother anyone. I've always been that way. It's my work that has sustained me all my life, no other person, only my work." And although Estrella always seemed confident and strong to me, she got a little emotional when talking about her work. She beamed when she described what she did, the long hours she put in, what it meant to her, and, most of all, what her beloved camera has meant in her life.

> From the day my husband abandoned me, my camera and me, my camera has been everything to me [she says with tears in her eyes]. My camera has helped me to support my children. I go take pictures at birthdays, weddings. With this one [a camera lying on a counter at her studio] on my shoulder,

> we go out and come back late, sometimes even at midnight. Because I, well, I live from taking photos. This is my life. For a birthday or something like that, people call me, so I can earn my cents. I've been taken pictures for fifteen years, and I'll continue until I can't see through the lens anymore [laughs]. People call me to take photographs because they like me, they love me, appreciate me.

However, although she loved her work and always mentioned the satisfaction it has brought to her, Estrella stressed the absence of her first husband in shaping her work life. She always implied that it had been "by force" and not by choice that she took her camera out for the first time. The long hours were tiring, and she felt enslaved by her work. She also mentioned that she would have liked to have met a responsible man so that she would not have had to work this hard. Later on she intimated, "Sometimes I feel bad because the burden is all mine; I'm in charge." Even though being in charge of "everything," even of construction at home, was sometimes overwhelming, her image as a hard worker, a *decent* hard worker, who never neglected her household responsibilities, was something very important for Estrella to cultivate, because she knew what it meant in San Alejo.

> Even when I get home at midnight, I come to see if things were done at home, to see what food needs to be bought the next day, to see if uniforms are in place, eesh, you name it. Then the next day up early and work again. Because I'm alone, I also supervised the building of those extra rooms [in the house]. I supervised the workers. I had to see the work they were doing because I was paying them from my own work. People know what I have sacrificed, that I live a very busy life earning a decent living for my children. I live enslaved, but I am respected. I know there are bad tongues out there because I have to walk alone at night, my work requires me to go out and be in the streets, so naturally there is gossip, right? But I can tell you, I am not ashamed of anything.

Others in town did, indeed, respect Estrella and admired her for remaining "a decent woman," even when, as a single woman, she needed to work outside the home because she had children to support. Those who spoke of Estrella's "decency" made it sound as if work for pay and motherhood did not go together. A physician who charged her half-price for consultations mentioned that Estrella was "recognized in town for earning her money the hard but decent way," and this is why he did not charge her full price. To reciprocate, when Estrella cooked a dish that the physician liked, she took some of the special food to him.

WOMEN WHO WORK OUTSIDE THE HOME

Women who worked outside the home in San Alejo often had a good deal of negotiating to do, not only because they had to remain in charge of the household and all its chores (or at least make sure the chores were done), but also because they had to keep up the appearance that they were still devoted, responsible "women of the house" whose pecuniary activities would not compromise their roles as wives and mothers. Indeed, as Dary Fuentes observed in her fieldwork in eastern Guatemala:

> The women see their work in the field as normal, but they would not even conceive of the possibility of a man doing household chores. This gender division of labor . . . is internalized by the women: "the place of man is in the field," one woman said, and "they would stop being men," said another one, when she was asked about the possibility of her husband helping her with chores at home. (1994: 103)

Women who worked outside the home therefore lived with the contradiction (and burden) of having to be in charge of both the productive and reproductive tasks, and often they seemed uncomfortable with having to work for pay (and would provide a list of justifications for doing so), a situation that underscores the internalized practices of gender socialization and the clearly demarcated roles and inequalities that are formalized in legal codes and in ideologies and practices that end up making them participants in their own domination. For instance, Gracia María always felt guilty about working: "What I lament about having to work is that one comes back very tired to the house and then has less time to dedicate to the children. I tell my sister-in-law that you end up dedicating more time to the children of others than to your own when you work [outside the home]. One must be so patient because the children ask so much when one comes home. It's not worth it. But if financially you need to, what can you do? One suffers because one knows that women are supposed to be with the children, right?" Gracia's thoughts about herself are in sharp contrast to her descriptions of her husband as being completely unaware of what was going on with the children (see chapter 4).

In Delfina's case, it was her husband who made sure that she felt guilty about working outside the home, especially because he thought she did not need her teaching job. She laughed as she described the lengths he went to in order to "make my life unbearable, just because I work and I like my job." When their daughters were toddlers, Delfina decided to go back to work, but her husband was opposed to it and decided that they would fire the housekeeper and the cook, "to castigate me for leaving the girls at home and wanting to go to work." As the daughters grew older, he decided (mostly in response to his own mother's pleas) to hire a couple of housekeepers to help out but not to do any of what he considered Delfina's duties, such as serving his meals, cooking certain dishes the way he liked, or deciding what to prepare daily. In my notes from one visit to Delfina, I wrote the following: "Her husband looks upset today—meals not hot enough when she served him." Sometimes her daughters wanted to help Delfina cook, but their father would order them to leave the kitchen and go next door to his parents' house. "One time," Delfina explained, "the girls were like nine or ten and they were helping me wash some dishes because the *muchacha* [housekeeper] was not here, and he said, 'No, you go to the other side [his parents' house] because your lazy mother doesn't need any help. This *tal por cual* [good-for-nothing] only serves to put you to work.'" When Delfina shared these experiences with her friends and colleagues at work, they were receptive because they had similar stories to share. Her friends had told her that based on their experiences, she might be having these problems because she lived right next door to her in-laws, although Delfina said, "My mother-in-law has been of tremendous help to me; she's interceded on my behalf with him [the husband], because she sees the situation and how unjust and malo he can be with me." Delfina emphasized that her life had been "hell" since she decided to go back to work and that her husband pointed to her work as the cause for everything that did and could go wrong in their family. But somehow, she intimated, smiling, "I don't know why, I don't know where this comes from, but from deep inside of me, I refuse to stop working. I cannot stop going to work regardless of what he says." A nurse at the health post described Delfina as "rebellious" and said she was known for having a "tough temper," which in the end caused her suffering.

In contrast to Delfina, many San Alejo women simply went along with their husbands' wishes and stopped going to work, even if it was against their will. Ivette is a case in point. Since she got married she stopped working as a cashier at a supermarket. When her daughter turned one year old, Ivette wanted to start working again, but her husband refused to allow it. "He told me not to, that I couldn't because I needed to take care of the girl. He didn't want me to work anymore. He said, 'Who is going to take care of the girl?' because it is not the same thing when the mother takes care of the children, right? And so that's why I have not gone back to work," she explained. Lila was in a similar situation; her husband sent remittances regularly from the United States and did not see a reason why Lila should work outside the home. Others in town assured me that Lila was happy and lucky to receive remittances. Lila described her situation with a tinge of anxiety mixed with sadness: "No, I've never worked, never. I've always been, well, we have always been dependent on him, whatever he decides, that's how it is around here. He doesn't like me to work, and since I have no diploma or anything, I cannot find work in something that is easy. I got to sixth grade, and my husband got to the seventh, but for a man that's fine. Not for a woman. So I have nothing to defend myself with, no degree. And he tells me, 'Look, you have no education, just dedicate yourself to the children.' And the truth is, he's right."

Not all men, of course, were opposed to their wives working outside the home. But even those who *allowed* their wives to earn an income made sure that everyone knew it *complemented* their earnings and should not be compared or thought to be greater (even if this was sometimes the case). This was especially true among those who were seen as not needing to work for pay. Emilia's work at the health post was very rewarding for her, she said, and she would never consider quitting, even if her husband was not completely happy about it. Emilia's husband, for his part, knowing well that Emilia would continue to work at the clinic regardless of what he wished, diminished the importance of her work by speaking of it as a hobby or something that brought in some income but never an "important" amount. Thus Emilia was convinced that her work and income were not consequential: "He knows, and well, yes, me, too, that what I do is minimal, small, but he knows that even in a minimal way I am contributing with something. So he says that it's probably good that a wife works, so she can help out a little, a job that is more like a distraction." It always seemed to me that by diminishing Emilia's financial contribution to the household, her husband minimized the fact that she was working outside the house largely against his will. However, like Delfina's husband, Emilia's husband made sure that Emilia felt guilty about dedicating time and effort to her job, pointing out that she was neglecting her household duties as a result, even when they had a muchacha who did most household chores. "He lets me work," Emilia commented, "but the problem is when I take a little bit more time at work, like when we have meetings in the city and I have to stay there longer, then he gets upset. I know that even if I'm at an important meeting, I have to fly out of that meeting to be home at the time he thinks I should be home. Or else, God save me, he explodes. So I have to be super careful with my time."

Image and gossip, already discussed at length earlier, were always in the minds of the women who worked outside the home, as well as in their husbands' minds, and it posed challenges for the women who earned more than their husbands did. With tears running down her cheeks, Andrea explained that her stepfather/partner, who no longer worked for pay, offended her with insinuations about where she obtained the money she earned from selling tostadas at the park. "He offends me really badly; he tells a thousand and one things about what I am. He tells me that I am a whore, that this is how I earn my money. I reply to him, 'No, look, I have my arms to be able to earn my *pisto* [money] honestly and not by sinning. I have worked since I was very little, so I know how to work hard. But he offends me." And Hortencia, whose regular work generated more income than the sporadic work of her husband (now deceased), went through contortions to make sure that no one, especially her husband and his family, doubted that her earnings came from "honest work." At one point her husband even took money from her in order to have a good time—to drink, buy cigarettes, and go to bars with women—so that others would assume he was earning more money than she was and that it was his own money he was spending. Hortencia thought that these vices were precisely the reason he was unable to keep the very good job he had had as a driver for a wealthy family in town, for which he earned Q.600 a month. For a while she actually had to quit working, because her husband started to go through "*ataques de celos*" (jealousy fits) and suspected that she was having affairs with every man in sight. She still washed clothes without her husband's knowledge in order to provide food for her children. After his death she worked as hard as she could, instead of "*andar en malos pasos*" (doing the wrong things), to keep up her good reputation. However, she said, "I considered "*juntarme* [living together] with someone who is responsible for me, even if he can only provide corn and beans. But I would only consider getting together if he is a responsible man, so that what happened to me with my first husband won't happen ever, ever again [laughs]."

In many respects the lives of the female workers in the Altiplano stood in sharp contrast to what I observed in San Alejo. Views of women's work outside the home, women's income, and women's (and men's) work in the household differed significantly from what I heard and observed in San Alejo. Over and over, the women in the Altiplano talked about all the female members of their families who had worked alongside men to provide for the home. Women's work in the Altiplano was seen as "natural," commonplace, and expected, and not as complementary to men's; I was told on several occasions that women who are known for being hard workers are particularly appreciated. Thus their contributions and responsibilities in the family were not viewed as being so dissimilar from those of men; women's work for pay—in town, in other cities, and in different occupations—was not unusual. Marta, the mother of six children, explained in a matter-of-fact way that her income was integral to the maintenance of her household. Perhaps influenced from having spent the previous week in San Alejo, I asked Marta if she saw her income as supplementary to her husband's. With some surprise, and frowning slightly, she replied:

> You mean like to support the family? Well, no, we share expenses here. See, when I started living with him, we agreed that I was going to take care of some expenses and he would take care of others. So I'm in charge of everything in the kitchen; he takes care of everything that relates to the children and clothing, like the doctor and that. I work so I contribute my part. Sometimes I don't have enough, so I ask for meat or a chicken on credit, and I pay back later. Sometimes I need all the ingredients to cook, and it's all *fiado* [on credit] at the store. But it's my responsibility. I work and then repay my debts.

And when she got home from work too late to get a meal ready, her husband did not hesitate to get it started himself. "In fact," Marta assured me, "he knows how to make better tortillas than I do [laughs]! He helps a lot with everything at home. We cooperate with one another."

Amelia did not speak of her experience as out of the ordinary when she recounted how her husband would meet her on the road when she was coming back from their plot of land and hauling the corn harvest. She helped him on the land, and he helped her with her textiles. "He works in agriculture and I do my *tejido* [weaving]. Sometimes I help another señora when orders for the items are large; we both earn. So I can't just say, 'Give me money to eat.' I have to find a way to earn a living. He helps me, and I help him," she explained.[11] However, because the youngest of their three children was still small and Amelia had to take him with her to work, she said that the money she earned was "in accordance to my effort." My boy is with me," she continued. "I'm not alone. I can't work as hard with him, so my husband and I know that I earn accordingly." Amelia and her husband seemed to factor the care of their youngest son into their income calculations.

Gina also saw her earnings as being equal in importance to her family as the earnings of her husband; she realized that one person could not earn all the money needed to support the household. They were trying to build a house, and they knew it would take both their efforts to complete the project. This equal sharing of responsibilities was made evident to me when Erminia related the story of the building project she and her husband started. They had lost their house in the 1976 earthquake and decided to rebuild it on their own: "Since we have no money, we decided to do it ourselves. Yes, we both carried bricks and put up the walls; we both hauled water. We worked shoulder to shoulder to build this house. Thanks to God all that is in the past, but, yes, we did it together."

Thus women's contributions were not as unequally perceived in the Altiplano as they were in San Alejo, where there were sharp distinctions that cut across social classes. Whereas work for pay was also a necessity for the women in the Altiplano, it was a necessity that had become normalized and was part of life, given the Maya's profound historical disadvantages, and thus women's work acquired a different meaning there than in San Alejo. "Women never stop working," Carmen assured me in the Altiplano. "I've never rested in my life." She had actually worked throughout her pregnancies, even when it was risky due to possible complications. Azucena also had worked to earn a living from the time she was a little girl and all through her pregnancies, to the point that one of her employers asked her not to do certain tasks, like mopping the floors, in her ninth month, because she did not want to be responsible if anything happened to Azucena and the baby. But hard work and all, in the brutal context in which the Maya have lived, to be able to earn some money was a blessing, I was told. "I thank God that people want to hire me to wash, clean, make tortillas," Azucena said. And although she had never been a stranger to earning a living, her main problem was that her husband did not help her financially, so she had to work even harder to provide for her children. Meanwhile, as she always noted (and I saw), she had her mother to help her in tough times.

> My poor mama, she works very hard and she is old already. Instead of my helping her, she has to help me. She gives me everything she earns on Tuesdays, then on Fridays she buys me tomatoes, sugar, soap, firewood, Incaparina,[12] or some food for the kids. But sometimes it is not enough. She has been forced to sell her clothes in order to help me. She used to have some very nice *huipiles*, and she has sold them for me. I have sold all my

> cortes and huipiles, too; I even had to sell my wedding corte to pay for the hospital when I had the youngest. I only have two cortes left now. I have to feed the kids, and he [her husband] is a drunk who doesn't help. He sends Q.50 every three months.

Azucena also paid Q.6 at the health post to obtain some grains, rice, and corn from a nutritional program in town subsidized by a U.S. organization. Some of her acquaintances knew of her situation. "They have mercy and give me clothes, rags that I put on the children," she said. Although for the most part the men seemed to responsibly share in the household expenses, this was not always true in the Altiplano, as the case of Azucena demonstrates. And as in San Alejo, there were cases in the Altiplano of men spending money that could go to food, clothing, or medicine on "women, alcohol, and vices," as I was reminded on a few occasions. Thus one must remember that Maya men themselves have suffered deeply the consequences of structural, symbolic, and political violence in Guatemala, and this was manifested in their relations with those close to them. "It is very difficult," Azucena noted, "to have a family here, for everyone."

In spite of the differences, there were important similarities related to women's work in the two towns. In the Altiplano, too, work outside the home provided women with an opportunity to forge friendships, have conversations, obtain information, or simply share their everyday life concerns and happenings. Isa and her neighbor both did weaving for sale, and when one needed thread of a color she did not have she would borrow from the other. Sometimes Isa kept her neighbor's weaving while the neighbor was out of town, in case any potential buyers came by, and they gave work to each other, too. If the neighbor had an order for textiles that was too large to complete alone, she shared the order (and the profits) with Isa. They knew how to embroider different designs and had slightly different ways of making hairpieces, so Isa saw their working relationship as a mutually beneficial one. And when Isa did not have money to buy sugar, coffee, soap, or whatever she needed for cooking, she borrowed from the neighbor and paid her back with weaving. Isa emphatically noted that this neighbor was her only contact in her neighborhood, but it afforded the two women many opportunities to converse and share their views, plans, and worries, so Isa felt she had "someone." And, as in San Alejo, spaces for women to connect with one another did not happen automatically; often these relations were shaped by the women's reputation, potential as a competitor for work, and socioeconomic standing, among other factors.

CONCLUSION

Focusing on paid work outside the home has allowed me to unveil the complex links between home and work and to expose this sphere of life as a profoundly social process that involves the women's male partners, friends, neighbors, relatives, coworkers, and children. It also has permitted me to note the mutually constitutive forms of violence in this area of the women's lives, including (1) the symbolic violence that leads the women in San Alejo to downplay the value of their own work and assess their contributions through a prism of inequality and subordination; (2) the structural violence that shapes the kinds of work to which the women have access, the conditions of their work, and the wages they earn; and (3) the gender violence that delineates women's and men's views of the work women perform and diminishes the importance of women's monetary contributions. The practices I have discussed point to how normalized these aspects of work are, for those who live them do not question them and those who study them sometimes take them to be part of "tradition."

My examination has not been intended to provide black-and-white assessments of the importance of work for women's relations with their partners in the home; indeed, it has exposed contradictions that are part of life, such as being aware of men's diminished economic contributions to the household—because they also have suffered from shrinking opportunities brought about by neoliberal policies and existing inequalities—but upholding views of men as the undisputed heads of household, or upholding this image of men while also realizing men's diminished financial and physical presence, as many men have engaged in emigration and are therefore absent. The absence of a man in the home—economically or physically—highlights the primacy that men and their wishes, dreams, and position have in the lives of women.

Placing the meaning of work in the San Alejo women's lives in a multilayered context of violence is not meant to portray this aspect of life as one exclusively of suffering, though using the lens I have constructed here did allow me to unearth hidden forms of suffering in this aspect of the women's lives. A focus on this sphere of life, which calls attention to meaning-making aspects and to the socially embedded nature of women's work, also led me to attend to women's relations with other women and to the spaces and opportunities that can engender a collectivity. Thus women's work was not simply a self-contained experience but rather something akin to an engine for sociability for many women of San Alejo. As such, even though the structures of inequality and the gender ideologies that dictate women's and men's behaviors are key to understanding the women's experiences, my presentation also points to important forms of gendered agency. This discussion continues in the next chapter, where I focus on another sphere of life away from the immediacy of the family, a part of life that is central for understanding the San Alejo women's experiences of multisided violence: religion and the church.

CHAPTER 7

Church, Religion, and Enduring Everyday Violence

Yo he sido evangélica ya diez años, por la Gracia de Dios, y desde ese momento he tratado de vivir una vida mejor. Mi situación en hi hogar es [niega con la cabeza] bueno, como Ud. sabe, yo he tenido momentos en que hubiera querido salir corriendo desesperada, llorar, gritar. Pero mi pastor, en mi iglesia, me habla mucho y me dice, "Mire hermana, acérquese a la Biblia, tiene que esperar, esperar y tener paciencia," y así es que he aguantado mi situación.

[I've been Evangelical for ten years, by the Grace of God, and I have tried to lead a better life since then. My situation at home is [shakes her head], well, you know, I have lived moments where I would have liked to flee desperately and scream and cry. But my pastor, in my church, talks to me a lot and tells me, "Look sister, get closer to the Bible, you have to wait and wait and be patient," and this is how I have endured my situation.]

—Nena, thirty-nine years old

Yo sé que puedo contar con los miembros de la iglesia. Sé que están conmigo, y esto me da alegría. Puedo contar con mis hermanas. Yo tengo una existencia muy triste, y mis únicos momentos de alegría son con mis hermanas de la iglesia. Mi sufrimiento es tan grade que ya tengo ganado el cielo. Dios me ha dado una paz bien linda que viene de mi resignación y de mi aceptación. Y esto para mí es un favor, un regalo de Dios.

[I know I can count on the church members. I know they're with me, and this gives me joy. I can count on my sisters there. I have a very sad existence, and my only moments of happiness are with my sisters from my church. My suffering is so much that I have already earned heaven.

God has given me a beautiful peace that comes from resignation and acceptance. So to me it is a favor, a gift from God.]

—Andrea, twenty-three years old

There has been significant scholarly attention to religion in Latin America, especially to the role it has played in contemporary social change in the region, with a focus on the social justice work of the progressive Catholic Church and its base communities and on the conversion of millions of local residents to Protestantism. And Catholic and Protestant churches have played a pivotal role throughout the region before, during, and after the political conflicts of the past several decades; Central American countries, in particular, Guatemala and El Salvador, are emblematic in this regard. This involvement has ranged from calls for and active involvement in addressing issues of social justice to the military-religious alliances present in the Pentecostal movement of the 1980s in Guatemala (see Casaús Arzú 1998). Thus scholars have examined the broad societal effects of the role of Catholic and Protestant churches in the political life of these countries (see Peterson 1997) as well as the impact these churches have had on the micro-processes of everyday life, especially at the household level. In this chapter I focus on the place of the church in the women's quotidian lives but do not engage in the debates that have guided this type of research in the region. For instance, I do not argue whether it is the Catholic Church or Protestant churches (the latter being mostly evangelical and Pentecostal where I undertook fieldwork) that have had a greater effect on improving the lives of the women. Instead, I turn the lens to focus on how women see the church as a space to find solace and comfort and on how, in turn, church activities can contribute to upholding gender inequalities indirectly, which in the context of other social inequalities exacerbate suffering in the women's lives.

Here I examine another space outside the home that is intimately linked to the maintenance, but also the contestation, of structures of violence that affect life in the home. An examination of this sphere provides another window into how violence is normalized and embedded in social life and in institutions outside the home and beyond the realm of purely individual behavior. Thus, even though I build on the important literature that examines the role of the churches in effecting social change in the lives of women and the poor in Latin America, I devote most attention to what it means to the women in San Alejo to join a community of people in similar circumstances and the way in which church activities can sometimes reinforce structures of inequality with significant consequences for women.

The voluminous literature on religious congregations has highlighted how these have successfully provided opportunities for friendships to flourish and for members to find different forms of support and assurance (Damaris, Charbonneau and Carrasco 1999; Taylor and Chatters 1988), as sources of services for the needy, and as networks of assistance for the urban poor (Roberts 1968). Religious involvement also has been identified as an important source of social capital, because it generates networks and relationships that help members attain important goals in life (Coleman 1988; Greeley 1997). In Latin America, before David Stoll (1990) drew attention to the massive conversion to Protestantism occurring in the region,[1] Roberts (1968) had noted increased conversion to Evangelicalism in Guatemala associated with efforts to counter poverty and marginalization among the urban poor.[2] Indeed, Guatemala has had one of fastest-growing and largest evangelical populations in Latin America (Freston 1998; Smilde 2007; Whiteford 2002). But the "Protestant revolution" has not been contained in only a few countries, and scholars of the region have directed attention to the effects of conversion on all aspects of life in different contexts, including the benefits that the poor and women might derive from it.[3]

Women constitute the majority of religious practitioners in the region (Chesnut 2003), and there is now an important body of work that examines the links between the lives of women and the church and religiosity. This work focuses on the benefits that conversion to evangelical Protestantism can have for women and men (Brusco 1995; Burdick 1993; Chesnut 2003; Smilde 2007), especially by providing a solution to men's drinking and marital conflict (Brusco 1995; Chesnut 2003; Mariz 1994; Stoll 1990).[4] Scholarly investigations also highlight the minimal differences between progressive Catholic and Pentecostal churches in helping the poor overcome their predicament (Mariz 1994) and describe religious fundamentalism's perceived threats to women's rights (Tarducci and Tagliaferro 2004). Even though an important line of argument notes that Pentecostalism can be seen as a form of women's collective action, indeed, as a "strategic" women's movement (Brusco 1995), as a form of women's empowerment (Hallum 2003), or as providing women with networks of support and a source of self-confidence that amplify reciprocal exchanges (Muratorio 1982), at the same time it has been seen as reinforcing patriarchal values (Mariz and Machado 1997). Brusco (1995) adds that the effects of conversion, or of church and religious activities, must be understood within the specific social-historical trajectory of a particular sociocultural context. And Wood, Williams, and Chijiwa (2007) sound a word of caution against treating all Protestants, or all Pentecostals, even in the same context, as a homogeneous group.

With these cautionary notes in mind, I discuss, with prudence, the religious lives of the women I came to know in Guatemala, noting that I focus narrowly on their views of the church within an overall framework that exposes the multisided violence in their lives. Thus whereas I discuss the enormous benefits the women see in their church membership (already documented in the scholarship mentioned above), I also focus on how this sphere of life is linked to the structures of violence on which this analysis is founded. Following the observations that Mariz and Machado (1997) made in their comparative study of Pentecostalism and Catholic base communities in Brazil and Goldstein's (2003) work in the favelas of Brazil, I present a nuanced image that can be seen as "both sides" of the place of the Catholic or Pentecostal churches in the lives of female congregants. I discuss the women's own views and overwhelmingly positive assessments, but I also note that in the context of San Alejo religious participation (in either Catholic or Pentecostal churches) does not fundamentally challenge the prevailing social order or women's place in the gender hierarchy, does not alter existing structures of social and economic inequality, and does not provide women with an awareness of basic rights that could lead to genuine transformation in their lives. Thus from my angle in this examination religion and the church in San Alejo were sources of solace and comfort but also appeared to reinforce certain structures of inequality and contributed to sustaining the internalized dispositions and frameworks that led to the toleration of structures that produce suffering, and I would like to highlight this complexity. This examination allows me to take a closeup look at the mechanisms, found in religious spaces, through which the women endure the multisided violence in their lives.

WOMEN'S VIEW OF THE CHURCH

For many of the ladinas in San Alejo (as well as for the Maya women in the Altiplano), the church and religious participation occupied a central place. Unprompted, they would bring up themes related to the church or to their religiosity and faith. Here I draw attention to two areas that are intertwined but that I separate for the purposes of analysis and discussion. In our conversations the women noted that belonging to a church, speaking to a pastor or a priest, talking about their concerns with other women at church, and in general knowing that they could count on their coreligionists and religious leaders for some form of comfort helped to sustain them through their difficult moments. At the same time, it was the palliative nature of this comfort that helped to sustain structures of inequality and, ultimately, led to suffering. Often religious teachings and the leaders' interpretations contributed to normalizing the unequal structures that made possible the multisided violence I examine in this book. As Andrea, whom I quote above, explains, her pastor and sisters from church provided her with almost the only source of support and enjoyment in her life, but by encouraging her to be patient, to have faith, and to endure, this support helped to normalize her suffering and thus to misrecognize that her suffering came from the structural, symbolic, and gender violence in her life. Thus I first present the women's views of religious spaces as sources of comfort and consolation, as agents that can mitigate suffering, and as potential arenas where women can forge important links of solidarity. In a subsequent section I shed light on the other side of the coin, to show how this supportive aspect of the religious sphere ends up legitimating the women's pain and thus sanctioning violent structures that injure them.

At first impression, it seemed as if the women in San Alejo were "not religious" or simply "didn't care" about the church, as one woman told me. But on closer inspection, this town was steeped in religious traditions, culture, and outlook, and thus it provided a fundamental angle from which to examine the lives and experiences of women. Many women spent significant amounts of time with their coreligionists, talking with their spiritual guides and pastors, praying, and congregating, activities that provided them with important (sometimes their only) opportunities, besides their work lives, to share their situations with others. And even the "nonreligious," those who claimed not to have a religion or never to attend church, invoked prayer or other spiritual practices as examples of what helped them to carry on.

Mariana mentioned that her family and her husband's family were Evangelicals but that she never attended or visited any church.[5] She complained, "The evangelical religion is very strict and puts a lot of obstacles [laughs] to people going there, like they don't let women use pants, or wear makeup, wear accessories. I know these are material things, but they help us, women, to feel good and to be comfortable. So that's why I don't attend church." However, Mariana noted that they were going to "present" her sons at the temple, a ceremony to introduce the boys as members to the congregation, and she expected to make it a large social event. Vera, another woman from a well-off family, also mentioned that she did not go to church and, in fact, did not know of anyone who did, except for her husband's sister, who was in a wheelchair and was Catholic. Vera thought that her sister-in-law's condition was the reason she sought out the church. "The Mormons have been visiting," Vera mentioned, "but we are not ready to join any church." Vera seemed indifferent to all matters related to church and had not attended a service since she was a child, when her mother stopped going to an evangelical congregation. Like Mariana, Vera remained religious "privately," praying and observing rituals and religious activities outside of the congregation. Also like Mariana, Vera saw both the Catholic and the evangelical churches as "too strict" and out of sync with their views of what women should do, especially regarding proscriptions on attire and behavior. Vera also mentioned, as others did, that the Catholic Church "repels people," because it demanded that godparents for any sacrament be married in the church, and many in San Alejo were not.

In fact, this was a major reason for Estrella, the photographer in town, to have stayed away from church. "It's probably not correct for me to say this," she explained, "but I've been a good person. Even if it's just a little bit of water, I give it to my neighbors. I do what I can for others, and maybe that's why God blesses me so much. I've never lacked my beans and tortillas. I help others, so God helps me." She had been Evangelical, but her second husband was Catholic, so in the eyes of the Catholic Church he was still married to his first wife. Because he "lived in sin," the priest refused to baptize their son. Estrella was particularly annoyed because her husband, unable to have any children with his first wife, went to ask for "the miracle of a child" from el Señor de Esquipulas, a famous image of Christ believed to be miraculous, located about two hours from San Alejo. A few days after her husband's pilgrimage to Esquipulas, she became pregnant. "Our son is a gift from

God," she said, "born big, healthy, and admired by everyone at the hospital." Thus she resented the irony that when her husband asked for a miracle and obtained it, the church refused to recognize it by not baptizing the boy. In her words:

> So we can't baptize him. This priest says that we lived in adultery. And well, it's true, we understood this. But it bothered me that the priest refused to baptize him. I live with that thing in my heart that bothers me, but I always ask God, 'Please help me.' That's how I talk with God. I speak with him like that. "Look, God," I tell him, "can you please help me today?" Every day, every morning in my room, I ask for his help, like in a conversation. And this is my only help. It's only God with me. So I just keep religion to myself, to my private moments when I pray. It should be a private thing for everyone, don't you think? No, no churches of any kind for me.

Isabel, who was "in between" churches and had not made up her mind yet whether to convert to Evangelicalism at a church not far from her house, found something else about the Catholic church in San Alejo that bothered her. One afternoon we were sitting in the living room of her house talking about "accepting Christ," as the Evangelicals refer to conversion, and seeing that she was already sympathetic to what Evangelicalism had to offer, I inquired why she had not already accepted Christ. "Because there has not been an opportunity yet," she responded, "but I am enchanted [with Evangelicalism] because in it there are no criticisms, no bad talk about others, no judging of any kind. And what I like the most is that the pastor doesn't talk about things that don't belong to the church. I don't like that this priest talks about things outside church when one goes there for the mass, [one does] not [want] to hear about how the poor are doing or how badly they're living; everyone knows they're in bad shape, don't you believe that? I think he should just focus, like the pastor does, on what the Bible says and not on things that don't belong in church." Isabel, who lived in the center of town and was related to the well-known and wealthier families, said that at the evangelical church no one judged her, and this made her feel comfortable. Hortencia, however, who lived day-to-day on the outskirts of town, had the opposite impression:

> I do find consolation in God, but I don't go to any church. I'll be frank with you. Once I went to church and I wore my *caitíos* [small *caites;* footwear worn mostly by the poor], and people looked at me. I felt really bad, humiliated, so I said no. In my house no one judges me, in my house I pray to God, I pray to him crying or in any other way, and since I know he is everywhere, I know he will listen to me from wherever I am. God is great and has never left me abandoned. I know that if I have a big preoccupation,

> I only have to ask, and he sends me the people who love me, those I have helped, and they bring me this or that thing. So I don't count on religions [churches]; I only count on God and my neighbors and some people who have more or less helped me when I have asked.

Thus it seemed that the women's socioeconomic standing shaped their views of the church.[6]

The San Alejo women's complaints about the Catholic church prompted me to visit the priest sooner than I had planned. When the women brought up the church and religiosity in our conversations, I knew I needed to talk with the priest and the pastors, but the women's complaints about the Catholic church, in particular, the priest, sparked my interest and added a bit of urgency to my plans. When I went to visit one of the evangelical pastors, he received me immediately and told me he had been expecting my visit; he knew I was in town and had heard I was interested in "religious things." His expectation was probably due in part to some of the women in his congregation inviting me to their church and asking me to contemplate converting to Evangelicalism. However, when I went to the Catholic church to make an appointment to talk to the priest, I was surprised that his schedule was completely full for weeks. He was unavailable then, and he was going to be unavailable in the future, I was informed. Even after the receptionist made sure I was Catholic, it did not help to clear a slot in the priest's calendar. In fact, on learning that I would be in town one more week, the receptionist said that the priest would only have an opening available after my departure. This coincidence was just too curious, so I informed the receptionist I would try to meet the priest one day after mass. She told me he was extremely busy and never had time to talk to people after mass, but since I was Catholic I was welcome to attend the Via Crucis (Stations of the Cross) that the priest held on Fridays at 5:00 A.M.; she was sure he would be happy to talk to me at that time. So I did. I got to church earlier than five o'clock, observed the Stations of the Cross with the other congregants, and then talked with the priest briefly. He was quiet and a bit shy, but he seemed friendly. He was rushing off to say mass in the next town, so we agreed that I should come a little later in the day to talk. He said he would inform the receptionist that we had met and that I would be making an appointment to see him. Later it became obvious that my initial difficulties gaining access to the priest had more to do with his tepid relations with ladinos in town than with his demanding work schedule.

The meeting early that morning did not clarify for me why some of the women complained about the priest, except for a glimpse provided by his brief reference to making sure that the poor in San Alejo, who work from dawn to dusk, should have a chance to hear the Word of God as the reason he started his work so early in the day. Indeed, the priest's words matched the backgrounds of those who were present at that early morning service; they were mostly the poor people in town. Later it was the self-appointed historian of San Alejo who explained to me why "the people don't like this priest." In his words: "I don't think it's escaped you that we have a Maya as priest, and this has presented us with challenges here. Look, like you, I've been Catholic for generations, but having this priest here has been problematic. [Catholic] people from here were already inclined to convert, let's say, but having a Maya priest, who's more concerned with providing social services than with taking care of the church's religious matters, is not good. Aleja a la gente [He pushes people away]." The historian inadvertently pointed to a key difference the church can make between normalizing the predicament of marginalized groups by reinforcing the necessity to endure on the one hand and inspiring them to respond to abuse and exploitation on the other. Disappointed in the social justice approach with which the Catholic priest conducted business, the historian opined, "The church should teach those people [the poor and the Mayas] to be patient with their situation, not to protest and start thinking that they can also have what others have, no? Otherwise it becomes a political and not a spiritual church [smiles]. Don't you think so?"[7]

Ofelia, who worked at the health post, made similar comments: "One sees that he [the Catholic priest] says a lot of masses for the poor people, or anything that they ask him, he gives them attention; but the people who are not *pobrecitos* [poor]? No, he gives them excuses. If for any reason he says mass for people who are not poor, it's a wedding or something like that. He treats people badly. So do you blame the people for not going to church?" The self-appointed historian also made a reference to the priest that left me startled. "And to be frank with you," he continued, "I have no idea who thought of sending this *padrecito* [little priest] to a town like ours; the only explanation is that he must have had a problem in the Altiplano and he was sent here as punishment [smiles]. It's obvious; the fact that he is Maya makes his work very difficult here. I'm not lying to you. This has left us with a segregated church; the people from here, old families, you understand?

And on the other hand, the priests' people." This man's words reverberated in my mind for a long time. Just as the injuries that come from exploitation, malnutrition, and other forms of structural violence shape the views women had of the church and their participation in religious activities, those that come from racism and other forms of symbolic and everyday violence also affect these views (and actions). As I discuss later, the poor people in town had decidedly different views of the Catholic priest and his activities.[8]

Turning to the Altiplano, some of the women there also mentioned that they did not go to any church, and like the women in a similar position in San Alejo, they would list all the religious activities in which they participated outside the confines of a congregation. In contrast to the critical opinions of the Catholic church (specifically, of the priest) that I heard in San Alejo, the women in the Altiplano had markedly more positive views of their local church. No doubt, this had to do with the different meaning the social justice work of the Catholic Church had for the women of the Altiplano. Consequently, the reasons for not attending church that the "nonreligious" women in the Altiplano gave had to do with their own situations, not with critical views of the church. For instance, Martina, a devout Catholic, said that although she believed in God she could not attend church: "El nene es muy chillón [The baby cries too much], and I can't go out with him, so I am always home with him." In lieu of not attending church regularly, Martina had built a large altar in the living room of her house. It contained small sculpted images of her favorite saints as well as votive candles, garlands, and flowers, and it occupied a good third of the front room space. With admiration for the large and ornate display, I asked how she came to build it. "This is how my faith in God is," she said, "and since I can't go to mass, I have this dedication to God in my house." Marta's situation was similar to Martina's. She could not attend church regularly, so she venerated the Blessed Sacrament at her home altar. I noticed that Marta's and Martina's altars, though much larger than others in town, were not an exception. Indeed, these home altars—of varying sizes and degrees of ornamentation—were rather common in the Altiplano, but I did not see any in San Alejo's Catholic homes.

In contrast to San Alejo, the strong presence and influence of the Catholic church in the Altiplano was undeniable, even among non-Catholics, Evangelicals, and the "nonreligious." Several times in my field notes I made reference to the presence of Catholicism; on one occasion I wrote, "The Catholic presence is superstrong here—people don't even notice it." Whereas several women in San Alejo said that they were not religious and kept their faith to themselves by praying in the solitude of their homes, I only came across one woman in the Altiplano, Lita's cousin, who professed not to have a religion. However, she still had both of her children baptized in the Catholic Church. A bit curious, I asked her why the children were baptized when she and her husband had "no religion." "Well," she said, "because we don't have any [religion], we thought that at least we should baptize them." As scholars have noted in other areas of Latin America (Brusco 1995; Freston 1998), in the Altiplano it seemed that Catholicism was the "default" religion, though this is declining in some areas. To confirm my assessment, a convert to Evangelicalism explained to me the importance of a child having godparents: "It is important for the patojos to have godparents because godparents will guide them and keep them from perdition. It's another set of parents for them. So it's good to have them." She paused for a moment, we were both quiet, and then as if to correct a mistake, she added, "So in my [evangelical] church we are all like *padrinos* [godparents] for all the patojos."

Like the San Alejo women, the women in the Altiplano who had converted to Evangelicalism were quick to describe the conditions under which they converted. And they mentioned events specific to that region of Guatemala, such as the direct political violence they had experienced or the 1976 earthquake that devastated the town. Marisela directly points to the violence in explaining her conversion.

> During the violence, around thirteen or fourteen years ago, we were working here when someone came to tell us that my husband's name was on a list with the army, so his sister and brother came [to the house] and told him that he needed to leave until the danger was over. So he went to Salcajá. I was pregnant; I had two months left, so he wasn't here when the baby was born. He said that he prayed and prayed at a Catholic church there [in Salcajá], but the army would come there, looking for people; one morning he had to flee the church. So he thought that it was better to pray at another church and switched. He became Evangelical. And I used to go visit him, and so he told me that it was better for me to accept Christ because he had switched, and so I did, too.

Erminia, a devout Catholic, explained that her entire family, except for her, had converted after the 1976 earthquake.[9] She referred to their conversion as having "gone" to another church. Her father had already converted before the earthquake, but her mother and her other siblings did so right afterward. In her words, "I trust that there is only one God and one true church, and that's why I'm staying in my church until I die." She also confided that her godparents had been very good to her, and when her mother "left for the *culto* (evangelical services), and I was left very sad, my godmother and godfather were with me." In addition, Erminia's church had a range of programs to serve women, children, the elderly, and the sick, and she was active in several of them. Erminia's sister, Flor, a jovial woman known in town for her *bondad* (kindness), told me that her evangelical church also had several programs to address different needs and that in fact she was a counselor in the youth program that informed the patojos about drugs, venereal disease, and HIV/AIDS. Thus perhaps in the context of the Altiplano, and in contrast to that of San Alejo, both churches provided avenues for women to enact what Jane Jaquette (1989) refers to as a new feminism that does not necessarily contradict women's role as caregivers and mothers. The work of both churches in the Altiplano in pushing for change and improvement in the lives of their members, therefore, seemed more aligned with what scholars have noted in other regions of Latin America but not with what I observed in San Alejo at the time I conducted my fieldwork.

BRIDGES AND SPACES FOR SOLACE AND SOLIDARITY

Through their churches the women of San Alejo had opportunities to create and maintain various ties, mostly with other women. Robert Wuthnow's (2002) analytic distinction of religious involvement in the formation of social capital is relevant here. He distinguishes between bonding—the interpersonal solidarity among people in small groups, local communities, and other settings over a period that occurs more easily in homogeneous groups—and bridging, which consists of less intimate, or "weak," ties between heterogeneous groups. Whereas bonding can be regarded as social capital insofar as it provides emotional support, friendship, and assistance needed in times of crises, bridging provides the means to stem divisiveness, and to encourage civic responsibility and tolerance in the larger society. Furthermore, Wuthnow (2002) distinguishes two forms of bridging social capital. Identity-bridging social capital is based on networks that span groups defined along cultural differences, with the possibilities for learning through working together, and status-bridging social capital refers to networks that span vertical arrangements of power, influence, wealth, and prestige, which link rank-and-file members of society and elites. Wuthnow (2002) observes that religious involvement may generate status-bridging social capital, because places of worship provide spaces where relationships that cut across vertical social arrangements (e.g., friendships with high-status people) may flourish. Also, congregational leaders themselves are likely to be sources of status-bridging social capital, for they represent links to larger networks for the congregants. Although these insights are based on research in U.S. religious congregations and refer to the links between congregation-based ties and the generation of social capital, they are relevant to my study in that the women viewed their church-based ties as providing a range of support and access to other forms of resources (even if these did not always improve their conditions).

For Mirna, in San Alejo, active participation in the Catholic church provided vital support from people linked in various ways to the church, especially her comadres and compadres, her children's godparents. She was also grateful to other church members for keeping her in their prayers and for asking her how she was doing; she felt compelled to reciprocate whenever she could. And she was looking forward to a new free clinic for the very poor that the priest was about to open, because she and her children often went without any medical care at all. Thus, in her eyes, "the Catholic church gives me whatever I need; it's my *apoyo* [support]." María Ruth's family was in the *hermandades* (brotherhoods),[10] but she did not have time to participate in more activities because there were several children to care for at home. However, María Ruth went to mass every Sunday. Her children's godparents, all active in the church, had helped her in many ways, from providing her with advice and a kind word to clothes, shoes, and food for the children: "They have helped me a lot; they even help me with my husband and his drinking. They say that they will make sure that my oldest son doesn't turn out like the father. They are very Catholic and always make sure that the girls go to the groups at church so they are good girls." As is often the case, the godparents were better off financially, and María Ruth reciprocated their kindness by going to their house to clean or cook when their housekeeper did not show up to work. Although Susana went to mass every Sunday and felt she could count on the priest for advice and moral, even material, support in an emergency, she confided that she did not consider female church members close friends because they gossiped too much. But Teresa could not find enough words to explain how crucial the priest's advice had been to her when she was pregnant with her second child. Since the baby's father was married to another woman in town, Teresa "suffered humiliations," as she put it. Perhaps sensing that Teresa might consider an abortion, the priest made sure that she found dignity in her condition. In her words: "The priest said, 'Look, you can be cursed by others but blessed by God because there is nothing more blessed to God than a child. So have your child. Hold your head up and walk straight. Don't ever be ashamed to bring a child to the world.' So I was able to walk in the streets even when I knew people were eating me alive. He gave me strength."

Ivette, the ladina who lived in the Altiplano, said that being an Evangelical was key to her interactions with the Mayas around her, as this was one of the most important aspects of herself that she shared with others. Since she often felt different in the Altiplano, mostly because she did not speak Kaqchikel and did not wear traje, being an Evangelical made her feel closer to others and part of the family,

> Because everyone, my sisters-in-law, my husband, everyone, communicates through Christ; we are all brothers and sisters in Christ, so everyone helps me with whatever. The people from this town don't know me well, but I have the people from church who know me. If I'm sick, the sisters from church visit me. I'm in the church's choir, so if I don't show up they come to the house to see what happened, why I didn't go. And they pray for me. I go to the temple Sunday, Monday, Thursday, and Friday, so if I'm absent they notice. I don't receive material help, but the support and advice I get from them is more than pure gold. You should see how they have helped me calm my nerves.

In both the Catholic and the evangelical churches in San Alejo women generally found support from coreligionists as well as from the leader. Mercedes noted that it was the pastor's wife who was there for her in a difficult situation; she trusted this woman and felt that she had experience counseling others, and thus she could speak with her more easily than with others at church. In turn, Mercedes shared her knowledge, experiences, and views with other women from church, in particular, younger ones. She attended her temple on Tuesday, Wednesday, Thursday, and Sunday, which gave her ample opportunities to have significant contact both with the pastor's wife and with the younger women whom she counseled. Others mentioned that if they were ill the pastor and church members would take up a collection and bring them food or money for medicine and would check on them until they were well. Andrea confided that she did not have friends and felt isolated, a perception confirmed by others in town. She only talked with the pastors and sisters from church. In fact, she felt so at ease in that religious milieu that she frequented more than one evangelical church and attended several services per week. She went to these services for advice and comfort. "That helps me with my problems, with my nerves," she said. "It helps me a lot to hear others; they tell me to be patient, to have faith, not to despair, and that is comforting to me."

The organizational structure and size of the evangelical churches seemed to fit well with an orientation to providing individualized attention, which the women deeply appreciated. As is the case in other evangelical churches, the pastors in San Alejo had a personal relationship with the members and always seemed to be available at a crucial moment. The small size of these churches, compared to the larger congregations that characterize the Catholic Church, permitted this level of interaction and closeness. And although not all evangelical churches were of the same size, all were smaller than their Catholic counterparts, and the members seemed to know each other well. The frequency of attendance at services—three to four times a week—facilitated regular interaction, so the pastor knew the women rather well (and their needs, preoccupations, and goals), and the women knew of other women's situations. Thus Gloria turned to her pastor for all forms of guidance; he even "fixed" a problem Gloria had with a gossipy neighbor. The pastor not only counseled Gloria on what to do—he suggested avoiding and ignoring the neighbor—but also spoke with the neighbor's pastor, who in turn talked with the neighbor about the dangers of gossip. The gossip subsided, and Gloria was grateful to the pastor for his intervention. I had an opportunity to attend services at a relatively large evangelical church where Nena and some of the better-off women in town prayed and also to go to services at the house where Silvia and Mireya lived with their in-laws (and where I sometimes saw their daughter, Ivette). Their father-in-law was the pastor of a small church (the services were held in their living room) and also owned a barbershop, located next to the living room; sometimes when the living room proved too small they used the barbershop to accommodate congregants. It always seemed a bit artful to see the congregants sitting on the barber chairs, amid the combs and razors and faces reflected in the mirrors while singing songs of praise. Every time I visited I was welcomed, and I always found an open attitude when I inquired about their activities. It was this family who helped me out when I locked myself out of my room (the incident I mentioned in chapter 3).

Although the women found comfort and a convivial atmosphere in their churches, not all could go as often as they wanted to. They had to care for small children, do chores at home, and work for pay to sustain their families. Also, the services, especially at the evangelical churches, were frequently held in the evening and ended late at night, which posed additional challenges. Many women did not go out at night, either because they did not want to be seen walking in the streets then or because it was quite dangerous, especially on the outskirts of town. Thus the social context in which the women lived sometimes interfered with their religious participation. In this case some women were cut off from what perhaps was, in their eyes, their most important source of solace and support.

In the Altiplano many women were active in congregations and groups in both evangelical and Catholic churches. Erminia attended mass every Sunday but was also involved in a number of Catholic groups, including one that visited the sick and another that visited individuals in prison. She also worked with a group that took up collections of food, sugar, salt, and beans to take to the very poor in her church. Erminia drew on her religious beliefs to understand reciprocity: "One understands that one needs, and others need too. It's our duty to help others, our neighbors, everyone. God wants us to do favors. This is how I understand it. You help me, and I help you, but it is all God's help." One of her neighbors, Antonia, immediately mentioned Erminia when I asked to whom she turned for help and support: "As I told you, I go to my neighbor [Erminia]; sometimes she lends me a little, and when I have something I give her from what I have. This is how we live; in the church it is like this." Similar to the women in San Alejo, the women in the Altiplano who regularly attended church turned to coreligionists, leaders, and compadres and to church-based ties for a wide range of support. Isa said the priest had assured her that she should not hesitate to ask him or anyone in church for a favor. She had seen how the church had helped her in-laws not only with advice and emotional support during their crises but also with material and financial assistance, and when Isa's son was ill, she turned to the church for the comfort that comes from prayer but also for much-needed funds to purchase medicine. The Catholic prayer group had even gone to her house to pray for a sick child when Isa was not able to make it to church. She was visibly moved by these expressions of care. And Alberta had an endless list of concrete situations that demonstrated how much her church had helped her, mostly with advice and prayer, to deal with her husband's drinking. However, not all women who attended religious services regularly saw this space in the same way. For instance, Amelia, who confessed she was "in between" the evangelical and Catholic churches because she liked both, said that she entrusted all her troubles and tribulations to the Blessed Sacrament because it was the only one with the power to help and therefore the only one that should hear her problems. "I sometimes think that if I tell my problems to other people, they won't tell it like I told it to them. They will change it, and then I am left without a solution and probably only with gossip. So I only trust the Blessed Sacrament, and he gives me an answer."

In the Altiplano there were also specific links to the violence in the region that shaped the women's views of participation in church groups. Rosita said that she had received quite a bit of help from the Catholic church, especially from a group that helped widows of the violence with anything they needed in the house, such as repairs their disappeared husbands used to take care of. Indeed, this group had just come to fix a leaky roof in her dining room. However, she had declined to take part in the church's activities, especially in ministry groups. She was fearful to do so because of what had happened to people who had been active in committees and other community affairs; they were suspected of sympathizing with the opposition and had been disappeared or killed during the violence. This had happened to her husband and to his older sister, a woman in her forties who was active in church and was taken from her home one day in the early morning hours. Her badly tortured body was found three days later. This abduction prompted the family to move to Guatemala City the same day the sister was disappeared, and there her husband was disappeared a few months later, never to be found. Thus Rosita tried not to be involved in anything that required an organization or a committee, she said, due to the fear and sadness that she says will never leave her heart: "So I don't ask for advice, maybe that's why I continue to fail in what I do [smiles]. Receiving advice is good because it makes you want to live, but then you never know what can happen. When you've gone through what we went through, when I thought I was going to die from so much sadness and despair, you take life differently. I now realize that I didn't die, that I continued to make my tortillas and my weaving, that my children grew up. But there is a part of me that will never be the same. And this is the part of me that still has that fear inside."

Once, I wrote in my field notes about how serious, it seemed to me, people in the Altiplano took ties of compadrazgo, no doubt in reaction to the relatively looser ties of compadrazgo I observed in San Alejo. By this I do not mean to imply that compadrazgo ties were weak or had disappeared in San Alejo, because even the nonreligious or those leaning toward Evangelicalism had either baptized their children or had given them a set or two of godparents.[11] However, people in the Altiplano seemed to view being godparents as a lifelong responsibility, as the church mandated, and thus godparents seemed to be more involved in the lives of their godchildren than godparents in San Alejo. Asunción always mentioned their godparents when she described the children's activities. The godfather of one of her boys was a tailor and made the child clothes every year and brought him cookies once a month. "It is the duty of godparents," she explained, "to see that their godchildren are fine. A godchild means responsibility. So if one's godchild is ill, of course one goes to see him, to see what one can do." Although Asunción and others said that sometimes they felt *vergüenza* (shame) when asking godparents for help, as it was customary for the godparents to initiate the giving, they did it when the situation *aprieta* (presses). Isa explained the role that her son's godfather plays: "Me da un poquito de pena [I feel a little embarrassed] to go ask him for help. He is a professional; he is a *bachiller* [high school graduate]. And for Christmas or for the town's fiesta he always comes to give the boy a toy, a gift, clothes, or money, and not only to his godchild, but he also gives to my other children." Since godparents are involved in four of the seven Catholic sacraments, people in both towns ended up with multiple sets of godparents (e.g., for baptism, wedding, confirmation, and first communion) and thus with several people on whom to rely for advice and emotional and material support. When the godparents or the child's parents converted to Evangelicalism and became involved in those churches, these ties and the assistance they entail sometimes dissipated.

The women in the Altiplano who frequented evangelical churches always referred to the churches' importance in alleviating their problems. Toñita noted that even though she had never received any financial or material assistance from her church, she had obtained significant moral support, often delivered to her home by a pastor who made a point of doing home visits to the women who were in special need. And as scholars such as Brusco (1995) have noted, the women in the evangelical churches in the Altiplano made special note of how Evangelicalism helped them to deal with the problem of alcoholism. Some mentioned that their husbands had converted and as a result had given up drinking; others said that the church prayed for their husbands so that they would quit drinking. Flor, the health promoter who was an active member of an evangelical church, explained the deep connection she saw between what her church did to eradicate alcoholism—as a problem that affects women—and its religious mission: “Look, I have a cousin who was in Alcoholics Anonymous; he was there for about five years, and then he started drinking again. I have four brothers, two who drank and two who didn’t even drink but were affected. I won’t lie to you, because before God everything is clear and there is only truth, but with God’s great will, all of them stopped drinking when they started going to the evangelical religion. They never went back to drinking. Alcoholics Anonymous could not get these results, but the evangelical church did. Thanks to God we are happy now.”

Dalia, also in the Altiplano, said that her husband stopped drinking when he joined the evangelical church, and they were now trying to convince her brother-in-law to join so that he would stop drinking.[12] Her pastor also kept a close eye on what happened at home and was always there to help, mostly with advice or a kind word in a difficult moment or with prayer when they were ill. Hilaria was grateful for her pastor’s advice to be patient when as a “widow of the violence” (her husband was disappeared) she found herself alone dealing with her children’s behavior and discipline. “The pastor tells me that if one needs anything, we have to ask God with fervor, to have faith, to kneel and ask God and he will give us answers,” she said. She noted that because she and her in-laws always had a lot of work to do in the house and because they were the only Evangelicals on her block, they did not socialize much with the neighbors, which left them with more time to spend at the temple and with members of their church. However, as others did when talking about support and advice from coreligionists, Hilaria offered a word of caution: “I talk to the pastor and appreciate his advice, but with other people [from her church], no. There is no need to waste your time telling them your problems if they can’t help; it would be useless to only hear them say, ‘Ay, poor you, what can you do?’ but the pastor prays and gives advice and sometimes money for medicine. So it’s better to just confide in the pastor.”

Although central to the women’s activities, evangelical churches in the Altiplano were not only about praying and giving advice and comfort. They also helped materially. Gina, for example, received clothing for her eldest child, firewood when she had no money to purchase it, and medicine when someone in her family was ill. And her church even set up *jornadas de salud* (health-day campaigns) to bring medicine to the poor and to visit the sick in hospitals. Thus Gina was thankful to the church because the members provided help when her husband was unwilling or unable (due to his drinking and philandering) to provide for the family. In her words: "Before, when my husband was very irresponsible, they [the pastor and the church] helped me economically, with whatever they could, with corn, beans, firewood, whatever. They even gave me help to study corte y confección. They made sure that I didn't lack anything. They were my refuge." Like the evangelical churches in San Alejo, those in the Altiplano demonstrated a high degree of flexibility to accommodate culturally Catholic practices that were important to the members. Some women mentioned that their evangelical church had adapted the custom of pedidas. Yet, as Flor explained, "it depends on the church, of course. Not all Evangelicals agree. But in our case, our pastor goes with the elders, neighbors, family members to the pedida. You can think of this as *cofradías* [Catholic organizations], something like that we also have in our church. But not everyone agrees."[13]

SPACES WHERE SUFFERING IS NORMALIZED

Many women in San Alejo felt that faith and active participation in religious activities provided an important frame through which they found meaning in their everyday afflictions. In the context of my examination here, by providing meaning, consolation, a framework to understand their predicament, and sometimes opportunities to see others in similar situations, these religious spaces also contributed to normalizing the women's suffering and tribulations. In the absence of actions that would lead to genuine transformation in the women's lives and make women realize that avenues for change were possible, the comfort and solace provided by the churches served mostly to sustain various unequal structures, to internalize and to naturalize them. For instance, Andrea had sought out Evangelicals for comfort; this is how they helped her.

> The Evangelicals are good with advice; they say that one has to be patient, to pray with faith, if one really has faith, God listens. And they teach patience, tell you to be patient. One has to learn to accept. My suffering is so much that *ya tengo ganado el cielo* [I have already earned heaven], and God has given me a beautiful peace that comes from resignation and acceptance. So to me it is a favor, a gift from God that I have learned to accept my situation. The pastor always says, "Have patience with your father." Yesterday, when my father beat me in the kitchen, I was very hurt. Then the pastor

> and brothers and sisters in church told me, "Patience, patience, you already have earned heaven by living with him, remember this is happening only here, only in this world." Their words help my spirit.

In Mercedes's case, her "brother from church" (pastor) told her that whenever she felt depressed and sad about events at home, mostly when her husband would not allow her to do what she wanted, she should pray alone. If fact, this pastor even discouraged the women from sharing their concerns and troubles with other women, in order to avoid gossip. "I almost never like to tell others my problems," Mercedes explained. "What I do is tell God. The brother at church has told us that we should lock ourselves in our room and pray to God with all the strength of our heart, but it's better to pray alone because he is the only one who can solve everything. If we go to a neighbor instead, even if she has similar problems, it could be that she will fail us and start gossip and like that." Not only did this pastor discourage the women from creating a potential space for solidarity with other women by isolating them for prayer, but at the same time his advice (and that of others in the church) served to reinforce gender ideologies that kept women confined to strict roles and vulnerable. This was the case when Mercedes "begged" her husband to let her go to Chicago as her father was dying in that city.

> My husband didn't want to let me go, and I told him, "Look, he is my father, and it's likely that I won't see him ever again," so I called the pastor to intercede [with my husband] on my behalf. "Look, sister," he told me, "I cannot tell you that you should go or not go because in the Bible it says that the married woman is subject to her husband." The only thing I can do is to pray so that the Lord will soften his [her husband's] heart. "That's fine," I said to him. And I was praying when my sister called me to say that my father was in grave condition in Chicago, that the doctor said that he was only waiting for me. But now my problem was even bigger, because I could not leave without my husband's permission. And what about the house, the children? So everyone talked to him, and finally, like the brother [pastor] said, prayer helped and his heart softened and he let me go.

I noticed that in both the Catholic and evangelical churches, the emphasis on the individual, in terms of personal salvation (among Evangelicals) or responsibility for errors (sins for the Catholics), together with efforts on the part of the religious leaders to avoid gossip in the women's lives, seemed to contribute to a feeling of individual culpability and responsibility for the women's suffering. Thus rather than point to external sources of affliction, the solace and kind words women found in religious spaces in San Alejo turned attention on them, and it became *their* problem and responsibility to deal with difficult situations, an approach that also sustains forms of gender, gendered, and structural violence. This was conveyed in the advice the religious leaders (as well as the members) provided: pray, have faith, be patient, endure. If the women did not "pray with faith" or "with all the strength of the heart" it was likely that their problems would not be solved. It was therefore the women's problem—their doubts or wavering faith—that kept them from obtaining the favor from God. And coming with religious authority, these interpretations were key to normalizing the feelings of responsibility and culpability the women felt for their own predicaments. Thus Mirna described her confessions to the priest as an opportunity to recognize her errors (sins) and, of course, to repent; her "errors" included not being more tolerant, questioning her husband about his drinking, and even feeling lazy after getting very few hours of sleep due to all her duties and responsibilities at home. "When one goes to confession," she said, "you can see all the things that one is doing wrong, and one has a chance to reflect and correct them so that they don't lead us to perdition. Sometimes I feel like my thoughts alone can land me in jail, as I imagine very terrible things when I am frustrated. All that is bad, and confession helps me to think that one needs to change. So after I confess, I go to the altar to ask God for forgiveness for all my mistakes." María Ruth also noted the importance of the comforting words from the priest, and from her godparents and others at church, in her struggles with her husband's drinking and abusive behavior. She said, "[My coreligionists] have told us that this is bad, they have told him not to chupar; they give me advice, too, 'Look, do this, don't do this, go to pray,' so when he hits me I go to them and they tell me to be calm, to understand." The women were convinced that since they were advised to put up with the ravages of poverty, their husbands' drinking and philandering, and even gossip, this was "normal life." The problem then became a woman's own character and personality and how she handled these situations.

Women often sought out the churches they attended for help dealing with men's drinking (compounded by extramarital affairs and interpersonal violence, as noted earlier). Nena, who had money and resources to seek professional help for her husband's drinking, resorted to evangelical conversion in the hope that it would help. And in her view, it had. This was not because her husband had converted and given up drinking, because he never did either, but because she herself had changed, tried to live a better life, and, most important, belonged to a church that had given her the support she needed to continue to *endure*. With tears, smiles, sober statements, and a tinge of hope, Nena explained how her ten years in the evangelical church provided the help that doctors and professionals had been unable to give her, even if in the process her husband had not changed one bit, his health had continued to deteriorate daily, and basically nothing had changed at home. In her words: "I have searched everywhere for help and then I converted, by the grace of God, and this is what has helped me the most to continue to live with him. Sometimes my situation makes me want to run away, but no, I have my church, my pastor, and he talks to me a lot. 'Sister, come closer to the Bible,' he says, 'you have to wait and wait.'" Nena attended an Al-Anon group in Guatemala City at least once a month, but in her view nothing compared to the support she received from her pastor and church. However, her participation in the Al-Anon group allowed her to see other situations, and she thought of herself as relatively fortunate. "There, I see other problems," she explained, "like homosexuality, drug addiction, problems that are much graver than mine. This gives me a different perspective and to realize all the good things I have in the church and pastor and in my life." She had implored her husband to stop drinking but not to join the church, because she said he would never consider that. And while her husband would not quit drinking and his health worsened as a result, Nena shared an effective strategy she had learned at church.

> When I want to *desahogarme* [let it all out], I have learned to do that by talking with God; I tell him everything. When it comes to an idea I have about doing something and I need guidance, I consult with the pastor or with his wife, and they give me advice. 'Look, Pastor René, I am thinking of doing this and that,' and he tells me if it is good or not. Same with his wife; I trust her a lot. They give me advice with everything: house, husband, children, everything. I make sure I am not deviating from what I am supposed to do, what is supposed to be my purpose on this earth. And I realize I need patience.

I came across two cases in San Alejo that conform to what other scholars have observed regarding the place of evangelical churches in altering men's behavior to the betterment of women. Two men had converted with the specific purpose of putting a stop to their drinking, and they had achieved their goal. Both were the sons of the barber-pastor who himself had converted for the same purpose about a decade earlier. This pastor's sons were the husbands of Silvia and Mireya.

Mireya remembered how her father-in-law had asked his son to give himself to God because that would cure him. The son had done that two years earlier, and now he sang in church and traveled to other cities in Guatemala, including the town in the Altiplano where I was doing my fieldwork, because his sister, Ivette, lived there, to sing, and he was active in the church. Thus Mireya credited the evangelical church (and her father-in-law's intervention) with this major change in her life.

Nena explained that she did not rely only on the pastor and his wife for advice and support but mentioned the broader membership of the church in this regard as well. "Whoever it is," she said, "I pick up the phone and tell them what I need, and they are here quickly. No one has ever said no. This is probably why I feel so good at church. I've never experienced a scornful look or contempt from anyone about my situation, not even a bad look or some comment." Nena's sincere appreciation for the absence of such expressions points to their presence (and normality) in the lives of women in similar situations, as women are often seen as culpable for or at least complicit in their suffering. Nena recounted an incident when another woman who also had a husband who drank made a hurtful comment to her: "She tried to humiliate me here, in front of my house. We were talking and she tells me, 'Look, don't feel bad about living with a drunk because that's what your husband is, a drunk.' It made me feel ashamed, humiliated." Nena then took this opportunity to tell me about how the Bible and the Gospel have helped her: "But I am a Christian, I need to contain myself. I didn't respond the way I would have before. Because if there is an area in which the Gospel has helped me, it's in taming my temper. It has helped me to be more restrained, to control myself and not say what goes through my mind. I really have tried to change, to be another person. The Lord has helped me to be a better person, quieter, and really docile person." And she could not have been more grateful for her coreligionists' words of encouragement: "All my brothers and sisters in church tell me, 'Look, poor guy, your husband, be patient, *aguántelo* [endure, put up with him]; he is like that because of his illness. May God help him and you.'" Nena insisted that I accompany her to church so that I could see for myself what she had been telling me. I accepted her invitation and attended a service during which the pastor reiterated the advice to women that Nena had mentioned. One day I attended services when a Puerto Rican pastor visiting from New York City was the guest preacher. He talked about the virtues of a *familia unida* (intact, cohesive family) and the vital importance that women's tolerance, sacrifices, and understanding had for such families (as opposed to women who complain about their situations at home). According to this pastor, a familia unida was what God wanted from all of us. In a nod to the largely female attendance at the service and to underscore the importance of women to their families and the church, he observed, "In fact, it is virtuous women, those who don't deviate, who sustain us with their sacrifices, the ones who give us faith." To this, the San Alejo pastor raised his hands and invited the congregation to respond in agreement with a loud "Alleluia, hermanos [brothers and sisters]!"

Some women felt that because their situation was so serious and because they had been scorned for it, they could not turn to religious congregations to help them. A few months before she died of HIV/AIDS complications, Leticia said that she did not feel she could ask anyone at church for help. In fact, she had never talked to the priest about her condition, because she felt so humiliated and embarrassed about what people thought about her. However, rather than pray alone as women who did not attend religious congregations did, Leticia opted for going to church to pray. I asked her if she had opportunities to talk with people while she was there. "No, I don't talk with anyone," she said. "I stay there for a little while. I sit in the last pew in the back, say my prayers, put my troubles in God's hands, and leave. One doesn't go there to talk." As Leticia's disease progressed and the havoc it wreaked became more noticeable on her body, she avoided contact with most people, and though she was aware of the benefit of going to church she had stopped going to mass in the last months of her life—"*para no incomodar* [not to bother others]," Tita, her sister, said. Leticia's case stands in sharp contrast to that of Nena, a contrast that exposes the difference that social class makes in how women mobilize the social resources around them.

The messages of the churches and the experiences of the women in the Altiplano were similar to those I observed in San Alejo. With the exception of some circumstances that were specific to the Altiplano (to which I turn at the end of this section), the cases there seemed to mirror, and to make more vivid, those from San Alejo. Thus the churches in the Altiplano—both Catholic and evangelical—also conveyed similar messages of resignation, tolerance, and the importance of women's sacrifices for the good of their families, and these churches underscored the women's responsibility to disregard their own well-being in favor of a healthy and unified family. The churches also provided a framework to normalize unequal structures in women's lives. Thus Toñita explained that something that had helped her in her life and to understand her position in her family was the Bible: "We are Evangelicals and are close to the Bible, and it says that the man is the head of the woman, just as Christ is the head of the church. We have taken this into account, so when my husband tells me, 'We're going to put the boy in this or in that school,' it's fine I say, if that is what you think, with pleasure, we'll do that, and then we enroll the boy in the school he chooses." When her husband was out of town working, she was in charge of making decisions at home because her husband trusted her principles, she said. Flor echoed Toñita's views of the place of women in relation to men, which, she said, was the way it should be, as this is what the Bible said. But Flor introduced a caveat: "The one who makes most of the decisions is the head, the husband, but usually they [husband and wife] have to be in agreement."

As did the women in San Alejo, many in the Altiplano mentioned the advice they received and the comfort that came from prayer as important benefits they derived from attending church. Alberta turned to neighbors and people from church for help when her husband came home drunk wanting to start a fight. When that happened she and the children would run out of the house and return the next morning. She appreciated the encouragement of neighbors and people from church, who always had a kind word for her. "God willing, pray to God for all your problems, because only God can help you. Put yourself in God's hands so your problems are solved. But men don't listen; they fall for the bottle," she said. She had tried on numerous occasions to take him to the Catholic church she attended, and he went, but instead of listening to the advice the people there tried to provide, her husband criticized them for trying to interfere in his life. She had told him that people meant well, and she appreciated their advice because neither she nor her husband had living parents to turn to anymore. She noted that people from the church did not help them with material assistance, but for her it was their advice that was even more valuable.

Like Alberta, other women in the Altiplano took their husbands to church, or at least tried to, in the hope that their spouses would turn their lives around and discover the power of God (in Catholic churches) or of conversion (in evangelical churches). Once in a while this strategy worked and produced the expected results, but in many cases it did not. Occasionally the objective was attained but usually not due to a transformation in the men's faith. Thus Gina said that her parents always told her to take her husband to church because it would help stop his drinking. Her husband did stop, but the result she sought did not come from the church.

> My parents, they knew how the power of God works. They would call both of us [Gina and her husband] and would give us advice, to go to church. But you know that sometimes one goes to church as an obligation. Sometimes we would go to church, and then he would tell me, 'Look, I don't feel at ease here,' and he would leave me there and would go get drunk and I'm in church, sitting there. I didn't know what to do, what other solution to find for the problem. Well, I don't know if the prayer and advice helped. But my papa took my husband aside and explained to him what his behavior does, because my papa had been an alcoholic; I never knew that. So my papa made my husband realize what he was doing. This is how he changed.

Isa, in the Altiplano, also was encouraged to take her husband to church to "make him be a responsible husband," but in her case it was his parents who insisted on it. And although she credited prayer with the changes she eventually obtained, it took another kind of intervention to get results. According to her, her in-laws would tell her: "Go to mass and pray, and someday God will help you and he will change." But her husband continued drinking and generally "being irresponsible." Isa also prayed alone: "I prayed by myself that he would change. And I also prayed because I wanted to have a religious wedding; we weren't married before. I suffered for seven years; he was drunk all the time. And I was going to separate because I couldn't stand it. And now we've been married for five years in the church. So I feel that prayer and church helped me a lot." Then she added that her in-laws gave her husband an ultimatum: either he straightened out or they would take away from him the house in which he (and Isa) lived. Isa said that this probably made him reflect on his actions, and soon after that he started behaving well and never had problems again, "thanks to God." Mirian's mother advised her, "Pray for him and for the children so that they don't suffer." But in addition, her mother reminded her, "One of these days he will die and will have to answer to God for what he's done here on earth, and will get what he deserves." Mirian continued, "My mama tells me not to take into account anything he says, to ignore him, that I should care only for me and my children, that I should go out to work and to think that God will be the judge. God will see what's just and what's not."

As in San Alejo, religious leaders in the Altiplano sometimes discouraged the women from sharing their concerns and problems with other women from church so as to prevent gossip. One pastor in the Altiplano was adamant that people in the congregation not share intimate details about a difficult situation they were going through, and he encouraged them either to talk about it with him or directly with God but not with a neighbor. Toñita said that the pastor promoted respect among the members of the congregation because they were all brothers and sisters in Christ but not more than that. "The pastor always reminds us, 'Don't waste your time talking with others, that takes time away from prayer and from your own concerns,' and so we mostly talk with him. I also communicate with God and entrust my *penas* [worries] to him."

Even though prayer and advice did not always help the women achieve the expected outcomes, those who were active in a church did what they could in order to attend a service or a mass. Lita overcame obstacles in order to attend the services at her church, which she described as "my consolation, my support, what keeps me going in this life." She and her husband were both Evangelicals but they attended different churches. This posed difficulties because the services during the week were held in the evening, when it was dark out, and thus she could only go to the temple during the weekend. "We are divided," she laughed. "He goes to an evangelical church around here, and I go to the Centroamericana. He comes from work early and then goes. I would need to leave the house at 6:00 P.M., and the service ends at 8:00 P.M. and that's why I can't go. At night there is no light [electricity] over on this side of the street, all this area here, sí pues, no light, only dark. And it's dangerous for us to be out in the street at night. So I look forward to the weekend so I can go to my church."

There were also religious activities that were context-specific and applied only to the Altiplano. For instance, in Catholic churches there were special collections for the widows of the violence when these women had a special need. And situations like the incident of the Maya Catholic priest in San Alejo arose in the Altiplano, only in reverse, which highlighted the symbolic violence found in the daily practices of racism and exclusion of the Maya in Guatemala. Mirian explained that she lost faith in priests and the church and their potential to help after an incident in which she sought them out:

> We went to seek help from the priest, because people were talking, saying that we were doing witchcraft, just because I felt that we were obtaining results from our prayers. We went to the priest and he said, "Look, all these things, like the evil eye and all that, these are our things, it's all part of our culture, our Mayan culture, and I support you, but in order to see

if there is anything we can do, I would need to speak with Father Freddy, and I don't know if he'll support you." And Father Freddy [a ladino priest] then said, "Ah no, those are things from the devil," and my daughter and I came home crying because we were rejected. This is why we think that the church can't help us. We go to mass and pray, but we never talk to priests or put our trust in them because they can't understand. They think that our Mayan culture, our customs, are a thing of the devil.

CONCLUSION

In this chapter I have presented the women's assessments of the meanings they attach to religious participation, pastors, priests, and congregations, and their coreligionists in general, situating their assessments in the broader context of violence. Although I have not painted an optimistic picture that positions religious spaces as always favorable and deeply transformative, I have not argued that the religious activities in which the women engage are futile expressions or simply the "opium" that sustains them in oppressive situations. Such a picture would invalidate the spaces women create in their churches, which have tremendous meaning for them and allow them to receive solace and comfort. I simply do not place emphasis on the "empowering" potential of the women's religious activities or on what they did religiously in a context in which these practices were confined to women and did not alter in any way the violence in the unequal structures in which they lived.

I am aware that frameworks developed in the United States or in Europe are often used to assess the lives of women in poorer societies and how relying on lenses developed outside those societies can produce erroneous images. As Patricia Chuchryk (1989) notes for the Chilean case she studied, it is the women who should define what is transformative in their activities, and external assessments (and actions) should be based on the women's needs and concerns. Thus I do not use a yardstick that is out of sync with the specific realities of the women in my study to claim that their religious activities are not empowering or transformative because they do not conform to a certain standard and that they should oppose tradition in order to significantly challenge the status quo and the multiple structures of inequality in which they live. At the same time, I cannot argue that the women's religious participation (and what they do religiously) in San Alejo has led to empowerment or positive change, as noted for evangelical churches in other studies. Even if women congregate religiously and are thereby comforted in coping with their daily lives, generally speaking, these activities do not alter the fundamental frames and internalized dispositions that shape gender role expectations, do not help to get women out of poverty, do not bring needed medical care and dignified jobs, do not change the effects of gossip, and thus do not fundamentally alter the women's lives at home or in the community or push for gender justice. As such, religious participation, although perceived in a positive light by the women involved, seemed more akin to an analgesic that temporarily relieved certain kinds of pain than to a cure. This was especially the case in San Alejo. Even the potentially transformative progressive messages based on the teachings of liberation theology in the Catholic Church and its preferential option for the poor did not flourish in that context because the symbolic violence and the wounds to the self that come from racism stifled the priest's actions. Similarly, the potential for evangelical churches to bring real change to the lives of the women (and men), as has been observed in other studies of evangelicals in Guatemala (see Annis 1987), was hampered because the only evangelical churches that seemed to thrive in San Alejo were those with a strong Pentecostal bent that focus on individual salvation and a direct personal experience with God through prayer.[14]

My comments may not fall in line with positive assessments of religious participation noted in other studies, but when women turn to a pastor because their home environments are a torment or they cannot purchase food for their children, and their religious leaders and coreligionists advise them to endure and tell them that they already have earned heaven on account of their suffering, it is hard to make a case for genuine improvement in the women's lives. Or when the women are told to "pray with faith" but their problems continue, not only do they feel guilty for not being "true believers," but they also feel responsible for being unable to improve their situations. The same goes for the women who, desperately seeking a remedy for a curable ailment, go to church to ask for help because they have no money for medicine, and though they receive much-needed consolation and the benefit of a kind word, their children continue to lack medicine, the women and their families continue to be hungry, their health continues to deteriorate, or one (or more) of their children dies. In such situations it is difficult to make a case for improvement or empowerment coming from religious involvement.

I certainly do not mean to negate the observations about the benefits that women in other contexts have derived from their religious participation (and conversion), even in other regions of Guatemala. In many ways, when I started to examine this aspect of the San Alejo women's lives, it was the direction in which I thought my observations would take me. And I cannot deny that, as has happened elsewhere, in the process of coming together religiously, a shift may take place (Hallum 2003): women may begin to consciously demand gender equality and to struggle for their rights (Molyneux 1985) and to address the consequences of the multiple sources of violence that assault their daily lives, such as inadequate health care, poverty, exploitative working conditions, gender ideologies that diminish women's contributions to their households, and abusive relationships that also humiliate them in public. But that is not what these religious spaces provided for the women of San Alejo at the time I observed them. There, religion came closer to offering only a "'divine' explanation of the order of things in this world," in the words of Martín-Baró (1991d: 348). And as the fine scholarship that has examined these issues also has noted, religious activities, their expression and meaning, are context-specific and socio-historically bounded. Thus in the eastern Guatemalan context on which I base my observations, where I focused my attention on the lives of women in the context of violence, not with the specific objective to study religious participation (as studies of religious participation have done), I have come to see this sphere of women's lives less as a black-and-white picture and more as a space interwoven with other structures of inequality that contributes to sustain suffering and pain for the women involved. Finally, I do not mean to present a flat image of the work of these churches as simply a tool that reinforces patriarchy and women's subordination. The religious spaces in San Alejo and the general context of violence that I have set out to call attention to are mutually constitutive in a dynamic fashion. My portrayal introduces a cautionary note that highlights the complexity of the situation and points to both the benefits and the detriments of religious spaces; it shows how the women I came to know in Guatemala lived this aspect of their lives.

CHAPTER 8

Enduring Violence

REFLECTIONS ON THE STUDY OF VIOLENCE IN WOMEN'S LIVES

My primary goal in this book has been to shed light on the often hidden sources of violence and suffering in the everyday lives of Guatemalan women. I have argued that violence does not reside only in individuals' intentional acts to inflict pain on others. Instead, my analysis has pointed to the multiple sources of violence and away from the motivations of individuals, in an attempt to redirect the analytical gaze to the violence that comes from the economic, social, and political structures that generate suffering in the lives of women. Even as I have made use of individual cases of injurious acts to make points about structures of violence, because these acts concretize the violence I examine, I have emphasized that such actions are not solely the product of individuals' motivations but are shaped by the structures of violence in which people live. The kinds of violence I have discussed affect everyone in different ways, shaping the actions of those who act as well as the lives of those who suffer. I have told stories about how mothers, mothers-in-law, sisters, and female friends and neighbors actively participate in and normalize the infliction of pain on other women, not because they are violent individuals who behave aggressively, but because their lives are embedded in the same violent structures and the cognitive frames they use to guide their actions and understandings of the world are shaped by the social violence of institutions (Kleinman 2000) and are part of the "order of things." As Bourdieu and Wacquant (2004: 272) observed, "Of all the forms of 'hidden persuasion,' the most implacable is the one exerted, quite simply, by the *order of things*" (original emphasis). In the same vein, pointing to individuals as the source of women's suffering would undermine my analytic endeavor and defeat the purpose of my project, as the men also live in and their views and actions are shaped by the same structures of violence, and they too internalize power inequalities, systems of domination, and dispositions that sustain violent structures. As such, throughout the chapters of this book I have spotlighted the fundamental role that extrapersonal structures play in the production and reproduction of indignities, suffering, and violence in intimate spaces as well as in institutions. As Ellen Moodie (2006) did in her analysis of microbus crashes in El Salvador, I have broadened the analytic focus to include other categories of suffering that are undervalued in institutional discourses.

The forms of violence I have discussed are embedded in institutions, ideologies, and perceptions of behavior for women and men that seep through the quotidian, the normal, the familiar and generate fear, insecurity, and anguish in the lives of women, in ways that are not dissimilar in other contexts around the world (see Kristof and WuDunn 2009). It is through the comingling with formal structures that nonvisible forms of violence become normalized, routinized, and even legitimized and, as such, misrecognized. Each event in the women's life cycle that I examined—marriage, childbearing, entry into the labor force—added layers that allow us to see how women experienced multiple disadvantages, but each layer also permitted the women to speak about matters that remain invisible, naturalized, and silenced in their lives.

Out of necessity, however, this book has been about more than that, because while violent structures generate suffering they can also create spaces with the potential for gendered agency and sociability. Thus I also have discussed how women, as wives, mothers, workers, and religious individuals, turn to those familiar to them for succor but not without noting the complexities and contradictions involved in these everyday interactions, as they also take place within the same "social order of things" in which injurious interactions become normalized. Therefore, I do not present these social ties simply as sources of support, as they do not always take place on a terrain devoid of tension. Gossip, for instance, can create solidarity and boundaries in a particular group, but when it comingles with exclusion, inequalities, orthodox gender ideologies, and patriarchal structures, it emerges as a form of social control that permeates actions, perceptions, and expectations of behavior and generates fear, anxiety, and pain that exacerbates deeply unequal relations. However, noting the central place of the women's social worlds is fundamental for an understanding of how they respond to the conditions they face. It also makes evident that the social sphere is not separate from the economic or the political sphere. Highlighting the social, where friends, neighbors, family, coreligionists, and coworkers figure prominently, underscores the constructionist bent in attempting to separate the private and the public, because the social is where the private and the public, and the economic and the political, converge to blur artificial demarcations.

I have underscored the intertwined and tangled nature of the various forms of violence in the women's lives, those forms that are more easily recognizable as physical and even psychological violence and those that are less visible, by weaving in the material and social forms (exclusion, extreme poverty, gender inequality, unequal access to resources), because that is how these different forms converge in lived experiences. Structural inequalities based on class or ethnicity promote different forms of political, symbolic, and everyday violence (see Hoffmann and McKendrick 1990). Structural and symbolic violence intermingle and translate into everyday violence, which is expressed in social inequalities as well as in interpersonal conflicts. Those who are marginalized inflict this type of violence mainly on themselves, on their kin and friends, and on their neighbors (see Bourgois 2004a, 2004b). Focusing on violence in the home, David Gil (1986) observes that violence in human relations is rooted in institutionalized inequalities of status, rights, and power, not only between the sexes, but also among individuals of different ages and races. Examined this way, interpersonal, microlevel instances of violence are not simply the result of individuals' behaviors or choices, but, more important, they are the product of inequalities institutionalized in larger systems and justified through a host of frameworks, such as religion, ideology, and history (Bourgois 2001). And although I focus on the individual acts that instantiate the violence created by larger structures, I do not argue for a crude form of determinism either. As Farmer (1996: 271) observes, "Such afflictions are not the result of accident or force majeure but of human agency; human decisions are behind them, and sometimes the same decision makers are involved in the creation of different forms of suffering."

Political violence and structural violence, in the form of unemployment and underemployment and increased economic inequality arising from neoliberal market reforms, are intricately related and dictate the pace of everyday life in many corners of the world. The benefits of globalization that free trade proponents touted have not materialized; instead economic policies have contributed to intensify food insecurity in vulnerable communities around the world (see McGrew and Poku 2007). Political and structural violence are often so intertwined that in Guatemala, for instance, political violence has been an expression of structural violence "in the form of a brutal model of capitalist development combined with profound ethnic inequality to foil the development of an inclusive national project" (Grandin 2000: 8). Symbolic and everyday violence are intimately tied to political and structural violence. As Portes and Roberts (2005: 77) note more generally for Latin America, increased levels of delinquency (or common crime) "represent the counterpart to the deterioration of labor market opportunities and sustained high levels of inequality." And as in other "postconflict" societies that have experienced high levels of political violence, Guatemala has witnessed a "transition" from political to criminal violence, itself a "deeply class-bound discourse" (see Scheper-Hughes 1997: 477).[1] The targets today are not the perceived political opponents of the past but "ordinary" people, usually the poor and most vulnerable, who are victimized for acting on the conditions into which they have been forced.

The very notion of a "postwar" era in Guatemala can deflect attention from persistent linkages between violence, politics, and the state (Benson, Fischer, and Thomas 2008). The act of signing the Peace Accords might not have much meaning when the structures of inequality at the root of both the armed conflict and the multiple forms of visible and invisible violence have been left intact. Life in Guatemala today resembles closely what Quesada (2004: 292) described in Nicaragua during the years of the Contra War: "an unsettling hyperawareness of the fact that one resided in the heart of troubled terrain." This hyperawareness of residing in troubled terrain is not foreign to most Guatemalans today, especially to women from disadvantaged backgrounds, who on account of race and social class also bear the brunt of the effects of neoliberal structural adjustment programs a decade after the Peace Accords were signed.[2] And an examination of women's everyday lives within this terrain illuminates the naturalized assaults that Martín-Baró (1994: 130) referred to as "normal abnormality," where suffering becomes internalized and routinized, but the burden and the chronic nature of the suffering pose existential dilemmas for those who must endure it (see also Taussig [1992] on the "nervous system" and how terror is internalized in everyday life).

All the above forms of violence are deeply linked to and superimposed on gender and gendered forms of violence that reflect profound inequalities, patriarchal ideologies, and expectations of orthodox gender behaviors encoded in social institutions. Throughout this book I have illustrated the manifold expressions that gender inequality takes in the lived experiences of the ladinas and Mayas I came to know in Guatemala. Comparisons of women's class position (and race) in San Alejo with that of women in the Altiplano helped me to elucidate analytic points about gender and gendered violence and social position that otherwise would have remained obscured. And although this book focuses on the lives of ladinas, by making use of a comparative angle based on Maya women I also shed light on how Maya women experience visible, less visible, misrecognized, and normalized everyday violence in postwar Guatemala.

As I examined the different spheres of women's lives, I concentrated on exposing the misrecognized violence in women's everyday interactions with husbands, male partners, neighbors, friends, family members, and other women close to them and on how interactions with institutions contributed to the naturalization of gender and gendered forms of violence. A fundamental point is that the humiliations, insults, self-depreciation, internalization of inequalities, and self-culpability—the "private terrors" that women *habitually* experience—are part of the violence they suffer as women and that these often "invisible terrors" are intricately linked to overt, physical forms occurring in interpersonal violence in the home. This is in turn linked to the extrapersonal structures that assault the daily lives of each and every Guatemalan. Throughout this work, therefore, I have attempted to trace the links between the private fear and pain and the more overt forms of violence, relying on the women's own words to expose the normalized and silenced aspects of their suffering. Violence should be acknowledged even when it does not present itself in the form of visible wounds, bullets, and bodies. It is the thread that connects the suffering of the political target, hungry children, and women who suffer and *endure*—in the form of physical or psychological assaults, low pay, belittling, and gossip—often in silence. In the end, my examination can perhaps contribute a cautionary note to reflections on violence, to how we define and categorize it in its multiple expressions.

Like Goldstein (2003) in her discussion of sexuality in the lives of women in a favela in Rio de Janeiro, I remain alert to the reality that reporting on the conditions of marginalized populations can bring injuries to them. Like some of the themes in Goldstein's work, many of the areas I have discussed and the angle from which I have done so are "areas of knowledge production that can all too easily be used to control and revictimize marginalized populations." And, like Goldstein, I can say that "this project is generally challenging because of the ease by which the information here could be distorted" (227). Goldstein's words, as well as the reflections of other critical anthropologists who work with marginalized populations, have resonated with me ever since I started writing about the lives of the women I came to know in Guatemala. I opted for writing about the violence in their lives because an important aspect of my project is recognition—making visible the different sources of violence that assault the lives of women. The politics of recognition are a crucial component of any efforts toward gender justice. Thus I chose not to sanitize my discussions or to lessen the brutality that I have sometimes exposed. In doing so, like Goldstein (2003), I ask readers to avoid seeing the lives of the women I have presented through lenses clouded by ethnocentrism and classism.

In this vein, like Goldstein, I note that what I have presented here is not unique to Guatemalan women. The conditions I have exposed are a part of life for women in other contexts; they can also be found very close to us in wealthier nations. Moreover, Guatemala herself is not self-contained and is deeply connected to us. Long-standing U.S. foreign policy, militarization and state terror, industrial and agricultural exports, migration and immigrant labor, contemporary family separations through migrant deportations, and a host of other links make an examination of Guatemala a project that is deeply connected to us in the United States.[3] As Grandin (2000: 221) observed about Guatemala, "Colonialism, regional tensions, coffee export capitalism, and imperialism render such a bounded analysis untenable." Thus the broader forces that shape the lives of women in a rural town in Guatemala are not independent from those that affect our own lives. The lives of the women I discussed here should not be seen as independent from our lifestyles and consumer practices, our actions, and the policies and dealings of governments, especially the U.S. government, that have maintained close relations with Guatemala. Not everything we examine in other parts of the world should be treated as absolute differences,

Scheper-Hughes (1995) observed. The Guatemalan women's troubles, humiliations, and tribulations, their joys, desires, and dreams cannot be separated from our own, as if they belonged to exotic others. Their lives and ours have been and continue to be connected in multiple ways; we are all implicated in lives that seem far away from our own.

THE INTERTWINED NATURE OF VIOLENCE: FEMINICIDE IN GUATEMALA

Central America, especially its "northern triangle," formed by Guatemala, Honduras, and El Salvador, was just bestowed the dubious distinction of being "the most violent region" on the planet. According to the most recent United Nations Development Programme Human Development Report (2009: introduction), "Today Central America is the most violent region in the world. With the exception of wars in parts of Africa or Asia, this region registers the highest homicide rates in the planet. Moreover, unfortunately, the rates in question have been increasing in recent years in almost all countries in Central America." The same report notes that attention should be given not only to the actual number of homicides but also to the increased insecurity that people in the region experience and criticizes the *"mano dura"* (heavy hand) governmental approaches to dealing with violence that for a long time have created a false sense of security. In addition, in the case of Guatemala, President Álvaro Colom recently stated that his country is in a "state of calamity" (Council on Hemispheric Affairs 2009), a situation he links to food shortages caused by severe weather patterns that have created drought conditions and reduced agricultural production. However, the vulnerability of life in Guatemala today can hardly be the result of a recent drought or of a fresh crime wave; it is the legacy of a long history of violence and abuses, of profound socioeconomic inequalities, of the cheapening of life under such conditions, and of one of the most corrupt governments that sustain impunity. It is part and parcel of the still unaddressed but well-recognized inequalities and injustices and the sequel of violence left by more than three decades of state terror.

Throughout this book I have made the point that multisided violence is intertwined in the women's lives—private terrors, misrecognized and hidden, entwined with overt, sometimes public forms of violence. In fact, as part of my objective and to serve as a reminder that in reality all forms come together, I did not separate in my presentation the physical from the nonphysical forms of violence. Here, however, I would like to make one last connection to the forms of violence that were discussed explicitly in the women's narratives, reflections, and explanations. There is one especially cruel and terrifying form that loomed large in the minds, conversations, and actions of the women: the feminicide that is taking increasingly more women's lives in Guatemala with every passing year.

Victoria Sanford (2008) makes an important linguistic difference between *feminicide* and *femicide,* and it is one I adopt in this discussion. Diana Russell (2001: 3) defined *femicide* as "the killing of females by males *because* they are females—in the hope that naming these crimes will facilitate this recognition" (original emphasis). I use the term *feminicide* as Sanford uses it (see also Carey and Torres, forthcoming), because it "conveys not only the killings of women by men because they are women, but it also highlights the responsibility of the state in these assassinations, due to omission or because it executed the killing, to tolerance of the acts and their perpetrators, and to a lack of responsibility to guarantee the security of female citizens" (Sanford 2008: 64). There were 518 women killed in 2005 and more than 600 killed in 2006; by 2007 an average of 2 women a day were being killed in Guatemala, most of them between the ages of sixteen and thirty, an alarming trend that is fast approaching the peak in violent deaths reached at the height of the political conflict (Sanford 2008: 15–16).[4] José Steinsleger (2005) calls it the "feminicide iceberg": the bodies of the killed represent only the tip of the problem. Although these killings have been attributed to organized crime, to drug trafficking, or, more often, to gangs, in Sanford's view (2008) feminicide today can be considered a form of social cleansing.[5]

To be sure, I did not hear specific stories about feminicide among the women with whom I spoke, perhaps because when I stopped doing fieldwork there was less public awareness of these murders. So the links I make are not based on my empirical observations but follow naturally from my overall objective of unearthing links among different kinds of violence; the forms of violence I have examined, in my view, *pave the way for others to take place,* including the most visible and shocking murders we see today. The women with whom I spoke alluded to a few points in our conversations that are relevant to the connections I make. For instance, I noted that women were invariably fearful of going out at night, whether it was Estrella who had to take photographs to earn her family's sustenance or María Ruth who wanted to attend church.

It was simply too dangerous for women to do so, they would explain (see also Sanford 2008). But they were also afraid of going out during the day, especially when they had to travel by public transportation to work at a factory on the outskirts of town or to attend school, which signals a class-specific danger. The simple act of leaving the house can be frightening when one is in fear of violence both at home and in the street (Drysdale Walsh 2008). These were some of the indications of class-bound insecurity that women experienced; they are expressions of what it is to live in a context where feminicide, anywhere in the country, is a daily occurrence. The same occurred in the Altiplano, though initially I reasoned that the fear there was linked to the overt political violence that had enveloped western Guatemala in general. Feminicide is also one of the most concrete examples of what "postwar" Guatemala looks and feels like; it may be even more insecure and dangerous than "wartime" Guatemala (see Torres 2005).

I am not arguing that the different forms of violence I have discussed and the current wave of feminicide are directly related *causally,* for establishing causality in this case would be difficult (see also Ertürk 2005). But as Prieto-Carrón, Thomson, and Macdonald (2007) recently noted in their project on gender-based violence in Central America, femicide (their term) is an expression of gender discrimination and unequal power relations between men and women and of institutionalized discrimination against women. Carey and Torres (forthcoming) also note that the long history of legal and social practices embedded in Guatemalan institutions are *precursors* of the feminicides we see today. As well, the work of the the journalists Kristof and WuDunn (2009) in several countries in Asia and Africa has revealed how the multiple sources of violence come together in women's lives in shocking ways. And in my view, the daily acts of control, the women's self-recrimination for their own victimization, the humiliations, stigmatization, internalized submission, and multiple forms of social exclusion in education, health, and employment, as well as a general devaluation of poor women's lives and of the poor in general, are deeply linked to the brutal killings of women that are seen in Guatemala today. Once violence of the types Guatemala has witnessed is unleashed it can take many forms. The same gender ideologies and patriarchal structures and patterns of social exclusion based on race and class that make possible the intimate terrors in the women's lives also allow for a devaluation of women's lives *as women.* And this dehumanization is in turn linked to the state violence that created a climate in which life was cheap and institutions were not only indifferent to the plight of citizens but even victimized those who dared to complain.

Indeed, the U.N. rapporteur, Yakin Ertürk, noted that in the Guatemalan justice system there is a general lack of respect for survivors who seek justice, and the Guatemalan representative Alba Estela Maldonado Guevara (2005) stated that victims and those who have survived feminicide are subject to revictimization when they search for justice and are ignored and stigmatized by institutions. The impunity with which these institutions have reacted to the killings of women serves to normalize violence as it sends a message that the lives of the women are expendable. The law itself formalizes deep inequalities that embody violence: until recently, for instance, the law required women to ask for permission from their husbands if they wanted to work for pay, and it exonerated a violator if he married his victim, provided the victim was older than twelve. When women ask for assistance in cases of domestic abuse or when families seek justice after a woman has been killed, the institutions in charge of protecting them instead revictimize them. Steinsleger (2005) tells the story of a mother who could not recognize the body of her sixteen-year-old daughter who had been brutally killed. The investigator in charge of the case told this woman that her daughter had been killed because she was a *cualquiera,* a nobody. There was evidence of semen on the girl's pants, but instead of considering that the girl might have been raped, the investigator assumed she had been engaged in illicit sex and that this had led to her murder (as if this justified her horrific death). The mother explained that the following day a police officer told her these kinds of things happened to them because they were women.[6] Another study found that officials in the justice system relied on stereotypes when carrying out their work; in one instance an individual in the court said that women themselves were responsible for the violence in the home because they do not tend to their chores and do not obey their husbands (Morales, cited in Drysdale Walsh 2008: 54).

The U.N. rapporteur noted that, according to the Procuraduría de Derechos Humanos de Guatemala (Guatemalan Human Rights Office; PDH), 40 percent of cases of feminicide are filed and never investigated (Ertürk 2005), and in those that are investigated the women who were killed are considered culpable for their own deaths (see also Sanford 2008). Impunity, silence, and indifference are obviously part of feminicide (Sanford 2008: 62) but also part and parcel of the normalization of violence (Torres 2008).[7] In this way, as Walter Benjamin (1978) remarked, the founding violence of the state, or law-making violence, is indistinguishable from the legitimate exercise of state violence, or law-preserving violence. And when violence comes from the authorities, it is legitimized, which is the key to its acceptance as part of the "social order of things." One cannot lose sight of the power relations embedded in these violations. Farmer's (2003: 7) observation captures this point precisely: "Human rights violations are not random in distribution or effect. Rights violations are, rather, symptoms of deeper pathologies of power and are linked intimately to the social conditions that so often determine who will suffer abuse and who will be shielded from harm."

Human rights organizations, institutions, and laws have addressed the problem of the vicious killings of women (Torres 2008), all of these efforts initially proposed by Guatemalan women's groups (Drysdale Walsh 2008) with substantial impetus and funding from outside the country (Godoy-Paiz 2008). And although the signing of the Peace Accords left unaddressed the legacy of multiple social injustices (Torres 2008), Drysdale Walsh (2008) argues that the Accords produced an opening in civil society, and women began to demand the creation of specialized institutions to address violence against them. As a result, these organizations have exposed key links between Guatemala's violent past and today's wave of crimes against women.

For its part, at the instigation of women's groups and with outside pressure, the Guatemalan government started to "do something" about the direct violence against women. It created the Unidad de Homicidios contra Mujeres (Unit for Homicides against Women), part of the Servicio de Investigación Criminal (Criminal Investigation Service), with three desks and three computers, as well as the *Plan Nacional de Prevención y Erradicación de la Violencia Intrafamiliar y contra las Mujeres* (National Plan for the Prevention and Eradication of Intrafamily Violence and Violence against Women), but provided no budget for these endeavors (Steinsleger 2005). And after much pressure and debate, the government also approved the Ley para Prevenir, Sancionar, y Erradicar la Violencia Intrafamiliar (Law to Prevent, Sanction, and Eradicate Violence within the Family), based on the Convention of Belém to Pará, Brazil, 1994, which was ratified by Guatemala; the Ley de Dignificación y Promoción Integral de la Mujer (Law for the Dignification and Integral Promotion of Women); and the Ley contra el Femicidio y Otras Formas de Violencia contra la Mujer (Law against Femicide and Other Forms of Violence against Women) (Godoy-Paiz 2008).[8] The engrained injustice and impunity and the undermining of the law by the authorities in charge of upholding them underscore the limitations of these legal efforts. This predicament leads Godoy-Paiz (2008: 38–39) to ponder, "With the passing of laws in the area of gender-based violence, a woman in Guatemala now has the formal right to a life free of violence. However, what does it mean to her if she is unable to freely walk around her neighborhood without fear of attack or leave her home without being subject to family and/or community control?" In fact, the contrast between increased postconflict legal protections for women and the growing rates of violence against women points to the shortcomings of a strictly legal solution that focuses narrowly on attributing culpability to individuals alone. As Godoy-Paiz (2008: 39) insightfully observes, "A strictly legal, formal rights-based framework such as the one ascribed to by the Guatemalan State treats violence as an act involving *an* individual perpetrator and victim. This approach is problematic as it ignores the social conditions that give rise and sustain relations of domination." Kleinman (2000) notes that programs that focus on one or another outcome designed to alleviate the suffering that comes from the multiple *violences* in everyday life regularly fail.[9]

Given the climate of impunity and general inattention to this issue, many of those working in NGOs to address the vicious killings have been threatened, kidnapped, tortured, and killed. The recent kidnapping and torture of a professor of dentistry at the Universidad de San Carlos led to a public announcement by the Comisión Universitaria de la Mujer (University Commission on Women) that linked and condemned all forms of violence and aggression against women:

> *Las mujeres universitarias sancarlistas nos unimos al repudio de la violencia que afecta, cada vez más, a la sociedad guatemalteca. . . . Los actos de violencia en el presente representan la continuidad del autoritarismo y la represión que durante cuarenta años marcaron la historia del país, cuyas secuelas no han sido superadas. De manera que las agresiones, asaltos, asesinatos, feminicidios y otras formas de violencia, apenas inmutan a una ciudadanía que vive con temor porque, además, las autoridades encargadas de la seguridad no dan una respuesta acorde a las dimensiones de esta problemática. . . . Llamamos a la comunidad universitaria, a la ciudadanía consciente para que se exprese y sume su voz condenando la violencia y haciendo todos los esfuerzos para erradicarla.*[10]
>
> [The San Carlos University women join in the repudiation of the violence that affects, more and more, Guatemalan society. . . . The acts of violence today represent the continuity of the authoritarianism and the repression that for forty years marked the history of the country, whose sequel has not been surpassed. Therefore, the aggressions, robberies, murders, feminicides, and other forms of violence barely upset a citizenry that lives with fear because the authorities responsible for the security have not responded in accordance

> to the gravity of the problem. . . . We call on the university community, on the conscious citizens, to express and add their voices to condemn the violence and to make all efforts to eradicate it.]

At the beginning of this book, I noted that the division of labor in violence research has led to a focus on the infliction of injuries at a personal level (see Collins 2008), while other forms of violence, such as those that are found in social structures away from individuals, have not received much attention (see Jackman 2002). Although some forms of violence, such as political violence, civil unrest, labor violence, and armed conflict have been studied, important links with micro-expressions of violence at a personal level are not always made. As Jackman insightfully observes:

> As scholars have rushed to the analysis of specific forms of violence that have generated urgent social concern, the systematic definition of violence has languished.Those few analysts who have attempted to cast a broader conceptual net have generally restricted themselves to a subset of violent behaviors, such as domestic violence (itself subdivided into child abuse, intimate-partner violence, and elder abuse), gender violence, civil violence, criminal violence, or some selective combination of these. . . . The result has been a series of partially overlapping conceptual amalgams, with inconsistencies and gaps both within and among them. (2002: 389)

It is my hope that here in these pages I have contributed to exposing the links between macro- and micro-expressions of violence, economic and political structures that lead to suffering, and the routine violence in Guatemalan women's lives. I hope that my focus on social spheres that connect realms of private pain to public expressions of suffering underscores the need to open up the analytic lens to include a wider range of the sources of suffering in examinations of violence. By this I do not propose a concept so broad and inclusive as to lose theorizing potential and meaning. Less visibly violent but equally harmful acts, where multiple forms of unequal power relations converge, must be recognized as violence for projects of gender justice, or projects for justice more generally, to succeed. Close attention to the words of women, to their stories, and to how they talk about their lives can lead to a rethinking of how we theorize and study violence. I have examined the quotidian moments in the lives of women who have endured violence but whose experiences have not received enough scholarly attention in the hope that my work will expose the normalization of violence, the pervasiveness of fear, and the injury of neglect.

Appendix

LIST OF STUDY PARTICIPANTS, SAN ALEJO

Name	Age	Education	Occupation
Alma	31	nurse	nurse
Andrea	23	0	food street vendor
Concepción	29	0	cusha seller
Dalila	24	6 months	meat seller
Delfina	35	teacher	teacher/housewife
Emilia	26	teacher	office clerk
Estrella	46	5	photographer
Gloria	23	3	housewife
Gracia María	32	8	housewife/teacher
Hortencia	34	0	food street vendor
Ileana	17	0	housewife
Isabel	41	5	small store owner
Ivette	30	0	housewife
Leticia	27	0	tomato picker
Lila	38	6	housewife
Lucia	42	teacher	teacher/business
Lucrecia	27	7	food street vendor
María Ruth	29	0	housewife
Mariana	25	2 yr college	housewife
Mercedes	51	5	housewife
Mireya	22	0	housewife
Mirna	28	6 months	food street vendor
Nena	39	teacher	teacher/housewife
Ofelia	28	6	office clerk
Silvia	20	3	housewife
Susana	26	2	housewife
Teresa	21	dress making	housewife
Tita	34	0	tomato picker/comadrona
Vera	20	teacher	small store owner
Victoria	29	6	housewife

*All self-reported information, in most cases at the time of the first interview.

LIST OF STUDY PARTICIPANTS, ALTIPLANO

Name	Age	Education	Occupation
Adela	33	2	weaver/housewife
Alberta	44	0	weaver/housewife
Amelia	20	1	housewife/weaver
Antonia	39	1.5	weaver/housewife
Asunción	34	3	housewife
Azucena	23	0	tortilla maker/domestic
Carmen	36	4	weaver/raises chickens/pharmacy
Constantina	34	0	domestic/cusha seller
Dalia	25	2	weaver/housewife
Eliza	22	2	weaver
Erminia	53	0	comadrona
Filita	30	9	dress maker
Flor	45	6	health promoter
Gina	28	0	dress maker /weaver
Hilaria	33	0	housewife/weaver
Isa	32	3	weaver/housewife
Julia	31	0	weaver/housewife
Lilian	33	0	housewife
Lita	39	0	weaver/housewife
Marcela	29	6	housewife/weaver
Maria	25	6	housewife
Marisela	42	0	weaver/housewife
Marta	36	6	tamale maker/seller
Martina	27	2	housewife/weaver
Mirian	29	0	housewife
Rosita	38	1	housewife
Toñita	41	1	weaver/housewife
Violeta	27	0	housewife

*All self-reported information, in most cases at the time of the first interview.

Notes

CHAPTER 1

1. Other scholars have made similar points about the consequences that living in extreme situations of poverty and social exclusion, coupled with family violence and other forms of gender violence, can have on the lives of women (see Godoy-Paiz 2007, 2008; Goldín and Rosenbaum 2009).

2. I follow Veena Das (1997, 2007) in that in this project violence is not an interruption of life, an act to be witnessed; violence is part of life, of the ordinariness of life.

3. See Sutton (2010) for an examination of the female body in Argentina as a window into multiple forms of power inequalities and structural violence in the wider society.

4. For a review of the scholarship that brings the "lived experience" of social suffering to sociological focus, see Wilkinson (2005).

5. For a good overview of the term *ladino* in relation to the history of ethnic relations in Guatemala, see Grandin (2000); for the particular area where I conducted fieldwork, see Dary Fuentes (1991, 1994).

6. Here I do not claim to present a summary of the scholarship and debates on ladinos in Guatemala that would do justice to the work that has been produced; I am barely touching the surface of this complex area.

7. See the special issue of the *Journal of Latin American Anthropology* 2 (1), edited by Charles Hale, for an in-depth discussion of the concept of mestizaje, its multiple meanings across geographic regions and within the same societies (Hale 1996), as well as the edited collection by Euraque, Gould, and Hale (2004).

8. Casaús Arzú (1998) also notes the other strategies, such as the social division of labor and urban-rural dualities, that have been used to cement Guatemalan racism based on marking differences between ladinos and indigenous.

9. See Carol A. Smith (1995) on how systems of race, class, and gender shape social identities in Guatemala.

10. According to Hale's (2006) recent study, ladinos sometimes viewed themselves as victims and as a minority in the context of the Maya's political gains in the past decade and a half or so.

11. Maya communities and topics related to the Maya have been so prominent in research about Guatemala that when I started talking about my research it was assumed that I was writing about the Maya, especially when I mentioned that I was looking at violence. "It's what everyone does in Guatemala," a colleague responded, when I corrected him that my focus was ladinas.

12. I had expected this to a degree because I did not know if they would speak about this openly. However, unprompted, several women shared details about these experiences with me.

13. The owner of the house where I lived in the Altiplano was one of a handful of ladinas in town. At first I was not sure how this would affect my contacts with the Maya women, but it worked well. This woman was the only ladina in town who was fluent in Kaqchikel, which she had learned, she explained, as an expression of respect for the majority of people with whom she interacted.

14. In alternating between the two towns and comparing the lives of the ladinas and the Maya, I do not want to suggest that only these two groups exist in Guatemala. I also do not want to reify the indigenous-ladino bipolarity I mentioned earlier, or to erase the presence of other groups, such as the Xinca, Garífuna, and whites, that are usually lumped together in the "nonindigenous" category (see Tarracena Arriola et al. 2002) in the Guatemalan ethnic landscape.

15. I am not suggesting that all women, regardless of ethnicity, will have the same experiences of violence or that women universally experience patriarchy or inequalities in the market or access to social services in the same way.

16. One exception is Analicia (see chap. 3). I did not interview or even meet her, but I came to know her entire family well, and she died of complications from HIV/AIDS during my fieldwork. Thus I gave her a pseudonym.

17. I obtained these reactions from a wide range of colleagues in different contexts. A woman I met when I was a visiting scholar in Paris was puzzled that, as a Salvadoran, I was doing work in Guatemala and not in El Salvador. She was not intrigued, however, by the fact that all the researchers of Central America she knew were either European or from the United States.

18. Some colleagues mentioned that my decision to do work in Oriente is "naturally" explained by the close similarities between this region of Guatemala and my native El Salvador. "Studying one is like studying the other" or "It probably feels very close to you," they observed.

19. Although at the time I started visiting these towns to do fieldwork there was quite a bit of attention to the alleged stealing of children in rural communities by foreigners (see Adams 1998), I was not suspected of this. It was my Salvadoran nationality that would stand out but for reasons other than the disappearance of children.

20. See Adams (1998) for the different constructions of the term *gringa* by ladinos and indigenous in Guatemala and how the term can embody border-crossing possibilities.

CHAPTER 2

1. A focus "that privileges the everyday shows how social institutions are deeply implicated in two opposing modes—the production of suffering, on the one hand, and the creation of moral communities that could address it, on the other" (Das 1997: 563).

2. Galtung (1990) argued that direct violence is an event, structural violence is a process, and cultural violence—which normalizes and makes possible structural violence—is invariable.

3. Scholars have provided different explanations for violence in Latin America, including several based on the culture of machismo. Some argue that warfare and ritual violence have been woven into the fabric of life in the region since antiquity (Chacon and Mendoza 2007), that a history of colonization through violence created political and economic relationships based on power (Rosenberg 1991), that violence in Latin America is the result of struggles for power (Sosa Elízaga 2004), or that it has cultural origins (Cueva Perus 2006).

4. Auyero's (2000) work is an excellent example. He links Argentina's deregulated economy and the rise of predatory delinquency and substance abuse in shantytowns.

5. An article in the *Economist* (2003: 37) asks, "Why is Latin America so unequal?" and notes, "Inequality is as Latin American as good dance music and magical-realist fiction. Like those other regional products, it thrives." Stereotypes and sarcasm aside, the article notes that inequality in the region is deep-rooted and has varied little over time, despite changes in economic policies.

6. The *Economist* article cited in note 5 above also notes that inequality in Latin America rose in the 1990s, during the period of neoliberal policies, in a disturbing way: previously more egalitarian countries like Argentina became more unequal, thus reducing intraregional inequality gaps.

7. The World Bank (2006) estimates that close to two-thirds of Guatemala's seven- to fourteen-year-olds work and attend school and that approximately 40 percent of those in this age group only work.

8. In the political climate of Guatemala when I started this work, any criticism of the status quo could be taken as a condemnation of the regime, subject to a heavy price such as being targeted as a "subversive." Thus I was not surprised that women would not question the system openly.

9. For a good chronology and different forms of state terror directed at Mayas and ladinos in Guatemala, see Ball, Kobrak, and Spirer (1999).

10. Wilkinson (2004: 231) describes the abusive wife of a landowner who punished a blind plantation worker by making him put his hands into an anthill. One needs to be reminded that this incident did not take place in a dark basement during a torture session; it happened on a plantation, in the context of everyday landowner-worker relations.

11. Lynchings, mostly in Maya communities, are thought to be the result of the residents' frustration with the failure of the government to deal with crime. There have been claims that the instigators of these lynchings were former members of the Civil Patrols (Amnesty International 2004). See Snodgrass Godoy (2006) for an analysis of this new form of violence.

12. Kleinman (2000: 228–29) calls attention to the "*violences* of everyday life" to warn against focusing narrowly on the violence in the lives of the poor and most vulnerable but to be cognizant of the violence present in the lives of the nonpoor and the middle class.

13. In their study of urban violence in Guatemala, Moser and McIlwaine (2001) conclude that the exponential rise in youth gang activity is related to the return migration of the youths and their families, mainly from the United States.

14. Some scholars disagree with Bourdieu's conceptualization. For instance, Carolyn Nordstrom and JoAnn Martin (1992: 8) observe that whereas Bourdieu focused on the unconscious replication of structures of domination, Jean Comaroff (1985) takes a more focused approach, noting that this occurs in the blurry area of semiconscious social and conceptual action.

15. Jean Comaroff and John Comaroff (1991: 24–25) offer a useful distinction between ideology and hegemony: "Hegemony is part of the dominant worldview that has been naturalized and comes to exist without question, as habitual, whereas ideology is the more explicitly recognized worldview of a particular group." The distinction they make is relevant to my discussion of gender ideals as forms of symbolic violence, as it underscores the different frameworks that shape worldviews, including views about gender roles and ideal images of women and men. "Hegemony, at its most effective, is mute; ideology invites argument," they observe (1992: 29). (See also Raymond Williams's [1977] interpretation of Gramsci's concept of hegemony).

16. Bourgois (2004b) links rape and gendered violence to structural and interpersonal violence, a point that is also relevant for my analysis.

17. Also, according to Torres (2005: 155–56), it is difficult to assess in this context whether female victims suffered politically motivated or domestic abuse. In many cases, the victim's husband/boyfriend, or father, had been apprehended, though he was not necessary the perpetrator. In this way the crime was made to look as if it was a case of domestic violence.

18. In her research on the murdered women of Juárez, Wright (2007) notes that these women are often seen as evidence of diminished values. Thus, instead of going after the perpetrators, a trend in the erosion of cultural values that the women supposedly represent is highlighted.

19. Torres (2008: 6) notes that a Guatemalan government–sponsored study of random murders found that only 3 in 553 cases had been prosecuted in court, a rate of under 0.2 percent.

20. Alejandro Portes (2009) notes that a number of scholars from the global South have become strong critics of emigration and its consequences for development trends in sending nations; the causal link between migration and underdevelopment is reversed. He notes, in particular, the 2005 Declaration of Cuernavaca, which lists the regressive consequences that emigration has had for the social and economic development of poorer countries, especially with regard to the increased precariousness of work, the loss of qualified workers, and greater economic dependency (see also Delgado Wise and Márquez Cobarrubias [2009] for a political economy of development perspective). In portraying the effects of emigration on the lives of women at the microlevel, and from

the women's point of view, my treatment of migratory processes here parallels these views.

21. I do not disagree with Mercedes's statement, but as I have argued elsewhere (Menjívar 2006a, 2006b) this apparent disintegration sometimes may constitute reorganization and accommodation. However, my point is based on the perceptions of Guatemalan immigrants *in the United States*, most of whom do not think that they have abandoned their families in Guatemala and who remember them by sending remittances, and Mercedes is speaking *in Guatemala*, where different meanings are attached to these separations.

CHAPTER 3

1. Green (1998) questions understandings of the body/mind dualism and aptly notes, "To categorize suffering simply as a manifestation of a clinical syndrome or as a culture-bound construct of reality dehistoricizes and dehumanizes the women's experiences" (5).

2. Sutton (2010: 213) cites the work of Marcela Lagarde to note that in patriarchal societies a dynamic of "bodily self-negation" occurs, which "creates the basis for the diminished rights of women as a group."

3. Population Reference Bureau, www.prb.org/datafinder.aspx. Retrieved November 5, 2009.

4. Asunción in the Altiplano had a similar experience. In her words, "I get injections when I feel weak, but last time I really thought I would die. Can you imagine, I was in my ninth pregnancy and I continued to have problems with him? But this time [during this pregnancy] after we had a big argument, I fainted. I fell on the floor, and I thought that was the end of me. Imagine, what kind of injections will have an effect if he continues behaving like that with me?"

5. In a study of headaches among women in Peru, Darghouth et al. (2006) observe that these are often understood within a framework that includes bodily, emotional, family, and social terms through which the women articulate individual and shared notions of suffering as part of larger contexts of social dislocation. Thus, headaches underscore the links between bodily and emotional pain and distress experienced at family, community, and larger social levels.

6. This is not unlike the expressions of patriarchal morality that Gloria González-López (2007) observes among the Mexican women in her study.

7. See Engle Merry (1997) for a discussion of the differences that context makes regarding the role of gossip as a form of social control; and Kramarae (1981) for gender inequalities in speaking rights in the context of social interaction.

8. Gossip also has been characterized as a tool to *resist* the control of the more powerful, as a "weapon of the weak" (see Scott 1985), but in the context I examine it, it becomes a form of *control* of the weak.

9. For an interesting examination of laughter within multiple hierarchies of power (e.g., race and gender) and violence that inform the social world of women, see Goldstein (2003).

10. See Drotbohm (2010) for an interesting reflection on what gossip means to the fieldwork process.

11. During my last visits to San Alejo, more and more women commented on the ambiguity they noticed in their partners' plans to return, which concerned them quite a bit. This ambiguity might not have had anything to do with infidelity but rather with the increasingly stiffer U.S. immigration laws that have made migrants' trips back home more irregular and unpredictable.

12. Socializing and visiting among women is important beyond the benefits that these activities bring to individual women (See Hansen 1994).

13. One day I stopped by to visit Julia, and her son told me she was ill. In effect, she was in bed but asked me to come in anyway and sit beside her. Her voice was weak, and she told me she had a terrible headache. She said that her nervios were killing her because of gossip. Someone had shared gossip about her at the market that day, and this, Julia was convinced, had been the cause of her illness that afternoon.

14. This situation is not unlike what I observed among Salvadoran immigrants in San Francisco (Menjívar 2000), where women would avoid establishing regular contacts, particularly with unrelated men, even if doing so cut them off from certain material resources. They feared such contacts would lead to unwanted sexual proposals and/or gossip that would damage their reputations.

CHAPTER 4

1. In their study of urban violence in Guatemala, Moser and McIlwaine (2001) refer to alcohol-related sexual violence as social violence. We agree, however, that these practices have a harmful effect on women that can be called violent, whatever the term used.

2. I want to note the close links between state violence and the lives of individuals; for state violence to be effective, it needs to be part of local lives and of individuals' cognitive repertoire. Individuals then make use of these repertoires to guide their actions and make sense of the everyday world around them.

3. For an excellent examination of "servitude," see Ray and Qayum (2009). These authors focus on asymmetries of power that bring out domination, dependency, and submission in the institution of servitude—not on "domestic work" as an occupation—in a way that is relevant to the case of San Alejo.

4. Dalia, in the Altiplano, said that this custom is disappearing there. "We women have to be *willing* to be robadas," she explained. "That term is now used almost in a romantic way."

5. In the Altiplano the *pedidas* (when women are asked for in marriage) were elaborate, and the groom's family would take gifts to the bride's family at least once. This more intricate custom did not exist in San Alejo, though people knew about it. The weddings were also more elaborate in the Altiplano; a wedding there could entail up to four days of celebrations.

6. In the Altiplano town of Santiago Chimaltenango women protested the sale of alcohol, with signs of "No More Alcholism" during a demonstration. A female leader in the town explained, "Men drink too much, they beat their wives, steel their corn, wood, beans, and their dishes in order to purchase *guaro*." The women were successful in stopping the formal sale of liquor, but

as this was halted the sale of clandestine alcohol, some imported from Mexico, went up substantially, as did its cost (Hurtado 2009).

7. I do not refer to this form of violence as domestic violence for two reasons. First, there is a substantial literature on the topic that tends to situate this issue within frameworks that highlight individual characteristics as explanatory factors (see Kocacik, Kutlar, and Erselcan 2007; Menjívar and Salcido 2002). It is my objective to move away from such approaches. Second, and more important, although the violence that I capture in this section happens mostly within the confines of the home and is concretized in individual actions (mostly of men), I do not want to misconstrue it as located only there; I want to emphasize the social spaces that intersect with the intimacy of the home in this type of violence.

8. See Gutmann's (2007) discussion of the socially constructed links between promiscuity and masculinity.

9. There was a similar case in the Altiplano. Julia, who remarked that tolerance was not one of her virtues, reacted like Nena when her husband started an affair: "I saw the woman in the street and knew it was her, and since I have no reason to have respect for her I took her by the hair and hit her, but she was carrying her baby girl, so instead I hit the girl." This mini-scandal angered her husband terribly, and he reprimanded her for interfering in his affairs, Julia recounted.

10. Cases in the Altiplano paralleled this situation; men who were in unions and then got involved with other women would feel little responsibility for at least one of the households. In one case in the Altiplano, when the husband started an affair he virtually stopped contributing to the household he shared with his wife and eventually resorted to selling the furniture and other items in order to sustain his drinking and partying with other women. Such instances demonstrate how the different forms of violence come together in this aspect of women's lives.

11. According to Haviland (1977), adultery is by far the most frequent topic of gossip, and it can lead to divorce, or to violence in the home (Van Vleet 2003). Thus married couples, especially women with a reputation to protect, often became the object of gossip and were therefore particularly attentive to others' talk, insinuations, and gaze.

12. The presence of godparents and compadres in the Altiplano was more notable than in San Alejo. The self-appointed historian in San Alejo explained, "It's that the Mayas take *compadrazgo* [lit, "co-parenthood"] much more seriously than we ladinos, so yes, your observations are correct. For the indigenous it means a lot more; for us it's a symbol, and not even that important anymore."

CHAPTER 5

1. Gutmann (1996: 26) argues that *macho* and *machismo* "have become a form of calumny, shorthand terms in social science and journalistic writing for labeling a host of negative male characteristics in cultures around the world."

2. Although prenatal care has increased in Guatemala, it remains low compared to other Latin American countries (INE et al. 1996 and WHO 2001, cited in Glei, Goldman, and Rodríguez 2003), especially in rural Guatemala, where

most births still occur at home, assisted by midwives with little or no formal training (Glei, Goldman, and Rodríguez 2003: 2447–48; Goldman et al. 2001).

3. Research examining factors that influence access to and use of prenatal care in Guatemala (Pebley, Goldman, and Rodríguez 1996) indicates that women with higher educational levels, ladinas, women living in predominantly ladino communities, those who watch TV daily, and those who live closer to health clinics are significantly more likely to use prenatal care (see also Glei and Goldman 2000).

4. According to Marini and Gragnolati (2003:2), Guatemala's prevalence of chronic malnutrition in children in 2000 was 44 percent, the highest in the region and one of the highest in the world.

5. Midwives *(comadrona)* are among several types of traditional health care providers in Guatemala, among both indigenous Mayas and ladinos, though there are important differences between the two groups in terms of how they use them (Pebley, Goldman, and Rodríguez 1996).

6. Heaton and Forste (2008) note that violence is the best predictor of poor nutrition and lack of female autonomy the best predictor of children's health; in general, the absence of domestic violence and male control lead to better child health.

7. Even though the Guatemalan penal code prohibits abortion except when the mother's life is at risk, "the convention here" (as explained to me in San Alejo) was that women were willing to sacrifice their lives for their babies' survival because, as one woman said, "being a good mother stands above the law for most women."

8. According to UNICEF (n.d.b), Guatemala's reported maternal death rate was 130 deaths per 100,000 live births, and the adjusted rate for 2005 was 290, one of the highest in Latin America and the Caribbean; these deaths are even more common in rural, poor, and indigenous communities. For instance, among indigenous women it was 211 per 100,000 live births in 2005 (http://prb.org/Articles/2003/MaternalMortalityinGuatemalaAPreventableTragedy.aspx; retrieved May 1, 2009). According to this report, the maternal mortality rate is an indicator of "the extreme harm women suffer during their reproductive lives . . . and the consequences of women's marginalized status." And maternal mortality continues to rank at the top for causes of death among young women of reproductive age in many poor countries (Kristof and WuDunn 2009; Shah and Say 2007).

9. WHO (2009) estimates that in Guatemala in 1999 (when I was conducting fieldwork) 91.9 percent of births to the highest wealth quintile of the population were attended by a physician, whereas only 8.8 percent of births to the lowest wealth quintile were attended by a physician.

10. Demographic and Health Surveys (DHS n.d.) data for 1999 indicate that in Guatemala 1.4 percent of births were reported as not having been assisted by anyone.

11. The programs in the Altiplano aimed specifically at children included one that paired children in the town with a "godparent" in the United States who would provide a monthly stipend, clothing, and other gifts to a child and his or her family; another program helped children in schools. Other programs

helped to provide medical care and food to children who were undernourished. All these programs focused on the Maya population and were financed from outside Guatemala.

12. In their study of beliefs about childhood diarrhea in rural Guatemala, Goldman, Pebley, and Beckett (2001) noted the importance of interpersonal and impersonal contacts for the diffusion of information and beliefs about the causes of diarrheal diseases, contamination, and hygiene.

13. In a review of forty-five studies of the effects of the presence of kin on child survival rates, Sear and Mace (2008) found that the presence of at least one relative besides the mother improves child survival rates, though not all relatives have the same benefits. Whereas maternal grandmothers tend to improve child survival rates, paternal grandmothers have mixed effects, and fathers showed little effect.

14. Poverty places serious constraints on the options for treating children's illnesses in rural Guatemala; indeed, education and ethnicity have little effect on treatment behavior when income is held constant (Goldman, Pebley, and Gragnolati 2002).

15. I do not want to give the impression that there are strict, clear-cut differences in the *use* of health care providers based on socioeconomic standing, but I do want to point out the sharp differences in the *range of options* that people of different economic standing have. The poor had very limited, if any, real options; the wealthier had a wide range.

16. In 2000, 15 percent of deaths among children under the age of five were attributed to pneumonia and 13.1 to diarrheal diseases (WHO 2009).

17. In mentioning the heterogeneity in women's experiences I would also like to note that gender ideologies for men, masculinities, and experiences of fatherhood are not homogeneous either. A study comparing men's "modern thought" across Central American countries, controlling for socioeconomic position, education, place of residence, and religion, found significant differences by country (Ortega Hegg 2004). However, my study is women-centered, and women's lives dominate my writing; therefore, I do not devote the necessary time and space to these nuances in experiences of masculinities and gender expectations among men and fathers. But focusing on the everyday experiences of women, Dorothy Smith (1987) observed, provides an important point of departure to undertake sociological analysis of broader issues.

CHAPTER 6

1. I am not arguing that paid employment is a panacea here. In this respect, see Gutmann's (1996) reflection on the link between work and family based on his interpretation of Engels's thinking on this topic, which lies at the root of perspectives about the emancipatory potential of factory work for women. Gutmann (1996: 162) notes that Engels's emphasis was not on the liberating potential of work per se "but rather on the stultifying confines of modern capitalist families. Engels's point was not that remunerated employment in itself liberates women, but that liberation will never come about as long as women remain in cloistered domesticity."

2. Research in Guatemala (see Quisumbing, Hallman, and Ruel 2007) notes that the provision of formal day care may be even more important to a mother's decision to work outside the home in areas where formal sector work is dominant.

3. See Kleinman's (2000) discussion of the violence that stress itself does to individuals.

4. I also observed this difference in the Maya and ladina Guatemalans in my research among these immigrants in Los Angeles (Menjívar 1999).

5. Reflecting on what they thought was apathy toward participation in business activities on the part of ladinos, several ladinos and ladinas in San Alejo noted that the Maya did well in business, regardless of age or gender. "The Mayas are good commerce people; look at the markets they have there in the Altiplano. They buy and sell anything and from a very early age they are already selling," the self-appointed historian of San Alejo observed. "The Mayas are *chispudos* [smart] in all matters of business," a worker at the health post noted.

6. In recent years Maya women, as well as Maya youth, have not had to travel to Guatemala City for employment in maquilas, as the maquilas are now coming to rural areas. Green (2003) identifies this phenomenon and calls attention to the exploitative nature of this work and to how it intensifies inequalities and intergenerational tensions.

7. There are several rights organizations that monitor abuses in these garment and assembly factories, not only in Guatemala, but also in other parts of Central America and in other countries where maquilas operate.

8. Even though men also wove, the women tended to perform the more laborious forms of weaving, often without using a machine or an industrial *telar* (loom).

9. The sequelae of state violence seeps through and emerges in different forms in the lives of those who lived it. Gina explained that even though foreign aid has opened up these work opportunities in the Altiplano, people do not always trust it. In her words, "People say that before the violence came, there was aid that came to us, but unfortunately, after the aid, the *matazón* came, so people now don't always believe that this aid can be only for our well-being. Yes, people work in those projects; there is a big one with the church from Norway. Like that bridge you see, it hadn't been fixed, it was falling down, and so the neighbors who saw the need to fix it contacted that organization and it was fixed. The same with the school; since there are so many kids in need here, that organization was contacted and they opened a school. So it's good. But what I'm telling you is that, unfortunately, we have seen that after there is aid, violence can come. And so people are not so trusting anymore."

10. For the purposes of this study, by "school abandonment" I mean the practice of taking the children out of school; others refer to it as school interruption. Interruption implies that school will be continued, which was not the case among the people in this study. I call it "abandonment" because I only saw one case in which a girl was taken out of school and then returned but only to take a six-month sewing course. And referring to it simply as dropping out obscures the practices that elucidate how structural violence, entwined with other forms of violence, are embedded in the act of discontinuing education,

even when people are aware of the detrimental consequences this has for the children.

11. Dary Fuentes (1991) notes that in the Guatemalan Altiplano women, especially Mayas, also work in almost all stages of agricultural production, which means that in order to participate in agricultural activities they probably spend less time on domestic chores.

12. Incaparina is a popular protein drink developed by INCAP, consisting of cottonseed flour, or soy, and vegetables, plus vitamin and mineral supplements, and designed to treat protein and caloric deficiencies and malnutrition in infants, children, and adults.

CHAPTER 7

1. This conversion has been widely analyzed, and rather than ask whether (or why) Latin America is becoming Protestant, researchers are now focusing on the long-term implications of conversion for the region (Garrard-Burnett 1998).

2. In his classic study of the link between religion and socioeconomic advancement in Guatemala, Sheldon Annis (1987) noted that the factor most predictive of a family's upward mobility was Evangelicalism.

3. Although the Roman Catholic Church has been one of the most progressive forces for change in Latin America, the volume and pace of the phenomenon of conversion from the "default" religion of Catholicism to Evangelicalism represents one of the principal components of societal change in the region. And although evangelical Protestantism, with its attention to solving concrete problems, was portrayed as preeminently a practice of the poor (Freston 1998), it is no longer the case, as more middle-class and educated Latin Americans are now joining these churches (Castleberry 1999).

4. See Smilde (2007) for explanations of conversion to Evangelicalism for the purposes of obtaining nonreligious rewards.

5. Here I use the term *evangelical* as a broad umbrella concept, recognizing that it is not a homogeneous category, for there are important differences among the churches grouped under this category. It is the term the women in both towns often used to refer to the Christian churches that emphasize personal conversion (and salvation) and that hold biblical authority and the Gospel as central (see Brusco 1995). Although there were some mainline Protestant churches in both towns, the term mostly referred to Pentecostal churches (see Freston 1998 for a discussion of the Pentecostalization of Protestant churches in Latin America and Smith 1991 for a sociological distinction between neo-Pentecostals and traditional Pentecostals in Guatemala). Evangelicals also refer to themselves as "Christians."

6. I am not the first to note this. In her comparative study of Pentecostals and Catholics, Mariz (1994) noted differences that the church made in the lives of the poor in contrast to those who were already on their feet.

7. During these conversations with the self-appointed historian, which took place when I was visiting alone (without my assistant), he would usually note the background of the people we talked about. At one point, he asked me if my "assistant, the Mayan," would be coming later to join me, a reference that

took me by surprise because I had never thought of identifying individuals that way. But people in town told me that they "immediately notice" someone's background, including my assistant's and my own. They explained that if I were from there, I would do the same.

8. My experiences with these racist statements made me uncomfortable about what I was doing, the contradictions between my personal beliefs and my interlocutors' candid disclosures, and my position and reactions in a way that is similar to what researchers who study somewhat comparable situations have noted (see, e.g., Blee 2003). However, this is another instance of how symbolic violence permeates the lives and minds of those who live it.

9. Erminia wept as she narrated the conflicts that belonging to different churches has caused between her and the rest of her family. It did not help that hers was not the only family with these problems. As her relations with her siblings soured because of conversion (though the degree fluctuated from time to time), her relations with coreligionists strengthened.

10. A *cofradía* or *hermandad* is an association in the Catholic Church based on veneration of a particular saint, the Virgin, Christ, an aspect of the passion of Christ, or a relic with religious significance. With roots in Spain, these associations are highly organized groups whose leaders are charged with various tasks in the church, including keeping the vigil of the Blessed Sacrament. Members of the cofradías, especially in Maya communities, hold a great deal of power beyond the church in their communities (see Carrabús Pellecer 1998).

11. In efforts to accommodate the culturally Catholic, some evangelical churches allowed parents to have a modified version of compadrazgo so that the children would have godparents—"Just like everyone else," I was told. Thus both Vera and Mariana, whose families were either actively evangelical or had been active in the past, had godparents for their children. Whereas this flexibility on the part of some evangelical churches helps them attract and keep members, parishes of stricter evangelical churches disapprove of it.

12. In addition to changes in individual behavior that eventually benefit women, research has noted the important effects of converting to Evangelicalism in contexts of political violence (Annis 1987; Stoll 1990), for it provides a safe space to withdraw from situations of violence, in particular, for men to avoid conflict-ridden situations (Brusco 1995; Burdick 1993).

13. In both towns Catholic churches also incorporated practices, such as healing sessions, in their activities, and a few made the activities of Charismatic groups central to their missions, which resembled evangelical churches. Some evangelical churches accommodated practices such as pedidas and compadrazgo, even talking about their work using Catholic concepts and terms.

14. For an in-depth examination and explanation of the growth of Pentecostals among the Maya and rural and poor urban ladinos, see Wilson (1997); see also Smith (1991).

CHAPTER 8

1. For an excellent analysis of "postwar peace" and continued processes of exclusion, see the work of Silber (2004) on El Salvador.

2. A journalist from National Public Radio (June 4, 2009) reported from Guatemala that one of the most dangerous daily acts is to ride a bus, for anything can happen to anyone if the bus is robbed and/or the driver is killed. A woman the journalist interviewed said that people leave the house not knowing whether they will make it back and put themselves in the hands of God whenever they are in public. Daily life is especially dangerous for those who must rely on public transportation to go to work. This is not unlike the fear that Guatemalans lived with at the height of the political conflict in the 1980s.

3. For instance, in *Broccoli and Desire* (2006), Edward Fischer and Peter Benson examine the hidden and not-so-hidden connections between our lifestyles in the United States and Guatemalans' lifestyles in their own country. The authors dissect the links between Maya farmers in the Altiplano and supermarket shoppers in the United States, the "broccoli route," to show commodity chains in the global marketplace.

4. Men are also killed in Guatemala (see Torres 2008); in fact, the number of homicides in Guatemala between 2000 and 2005 was 1,715 among women and 17,713 among men (Sanford 2008: 27). The disproportionate numbers might indicate that relatively speaking there should not be a concern about women. However, within this overall climate there is a clear pattern of feminicide and "overkill" (see Torres 2005) among women.

5. Sanford (2008) notes important differences in the causes of death, location of the bodies, and signs of torture and "overkill" (Torres 2005) between crimes committed by gangs and those that are perpetrated in a context of social cleansing.

6. The director of Sobrevivientes (Survivors) in Guatemala, Norma Cruz, narrated a similar case in an interview with Drysdale Walsh (2008). The police, Cruz argued, not only do not apply the law but also undermine it. Even though the Ley para Prevenir, Sancionar, y Erradicar la Violencia Intrafamiliar (Law to Prevent, Sanction, and Eradicate Violence within the Family) says that the police can enter a home if someone is being attacked, when they were called to a case in which a woman was being hit by her husband the police refused to enter, saying, "If we enter, later they are going to denounce us because we violated his human rights and in a while the lady will be happy with the man because that is how women are" (Drysdale Walsh 2008: 54)

7. The case of the women killed in Ciudad Juárez, Mexico, has attracted international attention. But feminicide is also taking place and is even increasing in "postwar" societies. For instance, it has increased in El Salvador, and the characteristics of the killings, signs of torture and extreme violence, are similar to those in Guatemala (see Dalton 2007).

8. For an excellent and concise history of these laws, how they came to pass, and the depoliticizing of the process, see Godoy-Paiz (2008).

9. Programs like those that the Brazilian nonprofit Promundo has developed may provide an alternative. They design reading materials, posters, workshops, and multiple activities directed at children and youth to promote gender equality during key years of socialization, with the objective to prevent violence against women and children. Their work addresses how symbolic violence—images,

language, attitudes, treatment, everyday behaviors that go unquestioned—perpetuates harmful notions about the treatment of women. An example of their advice to children lists do's and don'ts—eat your vegetables, don't play with matches, respect women, do your homework—so as to make gender equality a "normal" behavior expected of children (www.promundo.org.br).

10. Pronunciamiento Público: http://docs.google.com/Doc?id=dggvxhqd_538fnvbjscv. Retrieved April 20, 2009.

References

Abreu Hernandez, Viviana M. 2002. "The Mothers of La Plaza de Mayo: A Peace Movement." *Peace and Change* 27 (3): 385–411.

Adams, Abigail. 1998. "Gringas, Ghouls and Guatemala: The 1994 Attacks on North American Women Accused of Body Organ Trafficking." *Journal of Latin American Anthropology* 4 (1): 112–33.

Adams, Richard Newbold. 1964. *Encuesta sobre la cultura de los ladinos en Guatemala.* Guatemala City: Centro Editorial "José de Pineda Ibarra," Ministerio de Educación Pública.

Alméras, Diane, Rosa Bravo, Vivian Milosavljevic, Sonia Montaño, and María Nieves Rico. 2002. *Violencia contra la mujer en relación de pareja: América Latina y El Caribe: Una propuesta para medir su magnitud y evolución.* Serie Mujer y Desarrollo, 40. Santiago de Chile: Comisión Económica para América Latina (CEPAL)/Naciones Unidas (ONU).

Amnesty International. 2004. "Guatemala." http://web.amnesty.org/report2004/gtm-summary-eng. Retrieved November 25, 2006.

———. 2005. "Guatemala: No Protection, No Justice: Killings of Women in Guatemala." http://news.amnesty.org/index/ENGAMR340432005. Retrieved November 25, 2007.

Annis, Sheldon. 1987. *God and Production in a Guatemalan Town.* Austin: University of Texas Press.

Auyero, Javier. 2000. "The Hyper-Shantytown: Neo-Liberal Violence(s) in the Argentine Slum." *Ethnography* 1 (1): 93–116.

Auyero, Javier, and Débora Alejandra Swistun. 2009. *Flammable: Environmental Suffering in an Argentine Shantytown.* New York: Oxford University Press.

Ball, Patrick, Paul Kobrak, and Herbert F. Spirer. 1999. *State Violence in Guatemala, 1960–1996: A Quantitative Reflection.* Washington, DC:

International Center for Human Rights Research, American Association for the Advancement of Science.

Barrett, Frank J. 1996. "The Organizational Construction of Hegemonic Masculinity: The Case of the US Navy." *Gender, Work, and Organization* 3 (3): 129–42.

Becker, Stan, Fannie Fonseca-Becker, and Catherine Schenck-Yglesias. 2006. "Husbands' and Wives' Reports of Women's Decision-Making Power in Western Guatemala and Their Effects on Preventive Health Behaviors." *Social Science & Medicine* 62 (9): 2313–26.

Benería, Lourdes, and Martha Roldán. 1987. *The Crossroads of Class and Gender: Industrial Homework, Subcontracting, and Household Dynamics in Mexico City.* Chicago: University of Chicago Press.

Benjamin, Walter. 1978. *Reflections: Essays, Aphorisms, Autobiographical Writings,* edited and with an introduction by Peter Demetz. Translated by Edmund Jephcott. New York: Harcourt Brace Jovanovich.

Benson, Peter, and Edward F. Fischer. 2009. "Neoliberal Violence: Social Suffering in Guatemala's Postwar Era." In *Mayas in Postwar Guatemala: Harvest of Violence Revisited,* edited by Walter E. Little and Timothy J. Smith, 151–66. Tuscaloosa: University of Alabama Press.

Benson, Peter, Edward F. Fischer, and Kedron Thomas. 2008. "Resocializing Suffering: Neoliberalism, Accusation, and the Sociopolitical Context of Guatemala's New Violence." *Latin American Perspectives* 35 (5): 38–58.

Binford, Leigh. 2004. "An Alternative Anthropology: Exercising the Preferential Option for the Poor." In *Violence in War and Peace: An Anthology,* edited by Nancy Scheper-Hughes and Philippe Bourgois, 420–24. Malden, MA: Blackwell.

Blackburn, Susan. 1999. "Gender Violence and the Indonesian Political Transition." *Asian Studies Review* 23 (4): 433–48.

Blacklock, Cathy, and Alison Crosby. 2004. "The Sounds of Silence: Feminist Research across Time in Guatemala." In *Sites of Violence: Gender and Conflict Zones,* edited by Wenona Giles and Jennifer Hyndman, 45–72. Berkeley: University of California Press.

Blee, Kathleen M. 2003. "Studying the Enemy." In *Our Studies, Ourselves: Sociologists' Lives and Work,* edited by Barry Glassner and Rosanna Hertz, 13–23. New York: Oxford University Press.

Borland, Elizabeth. 2006. "The Mature Resistance of Argentina's Madres de Plaza de Mayo." In *Latin American Social Movements: Globalization, Democratization, and Transnational Networks,* edited by Hank Johnston and Paul Almeida, 115–30. Lanham, MD: Rowman & Littlefield.

Bossen, Laurel. 1983. "Sexual Stratification in Mesoamerica." In *Heritage of the Conquest: Thirty Years Later,* edited by Carl Kendall, John Hawkins, and Laurel Bossen, 35–72. Albuquerque: University of New Mexico Press.

———. 1984. *The Redivision of Labor: Women and Economic Choice in Four Guatemalan Communities.* Albany: State University of New York Press.

Bosco, Fernando J. 2001. "Place, Space, Networks, and the Sustainability of Collective Action: The Madres de Plaza de Mayo." *Global Networks* 1 (4): 307–29.

Bourdieu, Pierre. 1984. *Distinction: A Social Critique of the Judgement of Taste.* Translated by Richard Nice. Cambridge, MA: Harvard University Press.

———. 1996–97. "The Goffman Prize Lecture: Masculine Domination Revisited." *Berkeley Journal of Sociology* 41: 189–203.

———. 1998. *Acts of Resistance: Against the Tyranny of the Market.* Translated by Richard Nice. New York: New Press.

———. 2001. *Masculine Domination.* Cambridge: Polity Press.

———. 2004. "Gender and Symbolic Violence." In *Violence in War and Peace: An Anthology,* edited by Nancy Scheper-Hughes and Philippe Bourgois, 339–42. Malden, MA: Blackwell.

Bourdieu, Pierre, and Loïc Wacquant. 1992. *An Invitation to Reflexive Sociology.* Chicago: University of Chicago Press.

———. 2004. "Symbolic Violence." In *Violence in War and Peace: An Anthology,* edited by Nancy Scheper-Hughes and Philippe Bourgois, 272–74. Malden, MA: Blackwell.

Bourgois, Philippe. 2001. "The Power of Violence in War and Peace: Post–Cold War Lessons from El Salvador." *Ethnography* 2 (1): 5–34.

———. 2004a. "The Continuum of Violence in War and Peace: Post–Cold War Lessons from El Salvador." In *Violence in War and Peace: An Anthology,* edited by Nancy Scheper-Hughes and Philippe Bourgois, 425–34. Malden, MA: Blackwell.

———. 2004b. "US Inner-City Apartheid: The Contours of Structural and Interpersonal Violence." In *Violence in War and Peace: An Anthology,* edited by Nancy Scheper-Hughes and Philippe Bourgois, 301–7. Malden, MA: Blackwell.

Brockett, Charles D. 1991. "Sources of State Terrorism in Rural Central America." In *State Organized Terror: The Case of Violent Internal Repression,* edited by P. Timothy Bushnell, Vladimir Shlapentokh, Christopher K. Vanderpool, and Jeyaratnam Sundram, 59–76. Boulder, CO: Westview Press.

Brusco, Elizabeth E. 1995. *The Reformation of Machismo: Evangelical Conversion and Gender in Colombia.* Austin: University of Texas Press.

Bunster-Burotto, Ximena. 1986. "Surviving beyond Fear: Women and Torture in Latin America." In *Women and Change in Latin America,* edited by June Nash and Helen Safa, 297–325. South Hadley, MA: Bergin & Garvey.

Burdick, John. 1993. *Looking for God in Brazil: The Progressive Catholic Church in Urban Brazil's Religious Arena.* Berkeley: University of California Press.

Burkhart, Ross E. 2002. "The Capitalist Political Economy and Human Rights: Cross-National Evidence." *Social Science Journal* 39 (2): 155–70.

Campbell, Rebecca, and Sharon M. Wasco. 2000. "Feminist Approaches to Social Science: Epistemological and Methodological Tenets." *American Journal of Community Psychology* 28 (6): 773–91.

Carey, David, Jr. 2006. *Engendering Mayan History: Kaqchikel Women as Agents and Conduits of the Past, 1875–1970.* New York: Routledge.

Carey, David, Jr., and M. Gabriela Torres. Forthcoming. "Precursors to Femicide: Guatemalan Women in a Vortex of Violence." *Latin American Research Review* 45 (3).

Carmack, Robert M. 2001. *Kik'ulmatajem Le K'iche' aab'/ Evolución del Reino K'iche'*. Guatemala City: Editorial Cholsamaj.

Carrabús Pellecer, Carlos Rafael. 1998. *En la conquista del ser: Un estudio de identidad étnica*. Guatemala City: Centro de Documentación e Investigación Maya, CEDIM/Programa Noruego de Pueblos Indígenas, FAFO.

Casaús Arzú, Marta Elena. 1998. *La metamorfosis del racismo en Guatemala/ Uk' Exwachiziik Ri Kaxlan Na'Ooj Pa Iximuleev*. Guatemala City: Editorial Cholsamaj.

———. 2007. *Guatemala: Linaje y racismo*. 3rd ed. Guatemala City: F&G Editores.

Castleberry, Joseph Lee. 1999. "It's Not Just for Ignorant People Anymore: The Future Impact of University Graduates on the Development of the Ecuadorian Assemblies of God." Ph.D. dissertation, Columbia University Teachers College.

Chacon, Richard J., and Rubén G. Mendoza, eds. 2007. *Latin American Indigenous Warfare and Ritual Violence*. Tucson: University of Arizona Press.

Chant, Sylvia. 1996. *Gender, Urban Development and Housing*. United Nations Publication Series for Habitat II, vol. 2. New York: United Nations Development Programme (UNDP).

———. 2003. "Families on the Verge of a Breakdown? Views on Contemporary Trends in Family Life in Guanacaste, Costa Rica." In *Through the Eyes of Women: Gender, Social Networks, Family, and Structural Change in Latin American and the Caribbean*, edited by Cecilia Menjívar, 112–51. Willowdale, ONT: de Sitter Publications.

Chant, Sylvia, with Nikki Craske. 2003. *Gender in Latin America*. New Brunswick, NJ: Rutgers University Press.

Chesnut, R. Andrew. 2003. "Pragmatic Consumers and Practical Products: The Success of Pneumacentric Religion among Women in Latin America's New Religious Economy." *Review of Religious Research* 45 (1): 20–31.

Chuchryk, Patricia M. 1989. "Feminist Anti-Authoritarian Politics: The Role of Women's Organizations in the Chilean Transition to Democracy." In *The Women's Movement in Latin America: Feminism and the Transition to Democracy*, edited by Jane S. Jaquette, 149–84. Boston: Unwin Hyman.

Cockburn, Cynthia. 2004. "The Continuum of Violence: A Gender Perspective on War and Peace." In *Sites of Violence: Gender and Conflict Zones*, edited by Wenona Giles and Jennifer Hyndman, 24–44. Berkeley: University of California Press.

Cojtí Cuxil, Demetrio. 1997. *El movimiento maya (en Guatemala)/Ri Maya' Moloj Pa Iximulew*. Guatemala City: Editorial Cholsamaj.

Colby, Benjamin N., and Pierre L. van den Berghe. 1969. *Ixil Country: A Plural Society in Highland Guatemala*. Berkeley: University of California Press.

Coleman, James S. 1988. "Social Capital in the Creation of Human Capital." *American Journal of Sociology* 94: S95–S120.

Collins, Randall. 2008. *Violence: A Micro-Sociological Theory.* Princeton: Princeton University Press.
Comaroff, Jean. 1985. *Body of Power, Spirit of Resistance: The Culture and History of a South African People.* Chicago: University of Chicago Press.
Comaroff, Jean, and John Comaroff. 1991. *Of Revelation and Revolution: Christianity, Colonialism and Consciousness in South Africa.* Vol. 1. Chicago: University of Chicago Press.
———. 1992. *Ethnography and the Historical Imagination.* Boulder, CO: Westview Press.
Comisión para el Esclarecimiento Histórico (CEH). 1999. *Memoria del silencio: Las violaciones de derechos humanos y los hechos de violencia* (Capítulo II). Guatemala City: Programa de Ciencia y Derechos Humanos and Asociación Americana del Avance de la Ciencia.
Connell, Robert W. 1987. *Gender and Power.* Cambridge: Polity Press.
Cosminsky, Sheila, and Mary Scrimshaw. 1987. "Women and Health Care on a Guatemalan Plantation." *Social Science & Medicine* 25 (10): 1163–73.
Council on Hemispheric Affairs. 2009. "While His Citizens Suffer, Guatemalan President Colom's Administration Spawns Setbacks." COHA Research Memorandum. www.coha.org/while-his-citizens-suffer-guatemalan-president-colom%e2%80%99s-administration-spawns-setbacks/. Retrieved November 30, 2009.
Cueva Perus, Marcos. 2006. *Violencia en América Latina y el Caribe: Contextos y orígenes culturales,*Cuadernos de Investigación, 33. México, DF: Instituto de Investigaciones Sociales, Universidad Nacional Autónoma de México.
Dalton, Juan José. 2007. "Grave ascenso de la violencia de género en El Salvador." *El País,* June 16. www.elpais.com/articulo/sociedad/Grave/ascenso/violencia/genero/Salvador/elpepusoc/20071116elpepusoc_2/Tes. Retrieved June 20, 2010.
Damaris, Rose, Johanne Charbonneau, and Pia Carrasco. 1999. "La Constitution de liens faibles: une passerelle pour l'adaptation des immigrantes centro-américaines mères de jeunes enfants a Montreal." *Canadian Ethnic Studies/Etudes Ethniques au Canada* 31 (1): 73–91.
Darghouth, Sarah, Duncan Pedersen, Gilles Bibeau, and Cecile Rousseau. 2006. "Painful Languages of the Body: Experiences of Headache among Women in Two Peruvian Communities." *Culture, Medicine and Psychiatry* 30 (3): 271–97.
Dary Fuentes, Claudia. 1991. *Mujeres tradicionales y nuevos cultivos.* Guatemala: FLACSO.
———. 1994. *Entre el hogar y la vega: La participación femenina en la agricultura de El Progreso.* Guatemala: FLACSO.
Das, Veena. 1997. "Sufferings, Theodicies, Disciplinary Practices, Appropriations." *International Social Science Journal* 49 (4): 563–72.
———. 2007. *Life and Words: Violence and the Descent into the Ordinary.* Berkeley: University of California Press.
Delgado Wise, Raúl and Humberto Márquez Covarrubias. 2009. "Understanding the Relationship between Migration and Development." *Social Analysis* 53 (3): 85–105.

Demographic and Health Surveys. n.d. "Stat Compiler/Building Tables with DHS Data." www.statcompiler.com/tableBuilderController.cfm?table_orientation. Retrieved March 27, 2009.

Dreby, Joanna. 2009. "Gender and Transnational Gossip." *Qualitative Sociology* 32 (1): 33–52.

Drotbohm, Heike. 2010. "Gossip and Social Control across the Seas: Targeting Gender, Resource Inequalities and Support in Cape Verdean Transnational Families." *African and Black Diaspora: An International Journal* 3 (1): 51–68.

Drysdale Walsh, Shannon. 2008. "Engendering Justice: Constructing Institutions to Address Violence against Women." *Studies in Social Justice* 2 (1): 48–66.

Dutta, Mousumee. 2000. "Women's Employment and Its Effects on Bengali Households of Shillong, India." *Journal of Comparative Family Studies* 31 (2): 217–29.

Eckert, Penelope. 1993. "Cooperative Competition in Adolescent 'Girl Talk.'" In *Gender and Conversational Interaction,* edited by Deborah Tannen, 32–61. New York: Oxford University Press.

Economist. 2003. "A Stubborn Curse: Inequality in Latin America" November 8, 37.

Ehlers, Tracy Bachrach. 2000. *Silent Looms: Women and Production in a Guatemalan Town.* Rev. ed. Austin: University of Texas Press.

Engle Merry, Sally. 1997. "Rethinking Gossip and Scandal." In *Reputation: Studies in the Voluntary Elicitation of Good Conduct,* edited by Daniel B. Klein, 47–74. Ann Arbor: University of Michigan Press.

Enloe, Cynthia. 2000. *Maneuvers: The International Politics of Militarizing Women's Lives.* Berkeley: University of California Press.

Ertürk, Yakin. 2005. "Integration of the Human Rights of Women and the Gender Perspective: Violence against Women. Report of the Special Rapporteur on Violence against Women, Its Causes and Consequences." Addendum, Mission to Guatemala. United Nations, Economic and Social Council, Commission on Human Rights (E/CN.4/2005/72/Add.3). http://daccess-dds-ny.un.org/doc/UNDOC/GEN/G05/108/17/PDF/G0510817.pdf?OpenElement. Retrieved June 12, 2009.

Escoto, Jorge, Ana Leticia Aguilar, Julieta Hernández, and Manfredo Marroquín. 1993. "El acceso de la mujer a la tierra en Guatemala." Fundación Arias para la Paz y el Progreso Humano, Agrupación de Mujeres Tierra Viva, Guatemala City.

Euraque, Darío A., Jeffrey L. Gould, and Charles R. Hale, eds. 2004. *Memorias del Mestizaje: Cultura Política en Centroamérica de 1920 al Presente.* Antigua Guatemala: Centro de Investigaciones Regionales de Mesoamérica (CIRMA).

Fabj, Valeria. 1993. "Motherhood as Political Voice: The Rhetoric of the Mothers of Plaza de Mayo." *Communication Studies* 44 (1): 1–18.

Falla, Ricardo. 1994. *Massacres in the Jungle: Ixcán, Guatemala, 1975–1982.* Translated by Julia Howland. Boulder, CO: Westview Press.

Farmer, Paul. 1996. "On Suffering and Structural Violence: A View from Below." *Daedalus* 125 (1) : 261–83.

———. 2003. *Pathologies of Power: Health, Human Rights, and the New War on the Poor.* Berkeley: University of California Press.

———. 2004. "An Anthropology of Structural Violence." *Current Anthropology* 45 (3): 305–25.

Fine, Gary Alan, and Ralph L. Rosnow. 1978. "Gossip, Gossipers, Gossiping." *Personality and Social Psychology Bulletin* 4 (1): 161–68.

Fischer, Edward F., and Peter Benson. 2006. *Broccoli and Desire: Global Connections and Maya Struggles in Postwar Guatemala.* Stanford: Stanford University Press.

Fitch, Kristine L. 1991. "The Interplay of Linguistic Universals and Cultural Knowledge in Personal Address: Colombian *Madre* Terms." *Communication Monographs* 58 (3): 254–72.

Floro, Maria Sagrario. 1999. "Double Day/Second Shift." In *The Elgar Companion to Feminist Economics,* edited by Janice Peterson and Margaret Lewis, 136–42. Cheltenham, UK: Edward Elgar.

Forster, Cindy. 1999. "Violent and Violated Women: Justice and Gender in Rural Guatemala, 1936–1956." *Journal of Women's History* 11 (3): 55–77.

Foucault, Michel. 1978. *The History of Sexuality: An Introduction.* Vol 1. Translated by Robert Hurley. New York: Random House.

Fraser, Nancy. 2007. "Feminist Politics in the Age of Recognition: A Two-Dimensional Approach to Gender Justice." *Studies in Social Justice* 1 (1): 23–35.

Freston, Paul. 1998. "Pentecostalism in Latin America: Characteristics and Controversies." *Social Compass* 45 (3): 335–58.

Galtung, Johan. 1969. "Violence, Peace, and Peace Research." *Journal of Peace Research* 6 (3): 167–91.

———. 1990. "Cultural Violence." *Journal of Peace Research* 27 (3): 291–305.

Garrard-Burnett, Virginia. 1998. "Transnational Protestantism." *Journal of Interamerican Studies and World Affairs* 40 (3): 117–25.

Gil, David G. 1986. "Sociocultural Aspects of Domestic Violence." In *Violence in the Home: Interdisciplinary Perspectives,* edited by Mary Lystad, 124–49. New York: Brunner/Mazel.

Gill, Lesley. 2007. "'Right There with You': Coca-Cola, Labor Restructuring and Political Violence in Colombia." *Critique of Anthropology* 27 (3): 235–60.

Gilligan, James. 1996. *Violence: Our Deadly Epidemic and Its Causes.* New York: G.P. Putnam's Sons.

Glei, Dana A., and Noreen Goldman. 2000. "Understanding Ethnic Variation in Pregnancy-Related Care in Rural Guatemala." *Ethnicity and Health* 5 (1): 5–22.

Glei, Dana A., Noreen Goldman, and Germán Rodríguez. 2003. "Utilization of Care during Pregnancy in Rural Guatemala: Does Obstetrical Need Matter?" *Social Science & Medicine* 57 (12): 2447–63.

Gluckman, Max. 1963. "Gossip and Scandal." *Current Anthropology* 4 (3): 307–16.

Godoy-Paiz, Paula. 2007. "Violence and Women's Everyday Lives in Guatemala." Paper presented at the annual meeting of the Latin American Studies Association, Montreal, Canada, September.

———. 2008. "Women in Guatemala's Metropolitan Area: Violence, Law, and Social Justice." *Studies in Social Justice* 2 (1): 27–47.

Goffman, Erving. 1959. *The Presentation of Self in Everyday Life.* New York: Anchor Books/Doubleday.

Goldín, Liliana R. 1987. "The 'Peace of the Market' in the Midst of Violence: A Symbolic Analysis of Markets and Exchange in Western Guatemala." *Ethnos* 52 (3–4): 368–83.

Goldín, Liliana, and Brenda Rosenbaum. 2009. "Everyday Violence of Exclusion: Women in Precarious Neighborhoods of Guatemala City." In *Mayas in Postwar Guatemala: Harvest of Violence Revisited,* edited by Walter E. Little and Timothy J. Smith, 67–83. Tuscaloosa: University of Alabama Press.

Goldman, Noreen, Dana A. Glei, Anne R. Pebley, and Hernán Delgado. 2001. *Atención prenatal en Guatemala rural: Resultados de la Encuesta Guatemalteca de Salud Familiar.* Guatemala: Instituto de Nutrición de Centro América y Panamá (INCAP).

Goldman, Noreen, and Patrick Heuveline. 2000. "Health-Seeking Behaviour for Child Illness in Guatemala." *Tropical Medicine & International Health* 5 (2): 145–55.

Goldman, Noreen, Anne R. Pebley, and Megan Beckett. 2001. "Diffusion of Ideas about Personal Hygiene and Contamination in Poor Countries: Evidence from Guatemala." *Social Science & Medicine* 52 (1): 53–69.

Goldman, Noreen, Anne R. Pebley, and Michele Gragnolati. 2002. "Choices about Treatment for ARI and Diarrhea in Rural Guatemala." *Social Science & Medicine* 55 (10): 1693–1712.

Goldstein, Donna M. 2003. *Laughter Out of Place: Race, Class, Violence, and Sexuality in a Rio Shantytown.* Berkeley: University of California Press.

Gómez-Barris, Macarena. 2009. *Where Memory Dwells: Culture and State Violence in Chile.* Berkeley: University of California Press.

González de la Rocha, Mercedes. 1994. *The Resources of Poverty: Women and Survival in a Mexican City.* Oxford: Blackwell.

González-López, Gloria. 2007. " 'Nunca he dejado de tener terror': Sexual Violence in the Lives of Mexican Immigrant Women." In *Women and Migration in the U.S.-Mexico Borderlands: A Reader,* edited by Denise A. Segura and Patricia Zavella, 224–46. Durham, NC: Duke University Press.

Gragnolati, Michele, and Alessandra Marini. 2003. *Health and Poverty in Guatemala.* Policy Research Working Paper No. 2966, Human Development Sector Unit, Latin America and the Caribbean Region, The World Bank. Available at http://ssrn.com/abstract=636328. Retrieved May 24, 2009.

Grandin, Greg. 2000. *The Blood of Guatemala: A History of Race and Nation.* Durham, NC: Duke University Press.

Granovetter, Mark S. 1973. "The Strength of Weak Ties." *American Journal of Sociology* 78 (6): 1360–80.

———. 1995. *Getting a Job: A Study of Contacts and Careers.* 2nd ed. Chicago: University of Chicago Press.

Greeley, Andrew. 1997. "The Other Civic America: Religion and Social Capital." *American Prospect* 32: 68–73.
Green, Linda. 1998. "Lived Lives and Social Suffering: Problems and Concerns in Medical Anthropology." *Medical Anthropology Quarterly* 12 (1): 3–7.
———. 1999. *Fear as a Way of Life: Mayan Widows in Rural Guatemala.* New York: Columbia University Press.
———. 2003. "Notes on Mayan Youth and Rural Industrialization in Guatemala." *Critique of Anthropology* 23 (1): 51–73.
———. 2004. "Living in a State of Fear." In *Violence in War and Peace: An Anthology,* edited by Nancy Scheper-Hughes and Philippe Bourgois, 186–95. Malden, MA: Blackwell.
Guadarrama, Rocío. 2006. "Identidades, resistencia y conflicto en las cadenas globales: Las trabajadoras de la industria maquiladora de la confección en Costa Rica." *Desacatos* 21: 67–82.
Guarnaccia, Peter J., Roberto Lewis-Fernández, and Melissa Rivera Marano. 2003. "Toward a Puerto Rican Popular Nosology: Nervios and Ataque de Nervios." *Culture, Medicine and Psychiatry* 27 (3): 339–66.
Gutmann, Matthew C. 1996. *The Meanings of Macho: Being a Man in Mexico City.* Berkeley: University of California Press.
———. 2007. *Fixing Men: Sex, Birth Control, and AIDS in Mexico.* Berkeley: University of California Press.
Guzmán Böckler, Carlos. 1975. *Colonialismo y revolución.* México, DF: Siglo XXI.
Guzmán Böckler, Carlos, and Jean-Loup Herbert. 1972. *Guatemala: Una interpretación histórico social.* 3rd ed. México, DF: Siglo XXI.
Hale, Charles R. 1996. "Introduction." *Journal of Latin American Anthropology* 2 (1): 2–3.
———. 2006. *Más que un Indio/More than an Indian: Racial Ambivalence and Neoliberal Multiculturalism in Guatemala.* Santa Fe, NM: School of American Research Press.
Hallum, Anne Motley. 2003. "Taking Stock and Building Bridges: Feminism, Women's Movements, and Pentecostalism in Latin America." *Latin American Research Review* 38 (1): 169–86.
Hammar, Lawrence. 1999. "Caught between Structure and Agency: The Gender of Violence and Prostitution in Papua New Guinea." *Transforming Anthropology* 8 (1–2): 77–96.
Hannerz, Ulf. 1967. "Gossip, Networks, and Culture in a Black American Ghetto." *Ethnos* 32: 35–60.
Hansen, Karen V. 1994. *A Very Social Time: Crafting Community in Antebellum New England.* Berkeley: University of California Press.
Haviland, John Beard. 1977. *Gossip, Reputation and Knowledge in Zinacantan.* Chicago: University of Chicago Press.
Hay, Douglas. 1992. "Time, Inequality, and Law's Violence." In *Law's Violence,* edited by Austin Sarat and Thomas B. Kearns, 141–73. Ann Arbor: University of Michigan Press.

Heaton, Tim B., and Renata Forste. 2008. "Domestic Violence, Couple Interaction, and Children's Health in Latin America." *Journal of Family Violence* 23 (3): 183–93.

Hite, Amy Bellone, and Jocelyn S. Viterna. 2005. "Gendering Class in Latin America: How Women Effect and Experience Change in the Class Structure." *Latin American Research Review* 40 (2): 50–82.

Hoffman, Kelly, and Miguel Angel Centeno. 2003. "The Lopsided Continent: Inequality in Latin America." *Annual Review of Sociology* 29: 363–90.

Hoffmann, W., and B.W. McKendrick. 1990. "The Nature of Violence." In *People and Violence in South Africa,* edited by Brian McKendrick and Wilma Hoffmann, 2–35. Cape Town: Oxford University Press.

Hume, Mo. 2008. "The Myths of Violence: Gender, Conflict, and Community in El Salvador." *Latin American Perspectives* 35 (5): 59–76.

Hurtado, Paola. 2009. "Aquí no queremos guaro ni bolos." *El Periódico,* Guatemala, October 25. www.elperiodico.com.gt/es/20091025/cartas/121367. Retrieved January 7, 2010.

Jackman, Mary R. 2002. "Violence in Social Life." *Annual Review of Sociology* 28: 387–415.

Jankowiak, William, M. Diane Nell, and Anne Buckmaster. 2002. "Managing Infidelity: A Cross-Cultural Perspective." *Ethnology* 41 (1): 85–101.

Jaquette, Jane S. 1989. "Conclusion: Women and the New Democratic Politics." In *The Women's Movement in Latin America: Feminism and the Transition to Democracy,* edited by Jane S. Jaquette, 185–208. Boston: Unwin Hyman.

Jonas, Susanne. 2000. *Of Centaurs and Doves: Guatemala's Peace Process.* Boulder, CO: Westview Press.

Kent, George. 2006. "Children as Victims of Structural Violence." *Societies without Borders* 1: 53–67.

Kil, Sang, and Cecilia Menjívar. 2006. "The 'War on the Border': The Criminalization of Immigrants and the Militarization of the U.S.-Mexico Border." In *Immigration and Crime: Ethnicity, Race, and Violence,* edited by Ramiro Martinez Jr. and Abel Valenzuela Jr., 164–88. New York: New York University Press.

Kleinman, Arthur. 2000. "The Violences of Everyday Life: The Multiple Forms and Dynamics of Social Violence." In *Violence and Subjectivity,* edited by Veena Das, Arthur Kleinman, Mamphela Ramphele, and Pamela Reynolds, 226–41. Berkeley: University of California Press.

Kocacik, Faruk, Aziz Kutlar, and Feray Erselcan. 2007. "Domestic Violence against Women: A Field Study in Turkey." *Social Science Journal* 44 (4): 698–720.

Kondo, Dorinne K. 1990. *Crafting Selves: Power, Gender, and Discourses of Identity in a Japanese Workplace.* Chicago: University of Chicago Press.

Kramarae, Cheris. 1981. *Women and Men Speaking: Frameworks for Analysis.* Rowley, MA: Newbury House.

Kristof, Nicholas D., and Sheryl WuDunn. 2009. *Half the Sky: Turning Oppression into Opportunity for Women Worldwide.* New York: Alfred A. Knopf.

Kurtenbach, Sabine. 2008. "Youth Violence in Post-War Societies: Conceptual Considerations on Continuity and Change of Violence." Project Working Paper No. 1 (October), Social and Political Fractures after Wars: Youth Violence in Cambodia and Guatemala. Faculty of Social Sciences, Institute for Development and Peace (INEF), Universität Duisburg Essen. www.prio.no/upload/prio/WP1_Concept_Postwar_Youth_Violence.pdf. Retrieved June 21, 2010.

López Estrada, Silvia. 2003. "Work, Gender, and Space: Women's Home-Based Work in Tijuana, Mexico." In *Through the Eyes of Women: Gender, Social Networks, Family, and Structural Change in Latin American and the Caribbean,* edited by Cecilia Menjívar, 172–98. Willowdale, ONT: de Sitter Publications.

Lovell, W. George. 2010. *A Beauty That Hurts: Life and Death in Guatemala.* 3rd ed. Austin: University of Texas Press.

Lucchetta, Sonia Lina. 2003. "Madres de Plaza de Mayo: Entre la casa y la plaza." *Revista Brasileira de Sociologia da Emoçâo* 2 (5): 271–95.

Maldonado Guevara, Alba Estela. 2005. *Feminicidio en Guatemala: Crímenes contra la humanidad. Investigación Preliminar.* Guatemala City: Publicación de la Bancada de la Unidad Revolucionaria Nacional Guatemalteca del Congreso de la República de Guatemala. www.congreso.gob.gt/uploadimg/documentos/n1652.pdf. Retrieved May 24, 2009.

Manz, Beatriz. 2004. *Paradise in Ashes: A Guatemalan Journey of Courage, Terror, and Hope.* Berkeley: University of California Press.

Marini, Alessandra, and Michele Gragnolati. 2003. *Malnutrition and Poverty in Guatemala.* Policy Research Working Paper No. 2967, Human Development Sector Unit, Latin America and the Caribbean Region, The World Bank. Available at http://papers.ssrn.com/sol3/papers/cfm?abstract_id=%20636329. Retrieved May 3, 2009.

Mariz Loreto, Cecília. 1994. *Coping with Poverty: Pentecostal and Christian Base Communities in Brazil.* Philadelphia: Temple University Press.

Mariz Loreto, Cecília, and María das Dores Campos Machado. 1997. "Pentecostalism and Women in Brazil." In *Power, Politics, and Pentecostals in Latin America,* edited by Edward L. Cleary and Hannah W. Stewart-Gambino, 41–54. Boulder, CO: Westview Press.

Martín-Baró, Ignacio. 1991a. "Towards a Liberation Psychology." Translated by Adrianne Aaron. In *Towards a Society That Serves Its People: The Intellectual Contributions of El Salvador's Murdered Jesuits,* edited by John Hassett and Hugh Lacey, 319–32. Washington, DC: Georgetown University Press.

———. 1991b. "Violence in Central America: A Social Psychological Perspective." Translated by Anne Wallace. In *Towards a Society That Serves Its People: The Intellectual Contributions of El Salvador's Murdered Jesuits,* edited by John Hassett and Hugh Lacey, 333–46. Washington, DC: Georgetown University Press.

———. 1991c. "From Dirty War to Psychological War: The Case of El Salvador." Translated by Adrianne Aron. In *Towards a Society That Serves Its People: The Intellectual Contributions of El Salvador's Murdered Jesuits,* edited by John Hassett and Hugh Lacey, 306–16. Washington, DC: Georgetown University Press.

———. 1991d. "From Religion as Opium to Religion as Liberating Faith." Translated by Maria Ines Lacey. In *Towards a Society That Serves Its People: The Intellectual Contributions of El Salvador's Murdered Jesuits,* edited by John Hassett and Hugh Lacey, 347–70. Washington, DC: Georgetown University Press.

———. 1994. *Writings for a Liberation Psychology.* Edited by Adrianne Aaron and Shawn Corne. Cambridge, MA: Harvard University Press.

Massey, Douglas S. 2007. *Categorically Unequal: The American Stratification System.* New York: Russell Sage Foundation.

Maynard, Eileen Anne. 1975 [1963]. "The Women of Palin: A Comparative Study of Indian and Ladino Women in a Guatemalan Village." Ph.D. dissertation, Cornell University.

McGrew, Anthony, and Nana K. Poku, eds. 2007. *Globalization, Development, and Human Security.* Cambridge: Polity Press.

Meldrim, Harmon Lester. 2005. "The Impact of Infidelity on the Offended Spouse: A Study of Gender Differences and Coping Strategies in a Religious Population." Ph.D. dissertation, Syracuse University.

Menjívar, Cecilia. 1999. "The Intersection of Work and Gender: Central American Immigrant Women and Employment in California." *American Behavioral Scientist* 42 (4): 595–621.

———. 2000. *Fragmented Ties: Salvadoran Immigrant Networks in America.* Berkeley: University of California Press.

———. 2003. "Introduction: "Structural Changes and Gender Relations in Latin America and the Caribbean." In *Through the Eyes of Women: Gender, Social Networks, Family, and Structural Change in Latin America and the Caribbean,* edited by Cecilia Menjívar, 1–10. Willowdale, ONT: de Sitter Publications.

———. 2006a. "Family Reorganization in a Context of Legal Uncertainty: Guatemalan and Salvadoran Immigrants in the United States." *International Journal of Sociology of the Family* 32 (2): 223–45.

———. 2006b. "Liminal Legality: Salvadoran and Guatemalan Immigrants' Lives in the United States." *American Journal of Sociology* 111 (4): 999–1037.

Menjívar, Cecilia, and Victor Agadjanian. 2007. "Men's Migration and Women's Lives: Views from Rural Armenia and Guatemala." *Social Science Quarterly* 88 (5): 1243–62.

Menjívar, Cecilia, and Néstor Rodríguez. 2005. "State Terror in the U.S.–Latin American Interstate Regime." In *When States Kill: Latin America, the U.S., and Technologies of Terror,* edited by Cecilia Menjívar and Néstor Rodríguez, 3–27. Austin: University of Texas Press.

Menjívar, Cecilia, and Olivia Salcido. 2002. "Immigrant Women and Domestic Violence: Common Experiences in Different Countries." *Gender and Society* 16 (6): 898–920.

Miller, Francesca. 1991. *Latin American Women and the Search for Social Justice.* Hanover, NH: University Press of New England.

Molyneux, Maxine. 1985. "Mobilization without Emancipation? Women's Interests, the State, and Revolution in Nicaragua." *Feminist Studies* 11 (2): 227–54.

———. 2006. "Mothers at the Service of the New Poverty Agenda: Progresa/Oportunidades, Mexico's Conditional Transfer Programme." *Social Policy & Administration* 40 (4): 425–49.

Moodie, Ellen. 2006. "Microbus Crashes and Coca-Cola Cash: The Value of Death in 'Free-Market' El Salvador." *American Ethnologist* 33 (1): 63–80.

Moran-Taylor, Michelle J. 2008. "When Mothers and Fathers Migrate North: Caretakers, Children, and Child Rearing in Guatemala." *Latin American Perspectives* 35 (4): 79–95.

Moser, Caroline O.N. 1996. *Confronting Crisis: A Comparative Study of Household Responses to Poverty and Vulnerability in Four Poor Urban Communities.* Environmentally Sustainable Development Series, 8. Washington, DC: The World Bank.

Moser, Caroline, and Cathy McIlwaine. 2001. *Violence in a Post-Conflict Context: Urban Poor Perceptions from Guatemala.* Environmentally and Socially Sustainable Development Series. Washington, DC: International Bank for Reconstruction and Development/The World Bank.

Morales de Sierra, María Eugenia. 2001. *Eugenia Morales de Sierra* v. *Guatemala.* Comisión Interamericana de Derechos Humanos, OEA, Informe No. 4/01, Caso 11.625, OEA/Ser.L/V/II.111 Doc. 20. www.cidh.org/women/Guatemala11.625.htm. Retrieved January 9, 2010.

Muratorio, Blanca. 1982. *Etnicidad, evangelización y protesta en el Ecuador: Una perspectiva antropológica.* Quito: Centro de Investigaciones y Estudios Socio-Económicos (CIESE).

Navarro, Marysa. 2001. "The Personal Is Political: Las Madres de Plaza de Mayo." In *Power and Popular Protest: Latin American Social Movements,* edited by Susan Eckstein, 241–58. Berkeley: University of California Press.

Nelson, Diane M. 1998. "Perpetual Creation and Decomposition: Bodies, Gender, and Desire in the Assumptions of a Guatemalan Discourse of Mestizaje." *Journal of Latin American Anthropology* 4 (1): 74–111.

———. 1999. *A Finger in the Wound: Body Politics in Quincentennial Guatemala.* Berkeley: University of California Press.

———. 2009. *Reckoning: The Ends of War in Guatemala.* Durham, NC: Duke University Press.

Nordstrom, Carolyn. 1992. "The Backyard Front." In *The Paths to Domination, Resistance, and Terror,* edited by Carolyn Nordstrom and JoAnn Martin, 260–74. Berkeley: University of California Press.

———. 1997. *A Different Kind of War Story.* Philadelphia: University of Pennsylvania Press.

———. 2004. *Shadows of War: Violence, Power, and International Profiteering in the Twenty-first Century.* Berkeley: University of California Press.

Nordstrom, Carolyn, and JoAnn Martin. 1992. "The Culture of Conflict: Field Reality and Theory." In *The Paths of Domination, Resistance, and Terror,* edited by Carolyn Nordstrom and JoAnn Martin, 3–17. Berkeley: University of California Press.

Olmsted, Jennifer C. 2005. "Is Paid Work the (Only) Answer? Neoliberalism, Arab Women's Well-being, and the Social Contract." *Journal of Middle East Women's Studies* 1 (2): 112–39.

Oquendo Maria, Ewald Horwath, and Abigail Martinez. 1992. "Ataques de nervios: Proposed Diagnostic Criteria for a Culture Specific Syndrome." *Culture, Medicine, and Psychiatry* 16 (3): 367–76.

Ortega Hegg, Manuel. 2004. "Masculinidad y paternidad en Centroamérica." *Revista Centroamericana de Ciencias Sociales* 1 (2): 59–74.

Oxfam Novib. n.d. "Fighting Violence against Women: Guatemala." Oxfam International. www.oxfam.org/en/programs/development/camexca/guatemala_violence. Retrieved October 31, 2009.

Parenti, Michael, and Lucia Muñoz. 2007. "Gender Savagery in Guatemala." Global Research, July 13. www.globalresearch.ca/index.php?context=va&aid=6314. Retrieved October 15, 2009.

Paz Antolín, María José, and Amaia Pérez Orozco. 2001. "El empleo femenino en la maquiladora textíl en Guatemala y las transformaciones en las relaciones de género." *Anuario de Estudios Centroamericanos* 27 (2): 35–55.

Pebley, Anne R., Noreen Goldman, and Germán Rodríguez. 1996. "Prenatal and Delivery Care and Childhood Immunization in Guatemala: Do Family and Community Matter?" *Demography* 33 (2): 231–47.

Periódico, El. 2010. "Personas decapitadas aún sin identificar." Guatemala, June 11. www.elperiodico.com.gt/es/20100611/pais/157136/. Retrieved June 14, 2010.

Peterson, Anna L. 1997. *Martyrdom and the Politics of Religion: Progressive Catholicism in El Salvador's Civil War.* Albany: State University of New York Press.

Portes, Alejandro. 2009. "Migration and Development: Reconciling Opposite Views." Paper presented at the Pardee Center Conference "How Immigrants Impact Their Homelands." Boston University, September 24–25.

Portes, Alejandro, and Bryan R. Roberts. 2005. "The Free-Market City: Latin American Urbanization in the Years of the Neoliberal Experiment." *Studies in Comparative International Development* 40 (1): 43–82.

Preston, Julia. 2009. "U.S. May Be Open to Asylum for Spouse Abuse." *New York Times,* October 29. www.nytimes.com/2009/10/30/us/30asylum.html. Retrieved October 29, 2009

Prieto-Carrón, Marina, Marilyn Thomson, and Mandy Macdonald. 2007. "No More Killings! Women Respond to Femicides in Central America." *Gender &Development* 15 (1): 25–40.

Quesada, James. 2004. "Suffering Child: An Embodiment of War and Its Aftermath in Post-Sandinista Nicaragua." In *Violence in War and Peace: An Anthology,* edited by Nancy Scheper-Hughes and Philippe Bourgois, 290–96. Malden, MA: Blackwell.

Quisumbing, Agnes R., Kelly Hallman, and Marie T. Ruel. 2007. "Maquiladoras and Market Mamas: Women's Work and Childcare in Guatemala City and Accra." *Journal of Development Studies* 43 (3): 420–55.

Ray, Raka and Seemin Qayum. 2009. *Cultures of Servitude: Modernity, Domesticity, and Class in India.* Stanford: Stanford University Press.

Reina, Rubén E. 1973. *La Ley de los Santos: Un pueblo pokomam y su cultura de comunidad.* Guatemala City: Editorial "José de Pineda Ibarra," Ministerio de Educación.

REMHI (Informe del Proyecto Interdiocesano "Recuperación de la Memoria Histórica"). 1998. *Guatemala: Nunca más.* Guatemala City: Oficina de Derechos Humanos del Arzobispado de Guatemala.

Rico, María Nieves. 1992. *Violencia doméstica contra la mujer en América Latina y el Caribe: Propuesta para la discusión.* División de Desarrollo Social, Unidad Mujer y Desarrollo, 10. Santiago de Chile: Comisión Económica para América Latina (CEPAL)/Naciones Unidas (ONU).

Roberts, Bryan. 1968. "Protestant Groups and Coping with Urban Life in Guatemala City." *American Journal of Sociology* 73 (6): 753–67.

———. 1995. *The Making of Citizens: Cities of Peasants Revisited.* London: Arnold.

Rosenberg, Tina. 1991. *Children of Cain: Violence and the Violent in Latin America.* New York: Penguin Books.

Russell, Diana E. H. 2001. "Introduction: The Politics of Femicide." In *Femicide in Global Perspective,* edited by Diana E. H. Russell and Roberta A. Harmes, 3–11. New York: Teachers College Press.

Rydstrøm, Helle. 2006. "Sexual Desires and 'Social Evils': Young Women in Rural Vietnam." *Gender, Place, and Culture* 13 (3): 283–301.

Safa, Helen I. 1995. *The Myth of the Male Breadwinner: Women and Industrialization in the Caribbean.* Boulder, CO: Westview Press.

Sanford, Victoria. 2008. *Guatemala: Del genocidio al feminicidio.* Cuadernos del Presente Imperfecto 5. Guatemala City: F&G Editores.

Savenije, Wim, and Katherine Andrade-Eekhoff. 2003. *Conviviendo en la orilla: Violencia y exclusión social en el área metropolitana de San Salvador.* San Salvador: FLACSO.

Scheper-Hughes, Nancy. 1992. *Death without Weeping: The Violence of Everyday Life in Brazil.* Berkeley: University of California Press.

———. 1995. "The Primacy of the Ethical: Propositions for a Militant Anthropology." *Current Anthropology* 36 (3): 409–40.

———. 1997. "Specificities: Peace-Time Crimes." *Social Identities* 3 (3): 471–97.

Scheper-Hughes, Nancy, and Philippe Bourgois. 2004. "Introduction: Making Sense of Violence." In *Violence in War and Peace: An Anthology,* edited by Nancy Scheper-Hughes and Philippe Bourgois, 1–31. Malden, MA: Blackwell.

Scott, James C. 1985. *Weapons of the Weak: Everyday Forms of Resistance.* New Haven, CT: Yale University Press.

Sear, Rebecca, and Ruth Mace. 2008. "Who Keeps Children Alive? A Review of the Effects of Kin on Child Survival." *Evolution and Human Behavior* 29 (1): 1–18.

Sennett, Richard, and Jonathan Cobb. 1972. *The Hidden Injuries of Class.* New York: Norton.

Shah, Iqbal H., and Lale Say. 2007. "Maternal Mortality and Maternity Care from 1990 to 2005: Uneven but Important Gains." *Reproductive Health Matters* 15 (30): 17–27.

Silber, Irina Carlota. 2004. "Mothers/Fighters/Citizens: Violence and Disillusionment in Post-War El Salvador." *Gender & History* 16 (3): 561–87.

Sluka, Jeffrey A., ed. 2000. *Death Squad: The Anthropology of State Terror.* Philadelphia: University of Pennsylvania Press.

Smilde, David. 2007. *Reason to Believe: Cultural Agency in Latin American Evangelicalism.* Berkeley: University of California Press.

Smith, Carol A. 1990. "Class Position and Class Consciousness in an Indian Community: Totonicapán in the 1970s." In *Guatemalan Indians and the State, 1540 to 1988,* edited by Carol A. Smith, with the assistance of Marylyn M. Moors, 205–29. Austin: University of Texas Press.

———. 1995. "Race-Class-Gender Ideology in Guatemala: Modern and Anti-Modern Forms." *Comparative Studies in Society and History* 37 (4): 723–49.

Smith, Dennis A. 1991. "Coming of Age: A Reflection on Pentecostals, Politics, and Popular Religion in Guatemala." *Pneuma* 13 (2): 131–39.

Smith, Dorothy E. 1987. *The Everyday World as Problematic: A Feminist Sociology.* Boston: Northeastern University Press.

Smith, Laura C., Kenya J. Lucas, and Carl Latkin. 1999. "Rumor and Gossip: Social Discourse on HIV and AIDS." *Anthropology & Medicine* 6 (1): 121–31.

Snodgrass Godoy, Angelina. 2005. "La Muchacha Respondona: Reflections on the Razor's Edge between Crime and Human Rights." *Human Rights Quarterly* 27 (2): 597–624.

———. 2006. *Popular Injustice: Violence, Community, and Law in Latin America.* Stanford: Stanford University Press.

Sosa Elízaga, Raquel, ed. 2004. *Sujetos, víctimas y territorios de la violencia en América Latina.* México, DF: Pensamiento Propio, Universidad de la Ciudad de México.

Steenkamp, Christina. 2009. *Violence and Post-War Reconstruction: Managing Insecurity in the Aftermath of Peace Accords.* London: I.B. Tauris.

Steinsleger, José. 2005. "Feminicidio en Guatemala." *La Jornada,* March 9. www.jornada.unam.mx/2005/03/09/020a1pol.php. Retrieved April 20, 2009.

Sternbach, Nancy Saporta, Marysa Navarro-Aranguren, Patricia Chuchryk, and Sonia E. Alvarez. 1992. "Feminisms in Latin America: From Bogotá to San Bernardo." *Signs* 17 (2): 393–434.

Stevens, Evelyn P. 1973. "*Marianismo:* The Other Face of *Machismo* in Latin America." In *Female and Male in Latin America: Essays,* edited by Ann M. Pescatello, 89–101. Pittsburgh: University of Pittsburgh Press.

Stoll, David. 1990. *Is Latin America Turning Protestant? The Politics of Evangelical Growth.* Berkeley: University of California Press.

Sutton, Barbara. 2004. "Body Politics and Women's Consciousness in Argentina." Ph.D. dissertation, University of Oregon.

———. 2010. *Bodies in Crisis: Culture, Violence, and Women's Resistance in Neoliberal Argentina.* New Brunswick: Rutgers University Press.

Tarducci, Mónica, and Bárbara Tagliaferro. 2004. "Iglesia Católica: Ni diversa ni laica." *Política y Cultura* 21: 191–200.

Tarracena Arriola, Arturo. 1997. *Invención criolla, sueño ladino, pesadilla indígena: Los altos de Guatemala: De región a Estado, 1740–1850*. San José, Costa Rica: Editorial Porvenir, La Antigua Guatemala: Centro de Investigaciones Regionales de Mesoamérica (CIRMA).

Tarracena Arriola, Arturo, with Gisela Gellert, Enrique Gordillo Castillo, Tania Sagastume Paiz, and Knut Walter. 2002. *Etnicidad, estado y nación en Guatemala, 1808–1944*. La Antigua Guatemala: Nawal Wuj/Centro de Investigaciones Regionales de Mesoamérica (CIRMA).

Taussig, Michael. 1992. *The Nervous System*. New York: Routledge.

———. 2005. *Law in a Lawless Land: Diary of a Limpieza in Colombia*. Chicago: University of Chicago Press.

Tax, Sol. 1942. "Ethnic Relations in Guatemala." *America Indígena* 2: 43–47.

Taylor, Robert Joseph, and Linda M. Chatters. 1988. "Church Members as a Source of Informal Social Support." *Review of Religious Research* 30 (2): 193–203.

Torres, M. Gabriela. 2005. "Bloody Deeds/Hechos Sangrientos: Reading Guatemala's Record of Political Violence in Cadaver Reports." In *When States Kill: Latin America, the U.S., and Technologies of Terror*, edited by Cecilia Menjívar and Néstor Rodríguez, 143–69. Austin: University of Texas Press.

———. 2008. "Imagining Social Justice amidst Guatemala's Post-Conflict Violence." *Studies in Social Justice* 2 (1): 1–11.

Torres-Rivas, Edelberto. 1998. "Sobre el terror y la violencia política en América Latina." In *Violencia en una sociedad en transición*, 46–59. San Salvador: Programa de Naciones Unidas para el Desarrollo (PNUD).

Tumin, Melvin. 1952. *Caste in a Peasant Society: A Case Study in the Dynamics of Caste*. Princeton: Princeton University Press.

Turpin, Jennifer, and Lester R. Kurtz. 1997. "Introduction: Violence—The Micro/Micro Link." In *The Web of Violence: From Interpersonal to Global*, edited by Jennifer Turpin and Lester R. Kurtz, 1–27. Urbana: University of Illinois Press.

UNICEF-UNIFEM-OPS/OMS-FNUAP. 1993. *Estudio exploratorio: Violencia intrafamiliar hacia la mujer en Guatemala*. GT3.1^bHQ/809/.3/G8/G8. Guatemala: Ministerio de Salud Pública y Asistencia Social, Programa Mujer, Salud y Desarrollo.

United Nations Children and Education Fund (UNICEF). n.d.a. "Globalis-Guatemala." http://globalis.gvu.unu.edu/indicator_detail.cfm?Country=GT. Retrieved October 3, 2009.

———. n.d.b. "At a Glance: Guatemala." www.unicef.org/infobycountry/guatemala_statistics.html. Retrieved April 20, 2009.

United Nations Development Programme (UNDP). 2003. "Millenium Development Goals: A Compact among Nations to End Human Poverty." Human Development Report, Human Development Index. http://hdr.undp.org/en/media/hdr03_HDI.pdf. Retrieved December 9, 2009.

———. 2009. "Informe sobre desarrollo humano para América Central, 2009–2010: Abrir espacios a la seguridad ciudadana y al desarrollo humano." www.idhac-abrirespaciosalaseguridad.org/documentos/informe.pdf. Retrieved November 30, 2009.

United Nations World Food Programme (UN WFP). n.d. "Guatemala." www.wfp.org/countries/guatemala. Retrieved June 6, 2009.

Van Vleet, Krista. 2003. "Partial Theories: On Gossip, Envy and Ethnography in the Andes." *Ethnography* 4 (4): 491–519.

Vite Pérez, Miguel Ángel. 2005. "La urbanización popular mexicana y la globalización económica." *Sistema* 187: 95–110.

Walter, Eugene Victor. 1969. *Terror and Resistance: A Study of Political Violence, with Case Studies of Some Primitive African Communities.* New York: Oxford University Press.

White, Luise. 2000. *Speaking Vampires: Rumor and History in Colonial Africa.* Berkeley: University of California Press.

Whiteford, Michael B. 2002. "Staying Healthy: Evangelism and Health Perception Differences by Gender in a Guatemalan Marketplace." *Annals AAPSS* 583: 177–94.

Wilkinson, Daniel. 2004. *Silence on the Mountain: Stories of Terror, Betrayal, and Forgetting in Guatemala.* Durham, NC: Duke University Press.

Wilkinson, Iain. 2005. *Suffering: A Sociological Introduction.* Cambridge: Polity Press.

Williams, Raymond. 1977. *Marxism and Literature.* Oxford: Oxford University Press.

Williams, Simon J. 1999. "Is Anybody There? Critical Realism, Chronic Illness and the Disability Debate." *Sociology of Health & Illness* 21 (6): 797–819.

Wilson, Everett. 1997. "Guatemalan Pentecostals: Something of Their Own." In *Power, Politics, and Pentecostals in Latin America,* edited by Edward L. Cleary and Hannah W. Stewart-Gambino, 139–62. Boulder, CO: Westview Press.

Wood, Charles H., Philip Williams, and Kuniko Chijiwa. 2007. "Protestantism and Child Mortality in Northeast Brazil, 2000." *Journal for the Scientific Study of Religion* 46 (3): 405–16.

World Bank. 2006. "World Development Indicators (People Section Tables 2.7 and 2.8)." http://devdata.worldbank.org/wdi2006/contents/Home.htm. Retrieved October 2, 2006.

World Health Organization (WHO). 2006. "Core Health Indicators." http://apps.who.int/whosis/database/core/core_select.cfm. Retrieved May 31, 2009.

———. 2009. "WHO Statistical Information System (WHOSIS)." www.who.int/whosis/en/index.html. Retrieved June 6, 2009.

Wright, Melissa W. 2007. "The Dialectics of Still Life: Murder, Women, and Maquiladoras." In *Women and Migration in the U.S.-Mexico Borderlands: A Reader,* edited by Denise A. Segura and Patricia Zavella, 184–202. Durham, NC: Duke University Press.

Wuthnow, Robert. 2002. "Religious Involvement and Status-Bridging Social Capital." *Journal for the Scientific Study of Religion* 41 (4): 669–84.

Young, Iris Marion. 1990. *Justice and the Politics of Difference.* Princeton: Princeton University Press.

Zepeda López, Raúl. 2005. *Las Violencias en Guatemala: Algunas perspectivas.* Colección Cultura de Paz, 10. Guatemala City: FLACSO/UNESCO.

Zur, Judith N. 1998. *Violent Memories: Mayan War Widows in Guatemala.* Boulder, CO: Westview Press.

Index

TEXT
10/13 Sabon

DISPLAY
Sabon

COMPOSITOR
Toppan Best-set Premedia Limited

PRINTER AND BINDER
IBT Global